MYRTLEFIELD

HOUSE

The Bible
and Ethics

Myrtlefield Encounters

Myrtlefield Encounters are complementary studies of biblical literature, Christian teaching and apologetics. The books in this series engage the minds of believers and sceptics. They show how God has spoken in the Bible to address the realities of life and its questions, problems, beauty and potential.

Books in this series:

Key Bible Concepts: Defining the Basic Terms of the Christian Faith

Christianity: Opium or Truth?: Answering Thoughtful Objections to the Christian Faith

The Definition of Christianity: Exploring the Original Meaning of the Christian Faith

The Bible and Ethics: Finding the Moral Foundations of the Christian Faith

The Bible and Ethics

Finding the Moral Foundations
of the Christian Faith

David Gooding

John Lennox

Myrtlefield Encounters

Cover design: Matthew Craig.

First published in Russian 1993–95. Adapted from a series of articles published in *Uchitelskaya Gazeta* in the former Soviet Union from 1993 to 1995.
Revised edition, 2015.
Published by The Myrtlefield Trust
PO BOX 2216, Belfast, BT1 9YR
w: www.myrtlefieldhouse.com
e: info@myrtlefieldhouse.com
ISBN: 978-1-874584-57-5 (pbk.)
ISBN: 978-1-874584-58-2 (PDF)
ISBN: 978-1-874584-59-9 (Kindle)
ISBN: 978-1-874584-60-5 (EPUB without DRM)

24 23 22 21 20 19   10 9 8 7 6 5 4

Contents

Contents

Appendices

Figures

Introduction

Changing Times and the Danger of Moral Chaos

Today, many parts of the world are convulsed with very grave problems—economic, social, ethnic and political. These problems are compounded by the fact that in many places the old ideologies that held nations, and indeed empires, together have lost their grip on people's thinking, or else have collapsed completely. There is therefore a real danger of moral chaos. New thinking, new planning, new teaching are desperately needed. But here a difficulty arises. With the demise of older ideologies and with nothing as yet to take their place, whole nations find themselves without any shared moral values to form a basis for their ethical standards. There is, therefore, no motivation for people to deny themselves in the interests of their neighbour and of society as a whole. And without this, however good any new planning is, the carrying out of the plans is liable to falter, or even to fail altogether.

Religion as a source of values?

In countries where the norms of behaviour were founded on some form of atheistic ideology, the natural reaction of many people in their disappointment and bewilderment at the collapse of those norms is to turn to religion. On the other hand it is not obvious to everyone that religion has the necessary answers either. It is notorious that in some parts of the world people are fighting, torturing and killing their opponents in the name of religion. And that surely shows an appalling perversion of human values; though, to be fair, it often likewise represents an equally appalling perversion of the actual tenets of the religion in whose name it is done.

Our responsibility

All this places a very heavy burden on those who do not want the upcoming generation to face life in societies devoid of values. And teachers in particular, at whatever level we teach, owe it to our students to communicate moral principles and ethical norms that can provide them with a sound and healthy basis for their future private, social and professional lives. Scientists may well be tempted to argue that teaching students morality and ethics is none of their business. And maybe it is not their direct responsibility. Certainly science as such cannot give us answers even to the moral questions which science itself raises. Science has given us the hydrogen bomb; science by itself cannot tell us whether it is morally right to use it. But science teachers ought surely to be concerned that their students be given adequate moral guidelines for reaching a responsible decision in such matters. Science, if altogether devoid of morality, might still make our students clever; but it might also make them clever monsters. And the same goes for subjects like economics and social sciences. Social engineering, based on an inadequate assessment of the intrinsic value of each individual human being, has been known in the past to carry out its schemes of population shift at the cost of millions of human lives simply for the sake of economic advantage.

The importance of immediate action

For most teachers, it is not primarily the moral health of the world, or even of their own nation, but rather that of their own students that concerns them. These young people cannot wait for guidance until their teachers have developed some moral philosophy of their own. That might take years, by which time they will be grown up and gone. We urgently need to give our children here and now sound guidelines on moral values and ethics, lest they grow up a 'lost generation' as the result of a vacuum in serious moral teaching. This is what made an experienced teacher who grew up in a Communist country tell us on one occasion: 'We were taught to believe that Lenin was kind, loved children and sacrificed everything for the good of society. Now that belief is gone.' Her remarks would resonate with teachers in many countries today, for the fact is that around the world the ideas that once seemed like solid foundations for our lives have crumbled.

Though still an atheist herself, this teacher added: 'That is why we have to turn to Jesus. Either the children will learn from his example, or they will turn to crime, drugs and alcohol.' Her observation, of course, is good as far as it goes. Certainly, if everyone took seriously Christ's command to 'do to others what we would have them do to us' and to 'love even our enemies', the world would become a happier place overnight.

The ethics of Jesus and truth

On the other hand, young people have minds of their own, and it is our job to see to it that they are encouraged to use them. If we try to teach them simply the ethics of Jesus they may well start asking us some fundamental questions. 'Love our neighbours as ourselves? Why should we? Did not Jesus himself, who preached and practised this kind of thing, get crucified as a result of not putting himself first and sticking up for his own rights? And shall not we too be worse off if we follow his example? If other people prosper in business by cheating and lying and profiteering, why should we always tell the truth, like Christ says we should? Is there some value in telling the truth for its own sake?' In other words, we can teach the ethics of Jesus adequately only if we also teach the fundamental and absolute values and beliefs on which he based his ethics.

What, after all, is the value of an individual human being? If I own a computer, and it does not work very well, I am free to smash it, if I want to. If my neighbour or my business rival does not suit me, why should I not destroy them too, if I can get away with it?

Even if I start now to follow the ethical teaching of Jesus myself, the world at large is still liable to be more or less as bad in fifty years' time as it is now. Is it worthwhile, then, trying to follow Jesus' teaching myself? What ultimate hope is there either for me or for the world?

Our programme

To be able to answer questions like these and to make sense of Jesus' ethical teaching, we need to be able to trace its roots in the Old Testament and to follow the outworking of its implications in the New. That means, in fact, teaching at least the main major lessons of the whole Bible. That is a daunting task, particularly for anyone who has never attempted it before and may not even have read the Bible.

Of course, it is also a very worthwhile task. Even from the point of view of world history and literature, no other book has ever had such a vast influence on world thought as the Bible. No one, indeed, could be regarded as fully educated until they have read the Bible and understood at first hand the secret of its impact.

But for all that, the task remains colossal. And therefore we propose in the following chapters to present a survey of some of the leading historical events and personages, ideas, poetry, moral values and ethics of both Old Testament and New. At various points throughout this book we have included explanatory notes, discussion questions and suggestions as to how the moral and spiritual implications of this material can be made relevant to a class of students or else used to enhance discussions among the members of a study group. References from the Bible are given at the start of most chapters, and we encourage you to read these passages whether you are using the material in groups or on your own.

Our sincere hope is that you may find this material helpful in these changing times, whether you are a teacher, a parent, a student or someone who is interested in taking a guided journey through the Bible.

David Gooding
John Lennox

PART 1

The Moral and Ethical Teachings
of the Old Testament

CHAPTER

Human Ethics and
Human Origins

Please read Genesis 1:1–2:3

We set out now to study the question of ethics, that is, how we ought to treat one another and our environment. But questions of ethics raise other prior questions.

Why should we behave?
The questions behind ethics

What exactly is a human being? Some people say that humans are nothing more than clever animals.[1] But in the wild, animals will kill off other animals when they are weak or ill. Would it be right for us to kill a baby if it is

1 In this book the terms 'humanity' and 'humans' are used for the more traditional 'man' to denote the entire human race, except in those places where it would conflict with the biblical texts.

born with some weakness or handicap? Or a grandmother when she begins to get frail? If not, why not?

What is the purpose for humanity's existence? We need to know this before we can judge whether we are living as we should. Suppose, for instance, a tribesman from an isolated village found a flute. Not knowing what it was made for, he might use it as a magic wand or as a stick to beat his dog with. But his fellow villagers would not be able to decide whether he was using it as he should or not, unless they knew what the purpose was for which the flute was made. Is there then any purpose behind humanity's existence on this earth?

How should we treat the environment? If we can make a lot of money for ourselves and our immediate children, at the risk of polluting the rivers and oceans and ruining the environment for future generations, why should we not do so? Why should we not exploit nature simply for our own present enjoyment? Who said that we must consider future generations? Whose world is it anyway? Does it not belong to us? Have we not a right to do what we like with our own property?

We probably know the answers that atheism gives to these questions; but now let us see what answers the Bible gives. Read again the passage from Genesis quoted above.

Everything begins with God

'In the beginning God created the heavens and the earth', says the Bible (Gen 1:1 NIV).

This tells us that the universe did not always exist: it had a beginning. And that is interesting, because in times past many scientists used to believe that the universe always existed. Some still do; but most think nowadays that the universe must have had a beginning.

God not only made the universe; the Bible says that he constantly upholds it by the word of his power (Heb 1:3). What we call the laws of nature are the outworking of his maintaining power.

This brings us to the conclusion that neither the universe, nor even our earth, belongs to us: they are God's. 'The earth is the LORD's and all that is in it' (Ps 24:1). We are simply tenants of God's earth: we do not own it. We must therefore find out from the Bible and respect the conditions that God has laid down for our tenancy.

The whole creation, including humanity, was made to serve God's pleasure and to do his will (Rev 4:11). So the way to decide if humans are living as they should is to ask 'How well is each person fulfilling God's will?'

How God made the world

The Bible spends much more time discussing *why* God made the world than *how* God made the world. It is important to understand the difference between these two questions, so let's consider an illustration.

Imagine a grandmother has made a cake for her grandson. The sciences, from dietetics and biology to chemistry, physics and mathematics, can analyse how her cake is made but no amount of scientific analysis can tell why she made it. Indeed, unless grandmother tells us that she made the cake for her grandson's birthday, we shall never know. Similarly, our scientific analysis can tell us a great deal about how the universe is constructed, but nothing about its ultimate purpose. If the Creator does not tell us, we shall never know why the world was made. The Bible, which is the Creator's answer, therefore concentrates on this all-important question.

However, the Bible does say some very interesting things about how God made the world. The most fundamental is that he made it by his word. Notice how many times Genesis 1:1-2:3 repeats the phrase 'and God said' (cf. also John 1:1-5; Heb 11:3).

When we speak, our words express our minds, thoughts and intentions. Similarly, in creating the universe by his word, God was expressing his mind, his thoughts and his intentions. That is why, the more we discover the way nature works, the more we are amazed at its marvellous rationality. The universe is not the product of mindless, purposeless forces, as the atheist says it is. Everywhere it shows evidence of order, purpose, rationality—God's rationality expressed through his creative word.

Another way of putting it is to say that we use words to carry information. The repetition of 'and God said' at each stage of creation indicates that the information needed to create the world came from a personal intelligence—God, and that a fresh input of information was necessary in order to obtain each new level of complexity. This is in complete accord with what science teaches us. This resonates powerfully with the scientific discovery that the biological world is not composed of mere matter but of matter which carries information—we speak of the genetic 'code' and the 'language' of DNA.

This rationality of nature is also seen in the fact that, as science shows us, the operation of the universe can be described in terms of laws, often formulated in terms of mathematics.

Besides dealing with questions of why and how, Genesis 1 carries implications for the dignity and value of man, which we shall discuss in the next chapter.

Science and the Bible

One of the greatest ever historians of science, Sir Alfred North Whitehead, has pointed out the vital contribution that the biblical worldview made to the rise of modern science. C. S. Lewis summarised Whitehead's view: 'Men became scientific because they expected Law in Nature, and they expected Law in Nature because they believed in a Legislator.'[1]

1 *Miracles*, 110.

CHAPTER 2

The Dignity of Human Beings

Please read Genesis 1 again

The Bible teaches that God is all-powerful. We might have expected therefore that the Bible would say that God created the world all at once. But it doesn't. Look again at Genesis 1. It says that God did not create the cosmos all at once. He made it in stages. In each successive stage, moreover, there came into being higher, more organised forms of matter, and ever more complex forms of life.

The Bible and science

A difficulty that many scientifically educated people feel about this account of creation is that, superficially read, it seems to imply that the whole universe was made in one earth week. Genesis 1 is, however, a highly sophisticated narrative that should not be read simplistically. Since we are ourselves interested in the ethical implications of creation, we should not allow debate about length of time to obscure the main lesson of the stages—that humanity is the pinnacle of creation. For further discussion of some of the issues involved, see John Lennox's book *Seven Days that Divide the World*.

The pinnacle of creation

We naturally ask what is the climax of this progressive process? And the answer is: human beings! As far as this world is concerned, humanity is the crown, the high pinnacle of God's creation. Humans were created to have dominion over the earth and over all other forms of life in it (see Gen 1:26). The earth was created to be a home for human beings.

It follows that humans are more important than anything else in the earth. When you go home, you instinctively realize that you yourself are more important than the building and its furniture. They exist for you, not you for them.

Jesus Christ pointed out one of the implications of this: if God has spent so much care on beautifying the trees and flowers, on feeding the birds which are part of humanity's earthly home, he will most certainly spend more care on humanity whose home earth is (Matt 6:25-30).

Moreover, we are more important than the great material forces on which we depend for our lives. We could not live, for instance, without the sun and its light. But we instinctively know that we are more important and significant than the sun is. That instinct is confirmed by the Genesis account. The sun was made for us; not we for it. It is our servant, not a god to be served, as many ancient people thought. We know that the sun is there, and how it works; the sun does not know that we are here, or how we work.

Humanity's value and inviolability

Time and time again Genesis 1 says that God saw that all that he had made, humanity included, was good.

This is in striking contrast with what many eastern religions teach. They hold that matter is a very inferior thing; that the Supreme Being himself did not create it and would never have done so; and that the human body and the material world were created by some lower and much less wise 'power'. Some famous Greek philosophers (and even some theologians) thought that the body, being made of matter, is the tomb, or prison, of the soul, and therefore defiles the soul that dwells in it. This idea has led to all kinds of unhealthy attitudes to life. The Bible, by contrast, teaches that the human body is, in itself, good; and all its natural appetites are good and are to be enjoyed (though, of course, controlled and not perverted).

The Bible also teaches that humans, as distinct from the animals, were made in the 'image' and 'likeness' of God (see Gen 1:26-27). This means, in the first place, that humans were made to be God's representatives, to act as God's viceroy among all God's other creatures on earth, to control and look after them, to be the ruler of the earth. This is high dignity and a great responsibility. Humans represent God to the other creatures. They must not, therefore, abuse them or cause them unnecessary suffering.

It means, also, that all human life is sacred and inviolable. You may destroy your computer if it does not please you, for it is only a machine. But you must not murder a human being, because, says the Bible, he or she is made in the image of God (Gen 9:6) and is of infinite value. A human's value, moreover, does not depend on being clever, or rich, or powerful, or beautiful, or healthy, but simply on this great fact that each human being is made in the image of God. That is why we must not kill children by abortion before they are born; nor children after they are born, if they seem weak or have disabilities; nor grandparents when they get old and troublesome. Nor must we despise any human being, however poor: 'Those who oppress the poor insult their Maker', says the Bible (Prov 14:31).

Moreover, God has made all the races of the world out of the first original pair of human beings (Acts 17:26). There are no inferior human beings. All people of whatever race are made in the image of God. All racism, anti-Semitism and oppression of ethnic minorities is wrong and an insult to God the Creator. Women, too, are equally made in the image of God as men are. They are of equal value to God; they must be treated with equal honour as men; they must not be oppressed or abused.

A lesson from creation

Though humans were made as God's representatives with dominion over the earth, Genesis 1 points out that God made the earth in such a way as constantly to remind us of our dependence on God.

Take one example. Light is a basic necessity for life and God gave us the sun as the source of light. Genesis 1 says more than this. It not only makes the basic distinction between light and darkness but also adds: 'And God called the light Day, and the darkness he called Night' (Gen 1:5). This statement is very striking for two reasons.

First, naming, and therefore classifying things, is generally regarded as one of the basic scientific activities, which we call taxonomy. Indeed God later gave Adam the job of naming the animals (Gen 2:19). This incidentally shows that Genesis, far from being opposed to scientific endeavour, clearly tells us that God has given us a mandate to do science. Thus it is very unusual for God himself to give names to parts of the world, as we find here.

Second, light and day are not quite the same, nor are darkness and night. God is here drawing our attention to the organisation of the world's lighting system. Since we live on a rotating planet 150 million kilometres from the sun, its light source, our light is rationed. Once every day, whether we want to or not, we spin out of the light and plunge into darkness. There is nothing we can do about it except to wait for light to be given us again. That is, we are helplessly dependent on a light source outside our world. God has not given us (as he has given to glow-worms and certain deep sea creatures) a light source within ourselves!

What is true of physical light, is even more true of that moral and spiritual light that we need to make sense of life, and to live as we ought. That spiritual light is not in human beings either, in spite of their considerable intellectual powers. Nor is it in all the collected wisdom of humanity. As the Bible says: 'I know, O Lord, that the way of human beings is not in their control, that mortals as they walk cannot direct their steps' (Jer 10:23). The lesson is that we need to turn to a source of light and wisdom that is outside ourselves and outside our world—the Creator himself. The New Testament writer John puts it this way: 'God is light and in him there is no darkness at all. If we say that we have fellowship with him while we are walking in darkness, we lie and do not do what is true' (1 John 1:5-6).

But we must now turn to consider what else the Bible says it means to be a human being.

The light of the world

Discuss what you think Jesus meant by his claim to be the 'light of the world' (John 8:12; 9:5).

Jesus also referred to the fact that physical life is outside humanity and drew a lesson from it. Read the account in John 11 (see especially verses 9-10) and discuss its meaning.

CHAPTER 3

What it Means to be Human

Part 1: Life and its Many Levels

Please read Genesis 2:4–24

There are two accounts of the creation of the human race in Genesis 1–2. The first, as we saw in our last two chapters, presents humans as the pinnacle of God's creation. It teaches that God created humans in his own image, as his representative, to look after and develop the earth in loyal dependence upon God. Thus humans have a unique value and dignity. We saw, too, that this God-given status had very important ethical implications.

The second creation account

The second account of creation, which we find in Genesis 2, complements the first account. It does not contradict it. Since it is written in an unfamiliar idiom, at first sight it may seem very simple to us as an account of the meaning of human life, compared with other philosophies of man. But in its simplicity lies its genius. Step by step, in language accessible to everyone, it builds up a vivid picture of human life as God intended it to be—full of wonder and meaning.

Clearly, if we are going to enjoy life as God intended, we shall first need to know what is meant by 'life' in all of its senses, physical, moral, spiritual and eternal. This is the aim of the second creation account—to give us a practical 'definition' of life at all of its different levels and give us a context in which to face the inevitable moral and ethical considerations which arise.

But let us take it in order. Not surprisingly, Genesis 2 starts by defining humans as material beings.

What we are made of

'God formed man from the dust of the ground' (2:7). So far as we know, the chemistry of matter is largely the same throughout the universe. Our bodies, therefore, are made of the same basic stuff as the rest of the universe. We are made, as some scientists say, of star dust. However, we are more than matter:

> [God] breathed into his nostrils the breath of life; and
> the man became a living being. (2:7)

We note that animals also are said to have 'the breath of life' (1:30), and they too are described as 'living' (1:20, 24). In this respect, therefore, humans are the same as the animals.

Physical life remains a mystery. We know what physical components have to be present if life is to be possible, although we do not really know what life itself consists of. There is no evidence that even the lowliest of micro-organisms have ever arisen by spontaneous generation out of lifeless matter by accident. As astronomer and mathematician Sir Fred Hoyle has asked us to imagine when thinking about the chances that life just occurred on earth:

> A junkyard contains all the bits and pieces of a Boeing 747, dismembered and in disarray. A whirlwind happens to blow through the yard. What is the chance that after its passage a fully assembled 747, ready to fly, will be found standing there? So small as to be negligible, even if a tornado were to blow through enough junkyards to fill the whole Universe.[1]

The wonder of life. Life, whether of plants, animals, or human beings, is undoubtedly one of the wonders of the universe. The eye, the wing of a bird, or the dance by which scout-bees communicate the direction and the distance of a source of pollen to other bees, are marvels of complex, ingenious engineering. The way all the parts of a baby in its mother's womb develop at the right time and in exactly the right place (it would be of no use for an eye to develop before there was a head for it to be in) is an astonishing example of precision design and finely tuned organisation—especially when we recall that the information required

1 Hoyle, *The Intelligent Universe*, 19.

for the development of a baby is all contained in two tiny cells derived from its parents.

Such things should move the normal mind to awe, delight and worship of the Creator's wisdom, like the Hebrew poet who wrote: 'For it was you who formed my inward parts; you knit me together in my mother's womb. I praise you, for I am fearfully and wonderfully made. Wonderful are your works; that I know very well' (Ps 139:13–14). The more we experience this wonder and awe, the more we shall value and respect life. Not to feel any gratitude to the Creator, says the Bible (Rom 1:21), is one of the first steps towards devaluing life, with all its ugly consequences.

Different kinds of life

What is the actual difference between plant life, animal life and human life?

What is it that makes human life human?

For example, a badly injured person can sometimes be kept alive by means of life-support machines and artificial feeding even when he or she is brain-dead. Would you describe such a person as 'being alive'? In the sense that a vegetable is alive, he is alive; but is this what we mean by human life? It looks, doesn't it, as if in one and the same human being there are different levels of life, and therefore of death?

Ethical implications

All of us, and young people in particular, need to be reminded that the human body and brain form a very delicately balanced system and so need to be maintained properly. Thus there is an inbuilt desire for food, which urges us to eat and so maintain our physical life. But sooner or later people may be tempted to abuse their bodies in a way that is both unhealthy and deceptive. They do it because it seems to promise happiness, wonderful thrills and freedom from boredom or worry, whereas in actual fact it may eventually destroy the delicate precision-engineering of the body and the brain, and lead to misery and even death.

Such warnings are vitally important. But, while *an ethical system that is built on the value of the human body as a biological machine is good, it is not enough.* Our bodies are not simply machines that came into existence by chance as a result of blind purposeless forces working on mindless matter. If that is all they were, we would still be fools to wreck them; but once we had destroyed them, that would be the end of it. But our bodies are more than that: they are a gift, designed and given to us by the Creator.

If some rich person gave me a new car and I ruined the engine by putting sand in it, I should certainly be a fool. In addition it would insult and anger the friend who gave it to me. Similarly, if we destroy our bodies, one day we shall have to answer to God for it. For according to the Bible, the death of the body is not the end of existence. There will be a resurrection; and we shall all have to give account to God of the things we have done in the body (2 Cor 5:10). If, furthermore, by misusing our own bodies we not only wreck them but ruin other people's bodies too, we cannot expect God to remain indifferent. And what shall we say about the millions of abortions that are carried out each year?

Of course we have all sinned against our bodies in some way or other. The good news is that there is hope. The God who made our bodies has a scheme for our forgiveness and for the redemption of the human body. Of that we shall have to speak in a later chapter. Meanwhile we now consider what else this second creation account means by 'life'.

For the classroom

Tell the students about the marvellous way the lungs are designed to work (look up videos online, if necessary). Then show them pictures of the horrific damage done by smoking. This will illustrate vividly the madness of destroying their lungs in this way.

Show them what an amazing chemical-processing plant the liver is, and then show them the effects of excessive consumption of alcohol and you may help save them from ruining their joy of life.

The same applies to the brain and the way its fantastically wonderful neural network can be destroyed by drugs.

Similarly, sexual promiscuity may lead to the dreaded disease of AIDS. In some countries in the West an increasing number of babies is being born already infected with drugs and AIDS while in their mothers' wombs.

Creativity and aesthetic sense

When God commissioned man to develop the earth, he first planted a garden in a part of the earth and placed him there to cultivate and guard it (Gen 2:5-15). Now there was nothing wrong with the uncultivated earth; but a garden results when someone takes a wild, uncultivated part of nature and arranges it with art and skill to make it a place of ordered beauty. Moreover, God placed in the garden not only trees that were good for food, able to satisfy man's physical hunger, but trees that were beautiful to look at, able to satisfy man's aesthetic sense.

This reminds us of the fact that *humans are able to appreciate beauty for its own sake*. People all over the world love a garden and are prepared to work hard to create one, not merely for the food it produces, but for its sheer beauty.

There is no evidence that birds and animals possess genuinely creative and aesthetic qualities. We never find animals doing the equivalent of creating a garden. A beaver will adapt nature by building a dam in the river. But it does this simply for the sake of survival and food. Animals and birds seem to be attracted by colour and song to their mates in the breeding season. But animals and birds do not seem to have either the interest or desire to create beauty for its own sake as humans do. Nor do they have the ability to create new things that their predecessors knew nothing about.

Of course, not all people make gardens. Nomads and many city dwellers do without them, either by choice or necessity. But nomads decorate their tools and utensils; city dwellers love flowers, art and beautiful clothes; and cities are often full of majestic architecture.

Creativity, then, and a sense of beauty are two characteristics which humans, in a limited way, share with their Creator. They are part of the image of God in us. They also form a magnificent element in human life.

The history of humanity is the story of ever increasing creative invention in almost every area of human activity. It has marked our progress in science, technology and mathematics as well as in literature, art and culture. It is the story of humans copying their Creator.

Another aspect of man's activity in the garden is that it was work. Work, in the sense of purposeful organising activity, is good for human beings. It plays a healthy and important part in developing life. A person without work to do can therefore rightly become very frustrated.

But what shall we say when, instead of producing beauty in a garden, humans ravage the earth and turn it into a desert, pollute the rivers, create a hole in the ozone layer and put the planet at risk, so ruining the very habitat that God made? Thus the biblical view would encourage us to do all we can to act responsibly towards the environment and avoid the destruction of the ecological balance.

The Bible has yet more to say in giving us its 'definition' of life, as we shall see in the next chapter.

CHAPTER 4

What it Means to be Human

Part 2: Life and Human Relationships

Please read Genesis 2:18–25

In the last chapter we noted that Genesis describes different levels of life, emphasizing particularly those features which mark man out as a creature made in the image of God and leading us to consider their ethical implications. We resume our considerations by thinking now of the higher levels of life to which Genesis draws our attention.

The creation of woman

Genesis tells us that when God made a woman as a companion for man, he first brought all of the animals to man. The man, Adam, named them all, thus demonstrating his superiority over them. No compatible companion for him was to be found among the animals. He was alone. He had no one to talk to, to appreciate the beauty. This profound story points to two more levels of life in which humans are different from the animals, and which make human life truly human and wonderful.

Language

First, there is language, to which our attention is drawn by Adam giving names to the animals. There is no evidence that animals and birds possess the ability to use language in the same way as humans do. Some creatures have a limited ability to communicate. But none of them has anything comparable with human language. The genius of human language lies in the ability to use an arbitrary (not onomatopoeic) sound to represent a thing, or a group of things, or even abstract ideas. So we use the sound (i.e. spoken word) *dog* in English (*sobaka* in Russian, *chien* in French) to denote either one particular dog, or the whole class belonging to that species. Similarly, most languages have sounds to refer to abstract qualities like justice, beauty and truth.

Language requires and facilitates the ability to think analytically, to group things into classes and categories, to think in abstract terms and to think and argue rationally. It enables us to express feelings and emotions in a far more sophisticated way than by physical acts, grunts or groans. Compare the wonder of love poetry with the few expressions of 'affection' which a lion can show to his mate! Animals write no books! But just think of the literary masterpieces which have been produced by authors like Tolstoy, Milton and Chinua Achebe.

Differences between human language and animal communication show us an important discontinuity between humans and animals. International linguistic research has shown us that only humans possess the ability to combine phonology and grammar. Even a five-year-old child can make up sentences which are totally new and which convey ideas that are spontaneous and creative. Furthermore, linguistic anthropologists analysing the languages of supposedly primitive jungle peoples find their structure to be as complex as modern English or Russian or ancient Greek. Linguistic research, therefore, does not appear to support the evolution of language between species.

Language, rather, demonstrates that humans are made in the image of God. It makes loving, self-conscious, personal communication and fellowship possible, not only between one human and another, but between God and humanity. God came down to the garden, we are told, and talked with man and man with God. This communication between Adam and his Creator was without fear; it was loving and intelligent.

It expressed the fellowship between them. Communication between a human and God is the highest level of human life. It is open to all of us. God speaks to us through the words of the Bible and each one of us can express the thoughts of our hearts directly to God in prayer. It is sad when a person who is physically alive cannot communicate with his loved ones around him, because of an accident or stroke. It is sadder still when a person in full possession of his faculties never speaks to God, nor allows God to speak to him. It means that such a person is dead at one of the highest levels of human life.

Words, language, meaning

Discuss together what everyone in your group thinks is unique about human language.

In the New Testament, Jesus Christ, the Son of God, is called the Word of God (John 1:1–14). Discuss what you think this title means.

Marriage

The second level of what it means to be really human to which this story points, is man's relationship with his wife. God recognised that it was not good for man to be alone. Man, made in the image of a loving God, needed someone to love. But love between a man and his wife was designed by God to be an infinitely higher thing than mere physical mating to produce offspring. Love involves not just a meeting of intellect, emotions, or physical attraction, but also a decision of the will. It means putting the needs and desires of the one loved before your own, and utter loyalty so that your chosen partner is completely secure in your love. Furthermore, in making man and woman, God shared his joy of creation with them. He did not go on creating individuals but gave man and woman the ability to procreate, to bring children into the world. He wanted them to know the joy and responsibility of having children.

God gave to Adam a woman of whom he could say: 'This at last is bone of my bones and flesh of my flesh' (Gen 2:23). He did not need to be told that she was different from the animals. She too, created in the image of God (1:27), was neither inferior nor superior to him, but delightfully different.

It is clear from Genesis that marriage was designed by God to be a very special, indeed, a sacred relationship. The lifetime bond of husband and wife, and their commitment to one another, was designed to give stability to that basic unit of society, the family (2:24). And if the individual cells in the organism of society were healthy, society would be healthy too.

We see today an increasing disregard for moral and spiritual standards which spreads through daily life like a cancer: spiralling crime rates, horrific child abuse, disregard for good and the pursuit of evil on an unprecedented scale. Much of it is directly traceable to the breakdown of the individual family cells. When society jettisons belief in absolute moral and ethical standards, and in the sacredness of marriage, we must not be surprised at the tragic results. The husband–wife relationship is not the result of the evolution of social conventions—it was created by God. Disaster will result if that relationship is tampered with.

Even children have a possession that is special for them, something they treasure and protect. Adults may have something in their homes, a special gift or piece of china. We would never treat them carelessly; they are too precious for that! Yet contemporary society often does just that. It treats marriage as a careless game and divorce as an easy option, mindless of the tragic effect on the family and children who are robbed of emotional stability.

If we ignore the instructions in the maker's handbook for a car or motorcycle and put water instead of petrol in the tank, we will seriously damage the engine. The instructions are given not to diminish our enjoyment of the car, but to make sure we enjoy it for as long as possible. Similarly, the instructions about marriage and relationships in the Bible are given by our Maker so that we may enjoy life to the full. We ignore them at our peril.

Thus pornography devalues sex and degrades human beings to the level of animals. The Bible condemns the abuse and misuse of sex not because God is some awful, boring tyrant who wants to stop humans having satisfaction and fun, but for the opposite reason. It is abuse that eventually destroys the possibility of real joy. God who invented human life and sexuality loves us, and because he loves us he has laid down the basic rules to enable us to get the maximum joy from life's relationships.

The Bible affirms marriage as God's good creation and speaks in praise of its health and beauty. It is used in the Bible as a picture of Christ's love for his people both now (Eph 5:22-33) and in eternity (Rev 19:7-9).

Equal yet different?

Think of ways in which men and women are designed to complement each other.

What relevance has the stability of marriage to the health of society?

Consider what the New Testament has to say about the attitude of Jesus to women compared with that of his contemporaries in John 4:1-42, and his attitude to divorce (Matt 19:3-12).

CHAPTER 5

Temptation, Fall and Alienation

Please read Genesis 3

It is everywhere evident that there is something wrong with humanity. The question is: What exactly is the cause of the trouble? Unless we diagnose the cause correctly, all attempts to deal with it will in the end prove inadequate; and all hope for building a permanently better world will be grievously disappointed. One view of the matter is that humanity's trouble and all the evil in the world is due to the fact that we have evolved imperfectly so far. Only give our species enough time and we will evolve into the perfect creatures we should all like ourselves to be. But the evidence of the last six thousand years is that while we have made vast strides in technology and science, the human race as a whole is not significantly less selfish, evil, cruel and corrupt than it ever was. In this lesson, therefore, we listen to the Bible's account of where the trouble stems from, as a basis for proceeding later to consider what hope the Bible holds out for the cure. But first we must consider another wonderful feature of what it means to be human, according to the Bible.

The power of moral choice

The fact of free will. Genesis tells us that all the trees in the garden of Eden were put there for man's delight and enjoyment, except one: the fruit of this tree God strictly forbade man to eat, and warned him that if he disobeyed and ate it, he would die. But the very fact that God had to warn man what the consequences of disobeying the prohibition would be shows us that God had made man in such a way that he was able to disobey God if he chose to. In other words, God had made man with a free will.

The necessity of free will for morality. Genesis is about to tell us that all the evil in the world is traceable ultimately to this, that man used his free will to disobey God, and so introduced into the world that evil principle and power which the Bible calls sin. The question arises: did not God foresee that man would misuse his free will? Of course he did. Why then did he give him free will in the first place? The answer is: because in his love God did not wish to create humans as biological machines, working simply by instinct and unable to make any genuinely free choice. If a bee stings a bus driver and causes a fatal accident, we do not take the bee to court and accuse it of having committed a crime. It had no choice: it stung simply by instinct. It would be very different if a passenger stabbed the driver: he might have an instinctive hate against the driver, but he still had a choice whether to stab him or not.

29

Moreover, God wanted a human to be an infinitely higher and more noble creature than even an animal. You can train a dog, for instance, not to eat a piece of meat unless its owner gives it the go-ahead. But if in consequence the dog refrains from stealing a joint of meat from the next door neighbour, it does so simply because past experience has impressed on its memory and nervous system that if it takes a piece of meat without its owner's go-ahead, this will be followed by punishment. The dog does not know what 'stealing' means, nor why stealing is wrong; it doesn't know therefore why the owner stops it from taking the next-door neighbour's meat. In creating humans God wanted creatures who could eventually be taught the reasons for God's commands and prohibitions, as a child can be taught by its parents the reasons for the parents' dos and don'ts; so that a human's obedience to God should be both intelligent and, because of free will, genuinely free.

The importance of free will for love. Above all, in creating humans, God wanted creatures that could genuinely love him; and that too meant that they must be given free choice and free will: love that is forced or mechanical is not true love. A human must therefore be genuinely free to choose to love God and to obey him, or to reject his love and to disobey him. If a robot came into your room, placed its arms round your neck, and said in its mechanical voice, 'I love you', you would either laugh at it or push it away in disgust. Why? Because you would know that the robot was simply doing and saying what it was programmed to do and say. It was not free to make a personal decision to love you; and certainly not free consciously to rebel against the instructions programmed into it by its maker. And God wanted humans to be infinitely more than a robot. Someone may say: would it not have been better if God had made humans as mere machines or animals? The answer is simple: which one of us would volunteer to give up our human free will and be turned into a machine?

Now an illustration. Fire is a very dangerous thing. A wise and loving parent, therefore, will forbid a young child to touch or light a fire, until the parent has had time to teach the child what destruction fire can cause if mishandled. So God forbade man, in his innocence, to eat from the tree of the knowledge of good and evil. How God would have eventually shown man the destructive results of disobedience and evil, and so have taught man to avoid evil, we are not told. For man chose to act independently of God, to disobey God; and so learned by grievously sad personal suffering the terrible consequences of evil. Why ever did man do it?

Man's temptation and fall

To many people the Bible's story of how the devil, impersonating a snake, tempted humanity to disobey God, seems a fairy story; but when we study the form the temptation took, we find it is all too true to life.

The devil's first ploy. He exaggerated God's prohibition in order to make God appear a cruel, tantalising spoilsport. 'Did God really say', he asked—though of course he knew that God had said no such thing—'that you must not eat from any tree in the garden?' The woman corrected him; but the devil's exaggeration is still believed by many people: they don't wish to know anything about God or even to think about him, because they imagine that belief in God would rob them of all pleasure.

The devil's second ploy. He denied God's word outright. 'You will not die', he said, 'if you disobey God. The reason for God's prohibition is that if you take the fruit, your eyes will be opened. You will be like God, knowing good and evil. You will no longer be dependent on God; you can decide for yourself what is bad and what is good. So strike a blow for moral independence and freedom. Decide for yourselves! Be your own boss! Don't let God decide for you.'

What of course the devil did not tell them was that by disobeying God's command and acting independently of him they would admit into their lives the powerful, evil force of sin which they themselves could not cope with. Once admitted, it would gradually enslave them and in the end destroy them. And still today many people are similarly deceived by the devil. Why else would they imagine they are striking a blow for personal freedom by destroying themselves physically with alcohol, drugs and sexual promiscuity, and by destroying themselves psychologically with envy, jealousy, rancour, malice, hatred, lying, cheating and all that ugly brood?

The devil's third ploy. He got the woman to look closely at the tree. She then noticed that it was good for food, pleasing to the eye, and desirable for gaining wisdom; that is, it could give her physical, aesthetic and intellectual enjoyment. And the devil suggested that if she had these three forms of enjoyment, she had all that was necessary for enjoying life to the full. She did not need God, and she need not listen to his word or worry about his prohibition. Many people think so still.

But it was, and is, a lie. The Bible says (Deut 8:3), and Jesus Christ repeated it (Matt 4:4): 'One does not live by bread alone, but by every word that comes from the mouth of God.'

An illustration. Suppose in your kindness you decide to befriend me, and to begin that process you invite me to dinner. I come to your table and I enjoy the food, and admire the pictures on the wall and the background music. But in spite of all your efforts to engage me in conversation, I persistently refuse to answer you or even to take any notice of you. And when at last you force me to explain my strange behaviour, I say that the physical enjoyment of the food and aesthetic and intellectual enjoyment of the paintings and the music are all that I am interested in. But as for you who provided these things, I am just not interested in you: as far as I am concerned you might as well be dead. What a fool I would be. Good as the food, the paintings and the music were, to take them and refuse friendship and fellowship with you would be to reject the highest significance and enjoyment of the dinner party.

The consequences of the fall

The result of the man and woman's disobedience was inevitable and instantaneous. Their enjoyment of life at its highest level was ruined. When next they heard the sound of the Lord God walking in the garden, they were afraid. Instead of welcoming God's presence, conversation and fellowship as life's supreme joy, they tried to hide from him. They felt naked. Now, of course, naked is how

God had made them and there was nothing wrong with that. But their disobedience had created within them a bad conscience; and they felt they were unfit for God's presence. They tried to cover themselves by sewing fig leaves together. But they sensed it was no use. So they hid from God among the trees. But that was no use either; for God summoned them to meet him and they had to come and stand before God. And what God then said and did, and how instead of destroying humankind for their rebellion, he showed them the way of forgiveness and gave them hope for the future—all that we must consider in the following chapters.

But still today it is one of the evidences that humans are fallen creatures, that the thought of God fills many people with uneasy feelings of fear and guilt, if not of vigorous resentment. The Bible calls that state of affairs spiritual death. According to the Bible this alienation from God is the root cause of all humanity's trouble.

CHAPTER 6

The Way of Hope and Recovery

Please read Genesis 3 again

Victory out of defeat

When humanity foolishly rebelled against God, it would have been understandable if God had decided to destroy them, and start again with a different kind of creature altogether.

But God did the very opposite. He not only continued with his original plan to have the human race as his vice-regal representative, but he announced that it would be through humans that the devil's attempt to ruin God's plan would be defeated. Addressing the serpent whom Satan had used to deceive the woman, he declared: 'I will put enmity between you and the woman, and between your offspring and hers; he will strike your head, and you will strike his heel' (Gen 3:15). These words doubt-less reflected the antagonism that would be felt between human beings and literal snakes all down the centuries; but God's promise used this antagonism to symbolize the age-long struggle that would ensue between the human race and Satan. Its major battlefield would be the hearts of men and women as God strove to win the human race back to his allegiance and Satan struggled to maintain humanity in his grip.

Looking back on this prophecy after the birth, life, death and resurrection of Jesus Christ, the New Testament claims that the promised seed of the woman referred in a special sense to him, since he was born of a human mother without a human father (Luke 1:35). He was truly human, though simultaneously God incarnate. Tempted by the devil in all respects like as we are, he overcame him (Matt 4:1–11; John 14:30; Heb 4:15), and maintained uncompromised obedience to God even to the point of death. And what is more, sinless himself he paid by his death the penalty of human sin, so that humanity could be reconciled to God and restored to paradise. In the course of this mighty conflict, then, the devil, like a snake, would strike at Christ's heel; but Christ as man would crush the serpent's head on humanity's behalf and gain the everlasting victory.

In a famous Old Testament passage (Ps 8), devoted to answering the question 'What is man?' the poet observes that God originally made man a little lower than the angels, but crowned him with glory and honour and put everything under his feet. Centuries later the writer of the Letter to the Hebrews in the New Testament repeats this statement and emphasizes that it means exactly what it says. 'Now in subjecting all things to them, God left nothing outside their control' (Heb 2:8).

Now granted that that was God's original intention, anyone can see that something has gone wrong. Evil and disease still stalk humanity. They are far from being undisputed master of the world. The writer himself admits it: 'Yet we do not see everything subject to them.' Must we then give up hope of regaining paradise? No, certainly not! For, says the writer, far from the plan having been abandoned, its fulfilment is already far advanced. For we see Jesus, who was made a little lower than the angels and became himself a man so that he could suffer death for everyone, thus making forgiveness and restoration possible. What is more, the man Jesus has already been crowned with glory and honour. His resurrection, ascension and glorification are the guarantee that the rest of God's plan will be fully carried out and humanity be returned to dominion over a sin-free universe.

But a question arises. If God intended right from the start to send Christ into the world as the Saviour of the human race, why did he not send him the very moment Adam and Eve sinned? Why wait centuries before sending him?

The necessity of discovering what sin involves

Consider an illustration. No one will go to a doctor to be healed, unless they are convinced they are ill. Some cancers begin as a tiny sore or as a minute spot in the skin; and because they seem unimportant, people suppose they will just go away. Only when, after months or years, they develop and show themselves as something serious, will the person concerned seek help from the doctor.

Now if, when Adam and Eve had used their free will to disobey God, God had intervened miraculously to prevent their sin having its painful consequences, Adam and Eve would never have realised what a serious thing it is to abuse free will. They would get the impression that it did not matter what they decided or how they chose: it all turned out the same in the end. They had to learn that their one sin of disobedience—let alone all the others which they went on to commit—was enough, not only to spoil their own lives, but to poison and pervert all their posterity. Only so would humanity come to hate sin, to repent of it, and to accept salvation when God offered it. And only so would humanity be trained thereafter to use free will in cooperation with God.

The immediate consequences of the fall

The Bible now points out some of the inevitable consequences of the fall, against which the human race would have to battle in the future.

Alienation from God. We have already discussed this in our previous chapter. Relationship with God would no longer be joyful and fearless but marred by a bad conscience and the awareness of God's displeasure against sin, even though God had made provision to cover the guilt of sin.

The brutalisation of human relationships. Childbirth would be accompanied by sorrow and fear; and men would tend to take advantage of women and domineer over them. Here are the beginnings of the mistrusts and passions that have since caused such damage to society. Here too, however, there is healing. Christ in his love for his people has made the ideal of love real, and in his strength it is possible for human relationships to be transformed and real harmony achieved within marriage, for Christian husbands to love their wives, and wives to respect their husbands. (See the way the Apostle Paul cites Genesis in Eph 5:31.)

Work becomes hard labour. Adam was originally set as lord over creation; but when he rebelled against God, his relation to the world around him changed. Work that before had been an unmixed pleasure, now began to involve struggle and hard labour. Life's tasks that had once been faced with joy in the full vigour of life and in fellowship with God, would look very different now that he was vulnerable to disease and prone to conflicting emotions and the inner pull of sin. His own inner world was disordered: he had lost control. And, as the New Testament points out (Rom 8:20–22), creation itself was subjected to frustration and groans. It is subject to thorns and thistles, blights and pests, and the ravages of pollution and disease. Yet here, once more, there is hope. In Romans 8 we are also told that believers in Jesus Christ are indwelt by the Holy Spirit, who gives us power in this life to overcome the pull of the sinful nature (vv. 9, 13), even though we still groan ourselves. More than that, a day is coming when God will raise believers' bodies from the dead through the very power of the Holy Spirit who indwells them (v. 11). This hope is no empty myth. For God has already raised the man Jesus Christ bodily from the dead. His triumph over death means that creation itself will one day be liberated from its bondage to decay and brought into the glorious freedom of the children of God (v. 21).

Banishment from Eden's paradise. Cut off from the tree of life, Adam would eventually age and die. He had already died spiritually. Physical death would constantly remind man that he was a fallen creature. It would become a warning and a foreshadowing of what the Bible calls the 'second death', that is the eternal death that all humans must eventually experience unless reconciled to God.

Meanwhile the way back into the paradise of Eden was barred, so we are told, by cherubim wielding swords, a reminder that humanity will never again know a paradise either on earth or in heaven until our sin is finally removed and humanity and nature are reconciled to God.

Inadequate diagnoses of humanity's trouble

Some people, of course, reject this diagnosis of what is wrong with our race. The ancient Greek philosopher, Socrates, thought that man's only basic trouble was ignorance. 'No one knowingly does wrong', he claimed. 'Educate man properly and he would cease to sin.' History has proved Socrates wrong. Marx held that humanity's only basic trouble was alienation from the means of production; once remove that alienation and humanity's difficulties would all be over: paradise would dawn. History has proved him wrong as well. The eminent historian Professor Herbert Butterfield said in his famous book *Christianity and History*:

> Amongst historians, as in other fields, the blindest of all the blind are those who are unable to examine their own presuppositions. . . . It must be emphasised that we create tragedy after tragedy for ourselves by a lazy unexamined doctrine of man . . . which history does not support.[1]

1 pp. 140 ff.

History teaches us, says Butterfield, that 'it is essential not to have faith in human nature. Such faith is a recent heresy and a very disastrous one.' History has proved, and will go on proving everyone wrong who tries to avoid what the Bible teaches and what Jesus Christ taught, that humans are fallen creatures and basically evil and sinful (Luke 11:13). People try to avoid this diagnosis because they do not like it—it seems too radical.

An illustration. If you have cancer, which would you prefer: (*a*) To be told that you have it, and that there is an operation that can cure you; or, (*b*) To be given a superficial diagnosis and a few aspirin, and die as a result?

And Jesus not only made a diagnosis, he offered a cure, a salvation that matched the diagnosis—a topic that will concern us in a later chapter.

Sin and death

In what way did Jesus fulfil the promise of Genesis 3:15?

Discuss ways in which you have discovered the seriousness and power of sin.

Trace the effects of the fall in modern society in each of the areas mentioned. How might faith in God make a difference both spiritually and morally?

'History is full of examples of human attempts to get back to paradise without God'—discuss.

What relationship do you think there is between the diagnosis Jesus made of sin and his death on the cross?

CHAPTER 7

The Way of Faith in God and in the Future

Please read Genesis 15:1–7

Some people, when they first read the Old Testament, experience surprise if not disappointment: after the first eleven chapters it is almost entirely concerned with the Jews. 'Why should God be interested solely in the Jews?' people ask. 'Were there not, all through the centuries, brilliant empires vastly greater than tiny Israel? Why do these other nations get such little attention? Was God not interested in them?'

Yes he was. The Bible says that God has made all people everywhere from one original pair (Acts 17:26); that he is the God of the Gentiles as well as of the Jews (Rom 3:29); that he does not show favouritism (Acts 10:34–35); and that his will is that everyone should be saved (1 Tim 2:3–7). On the other hand, the Bible says that God chose Israel to play a special role in history. To understand this, we must go back to Genesis' account of the fall.

The background to God's choice of Israel

Humanity's original sin, we remember, was to grasp at moral and spiritual independence from God; and though God immediately showed the way to forgiveness and reconciliation, it soon became apparent that their disobedience had injected into the human race a virulent poison of determined independence from God.

Cain and Abel (Gen 4:1–15). Abel responded by faith to God's instructions, brought a sacrifice approved by God and was accepted (Heb 11:4). Cain, in the very act of bringing his sacrifice to God, arrogantly rejected God's instructions regarding his sacrifice and in anger against God murdered his brother Abel.

Cain's descendants (Gen 4:16–24). In this period, city building, animal husbandry, metallurgy, technology, music and poetry flourished. But violence grew worse. It was even gloried in, and made the subject of popular song, much as violence nowadays is constantly represented on television and films as the action of super, tough men, even in societies that are otherwise technologically advanced and culturally sophisticated. Young people, taking these violent screen stars as role models, learn to admire and then to practise violence.

The generation of the flood (Gen 6:1–7). By this time the human race as a whole had become so corrupt as a result of occult and demonic practices, evil and violence, that the race was in danger of permanent physical and moral degeneration. We would be fooling ourselves if we imagined that contemporary examples of the same kinds of things did not abound today.

Now, a gardener will sometimes cut down a diseased plant in the hope that the stock of the plant will grow up to be more healthy. In the same way God brought a colossal flood on the world and destroyed the whole human race except for one family unit, that of Noah, so that the human race might have a new and potentially healthier start.

The city and tower of Babel (Gen 11:1–9). The tower was probably an early form of ziggurat. In its time it was a marvel of architecture and technology, an evidence that humanity, though fallen, was made in the image of the Creator. The tragedy was that this brilliant project was undertaken in a spirit of arrogant pride and independence from God. Similarly today, space travel is a magnificent achievement of humanity's God-given abilities. But it is sad to hear some of those involved boast that people have flown round the moon and not seen God anywhere. That is like a man claiming that he had watched a play created by Shakespeare and deducing, since he had not met Shakespeare anywhere in the play, that Shakespeare did not exist. God is not a part of his created universe, any more than Shakespeare is a part of his play. But what increased enjoyment there would be in watching such a play in company with Shakespeare himself and then in being taught by him to write similar plays ourselves. Why then do people imagine that a true understanding and enjoyment of the universe is only possible through independence or denial of the Creator?

The worst result of the fall (see Rom 1:19–23). This was that men eventually tried to expunge all thought of the One True God, Creator. As a result they fell into superstition.

They deified the mindless forces of nature, and worshipped the gods of the sun, moon, storm, fertility, etc. And since these 'gods' were the products of human imagination, they were conceived as behaving among themselves more immorally than humans. So the worship of these gods corrupted humanity yet more.

Modern atheists hold a similar view. According to them, the ultimate powers that brought the human race into existence are the impersonal, mindless, purposeless forces of the universe. They do not call them 'gods' as the ancient idolaters did, but they are referring ultimately to the same things. Thus atheists have no ultimate hope for the universe as a whole, nor for the individual after death. For, according to them, the same impersonal forces that produced men and women will one day mindlessly destroy both humanity and the universe. Thus rational human beings are the products, slaves and hopeless prisoners of non-rational powers.

The purpose of God's choice of Israel

God's problem. How could he rescue humanity from the hopelessness of independence from God? How could he demonstrate to the nations his own reality and the glory and hope of human life when lived in fellowship with God, so that the nations might be attracted, brought back to God and blessed?

God's answer to the problem. He would choose one man, Abraham, and from his descendants he would create a new nation through whom people from all nations would come back to God and be blessed (Gen 12:3; 22:18; 26:4).

The basis of God's choice of Abraham and Israel. It was not that they were better than other people. Abraham, before God called him, was an idolater (Josh 24:14–15); and Israel were reminded that they were a stiff-necked people and warned that when they misbehaved, God would discipline them more severely than other nations (Deut 9:6–24; Amos 3:2) because of the importance of their role.

The purpose of God's programme for Abraham and Israel. He raised them up, first as a living testimony to the existence of the One True God, and as a protest against idolatrous interpretations of the universe. In that, Israel was for centuries unique. Secondly, he raised them up as an example of what it means to live in fellowship with the living God, to experience his love, power, salvation, guidance and laws, so that people of all nations might come to see the attractiveness of knowing God personally. And thirdly, he raised Israel up as the channel through whom the Saviour of the

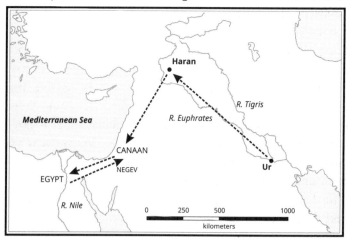

Abraham's Journey

world would come, so that the world would be able to recognize him when he came and find real hope in him.

The success of the programme. It is enough here to notice that through the Jewish nation and supremely through Jesus Christ, born of the seed of Abraham, uncountable millions of formerly pagan and idolatrous Gentiles have eventually been brought to living faith in the One, True and Living God. This is an undeniable fact of history; and the process is still going on in front of our eyes.

God's training of Abraham (Gen 11:26–25:11)

Arousing Abraham's hope. First, God revealed his glory to Abraham personally. He then led him to the land of Canaan, which he promised to give to him and to his seed, if for the present they were prepared to live as nomads without owning it.[1] Abraham was also told that for four hundred years his descendants would become slaves in a distant land, and only after that would God liberate them, bring them back to Canaan and give them the land as their inheritance. This certainly gave Abraham and his descendants a hope. But it was a long-term hope; and the practical question was: Dare they believe in it? Could they trust God sufficiently to adopt a nomadic lifestyle and continue living for some centuries simply on the basis of faith in God's promises? Adam and Eve in the garden had been unable to trust God's word. Millions since have likewise been unable. Could Abraham and his descendants? And would the promise eventually come true?

1 In fact, all Abraham ever did own in his lifetime was a small field with a cave in it that he used as a burial place for his wife, Sarah (Gen 23).

The testing of Abraham's faith (Gen 15–22). It was not very long before Abraham's faith in the promise met a fundamental difficulty. He was already old when God promised him this future inheritance. But he had as yet no son, and hence no hope of descendants to possess the promised inheritance. Abraham spoke to God, who promised him a son; and Abraham believed God the moment he made the promise (Gen 15:6). But God did not fulfil the promise at once. Now Sarah was barren; so to help God fulfil his promise, Abraham took a slave girl, and had a son by her. But God refused to regard this son as the one he had promised; and he made Abraham and Sarah wait until, as far as the physical possibility of becoming parents was concerned, their bodies were as good as dead. Abraham thus came to see clearly that his own powers were useless; if God's promises of descendants and inheritance were ever to be fulfilled in the future, God would have to do a miracle and bring new life out of virtually dead bodies. Abraham couldn't. And Abraham dared to believe; and the miracle eventually happened. The promised son was born. Also, centuries after Abraham's death, the long-term promise of the inheritance was also fulfilled.

The purpose of the testing of Abraham's faith. We recall that humanity's original sin, that caused the fall and ruined the human race, was to grasp at independence from God, and so to start the processes that would lead to death. Now God was teaching Abraham the first basic principle of the road back to true life and hope for the future: utter dependence on God, and faith in him and his promises.

The universal lesson to be drawn from Abraham's experience

History has demonstrated that God's promises to Abraham were true. His descendants eventually inherited the land of Canaan. And though from time to time God has subsequently expelled them from the land, as he said he would, his promises of their final restoration will also be fulfilled.

The promise that through Abraham and his seed all the nations of the world shall be blessed *has been dramatically fulfilled* through the birth of the Saviour of the world, Jesus Christ, the most famous descendant of Abraham and his son, Isaac.

Abraham's experience is not meant to teach us that any childless couple may have a child, if only they trust God. But it is cited in the New Testament as an example for all humanity. Abraham was justified by faith, says Genesis 15:6, when he learned to put his faith not in himself or his own works, but solely in the word of God who could bring life out of death. We too, says Romans 4:1-5, 19-25, can be justified and receive the gift of eternal life solely by faith, when we learn *not to rely on our own works*, but to believe in God who raised Jesus Christ from the dead.

The obedience of faith

Why do you think Cain refused to do what God said? Has this a lesson for us today?

What can we learn from the AIDS epidemic?

'Television and video can be morally corrupting.' Discuss.

How can the story of Noah help us to understand what faith in God involves? (See Heb 11:7.) What did Jesus use the story to illustrate? (See Luke 17:26–27.)

'Atheism is a cruel, long-term business'[1]—Jean-Paul Sartre. Discuss.

Why do you think Abraham believed God? How does the example of his faith help us to understand what faith really means?

1 *Words*, 157.

CHAPTER

Freedom and the Law

Please read Exodus 20:1–17

In this chapter we study the summary of the law that God gave to ancient Israel through Moses. The Ten Commandments have had a civilizing influence on millions of people, eventually spreading worldwide and being adopted by whole nations as the basis of their moral codes.

Our title 'Freedom and the Law' may well seem strange. To many people law is the opposite of freedom: freedom means being free to do what we like; law restricts or abolishes that freedom. But that is shallow thinking. In order to enjoy freedom we must have laws. If, for instance, we want to be free to walk the streets at night without fear, the State must lay down and enforce laws against mugging and murder.

'Yes,' someone will say, 'but the laws of the State are laid down with the consent of the majority of the citizens (except in a dictatorship). So the laws simply decree what we ourselves wish to be done (or not done). But the Ten

Commandments claim to be laid down by God. If then we accept this claim, we shall have to accept and obey these laws just because God says so, whether we like them or not. Will that not be the end of our personal freedom?'

But think again. We did not lay down the laws of nature. We respect them, of course, for if we don't, we destroy ourselves. But we do not normally complain that this removes our freedom. We know that life is not possible on any other terms. If we do not handle atomic reactors with sufficient care, the laws of physics produce a Chernobyl or a Fukushima. If we persistently smoke cigarettes we shall die, earlier than we need, of lung cancer. And what is true of the physical laws of nature is true of the moral laws laid down for us by the Creator. We had no say in the laying down of these laws either. Why should we? We did not create ourselves. However, our Creator has not laid down these laws in order to restrict our freedom; but in order to preserve our freedom and maximize our joy, as we shall now see by studying the example of Israel.

The basis of God's claim on Israel to keep his law

The preamble to the Ten Commandments (Exod 20:2). Here God not only introduces his law; he tells Israel why they should keep it: 'I am the LORD your God, who brought you out of the land of Egypt, out of the house of slavery.'

He thus reminds them that they had been slaves in the forced-labour camps of Egypt; and that it was he himself who had set them free. He was the God of liberation.

Having given them freedom from one form of slavery, he had no intention of imposing on them another. He was giving them his law to preserve and develop the freedom he had himself won for them. If they refused to keep his law, the nation, as he subsequently warned them (Deut 29), would sink into moral and spiritual degeneration and fall under the power of the neighbouring pagan nations.

Historical flashback. The story of how Israel came to be in Egypt, were eventually enslaved by the Egyptians, and how God set them free, is told in the Old Testament from Genesis 37 to Exodus 15. None of this was a mere accident of history. Indeed God informed Abraham long before it happened that his descendants eventually would be oppressed in a foreign country, and after that God would deliver them (Gen 15:13–14).

The nature of Israel's slavery in Egypt. As an ethnic minority they were oppressed by the Egyptians for political reasons. One of the pharaohs (the rulers of Egypt) attempted to get rid of them by genocide or ethnic cleansing. The Egyptian government refused to allow them to worship and serve God according to his instructions and their conscience. Such spiritual slavery is the worst kind of servitude people suffer: it imprisons and impoverishes not only the body but also the spirit.

The way God set Israel free. God did not require Israel to contribute to their liberation by fighting their own way out of Egypt. In their enfeebled state that would have been impossible anyway. God did all the liberating himself, first by sending his destroying angel to execute his judgment on Egypt. Then he used the forces of nature to overwhelm the Egyptian army at the Red Sea. All Israel had to do was to accept the liberation that God provided for them. They did not even have to merit deliverance by keeping God's law. Liberation, redemption, freedom—these were all free gifts. But after they had been set free they were commanded to keep the law which God laid down for them. This was not to restrict them but to enable them to enjoy their freedom to the full.

A lesson for all. The New Testament uses this experience of Israel's to illustrate the fact that sin has made captives of us all. We are chained to the past by the guilt of our sins. Unless that chain can be broken, we must eventually suffer the judgment of God. Moreover, like Israel, we cannot save ourselves, nor can we merit salvation by trying to keep God's law (Eph 2:8–9). But God has a deliverance for us too: he saves us from the guilt of our sins through the sacrifice of Christ, the Lamb of God—just as Israel was saved from God's destroying angel by the sacrifice and blood of the Passover lamb (see the story in Exodus chapter 12). And he saves us from the grip of Satan, by his own almighty power (Acts 26:18; Col 1:13). Then once we have experienced this liberation, and received our freedom, God will expect us to show our gratitude to him by keeping his commandments (John 14:21; Rom 8:3–4).

The principles of the Ten Commandments

The basic principle of love. Underlying all ten commandments is the basic principle of love: first, love to God; second, love to one's neighbour. The Old Testament book of Deuteronomy sums it up thus: 'Hear, O Israel: The Lord our God, the Lord is one. You shall love the Lord your God with all your heart and with all your soul and with all your might' (6:4–5 ESV). Accordingly, the first four commandments show how this love for God is to be expressed. The Old Testament book of Leviticus states the other great principle of law: 'You shall love your neighbour as yourself' (19:18). The last six commandments show how this love for our neighbour is to be expressed.

This shows us several important things:

(*a*) God's law is not some hard, legalistic code: its mainspring is love.

(*b*) God's law is balanced. Love for God must be followed by love for our fellow men and women. Love for people that is not based on love for God is not true love. As the New Testament puts it: 'By this we know that we love the children of God, when we love God and obey his commandments' (1 John 5:2). On the other hand, love for God that does not lead to love for our fellow men and women is not genuine love for God. The New Testament comments: 'Those who say, "I love God," and hate their brothers or sisters, are liars; for those who do not love a brother or sister whom they have seen, cannot love God whom they have not seen' (1 John 4:20).

(*c*) Love for God and people is not some sentimental feeling: it is an attitude of heart and will that shows itself in behaviour and action.

The first and second commandments (Exod 20:3–6). In these two commandments God demands his people's total allegiance. He says 'I the LORD your God am a jealous God' (20:5). In some languages 'jealousy' is a vice. But here it is a good thing. A man who really loves his wife will rightly be jealous of any rival. Just as adultery ruins the relationship between husband and wife, so disloyalty to the Creator ruins a creature's relationship with God and is an affront to his love:

(a) Paganism with all its many idols, its man-made gods, its deification of the forces of nature, obviously breaks these commandments.

(b) Atheism is doubly guilty. It rejects the One True God, and then exalts the forces of nature as the ultimate powers responsible for humanity's existence.

(c) Anything that we love or trust more than God is an idol. Covetousness, for instance, is idolatry (Col 3:5).

(d) Totalitarian governments sometimes demand from their subjects the absolute obedience that is due only to God. That is why they often ban the worship of God. To yield God's place in our hearts to a mere human government is to find ourselves enslaved to mere men. It is the very opposite of freedom (see the story of Daniel's three friends and their refusal to bow down to an idol in Daniel 3).

(e) History has shown the truth of Exodus 20:4–5. Nations that have substituted idols for God, or denied him altogether, have brought trouble not only on themselves but on succeeding generations.

The third commandment (20:7). God's name represents God's person and character, all that he is. This should be for us the highest, the most sacred thing of all—the ultimate value on which all other true values depend. When we blaspheme or swear, using God's name, or when we profess to believe in God and to be God's people, but live in a way that dishonours him, we degrade God in our own thinking and in the thinking of others.

The fourth commandment (20:8–11). This commandment reminded Israel that the world is God's world, for he made it. Our daily work was meant to be done in cooperation with God and to follow his pattern of creative work and rest. Regular rest from our normal work was designed by God to stop our daily work from becoming a slavery either for ourselves or for others. Such regular rest is necessary both spiritually, to give us time to remember and think about God, and to maintain bodily and mental health.

Commandments five and seven (20:12, 14) protect the sanctity of love, marriage and family life. In modern times, in many countries thousands of people have denounced these laws as restrictive and in the name of freedom have demanded sexual license. In some places even governments nowadays announce that the old idea of a two-parent family is obsolete. But the massive rise in crime and juvenile delinquency is directly attributable to the breaking of these two commandments.

Commandments six and eight (20:13, 15) protect the sanctity of life and of private property.

Commandment nine (20:16) protects the sanctity of truth. Interpersonal and international relationships, justice in business and in the law courts, psychological health, and sometimes a person's physical life, depend on people all telling the truth. If no one ever told the truth but everybody always told lies the result would be catastrophic social chaos, the shattering of all confidence. Without confidence, there is no security, peace, justice or freedom.

Commandment ten (20:17). The Hebrew word here translated 'covet' does not mean a passing feeling such as 'I should like to have a bicycle like my friend has'. It means 'to scheme to acquire' something that belongs to someone else. So Jesus said that not only is adultery wrong, but scheming in one's mind to acquire another man's wife is equivalent to the act of adultery (Matt 5:27–28). A vivid example of coveting is to be found in the Old Testament in 1 Kings 21.

Provision for failure

Jesus said that the first and greatest commandment is that we should love the Lord our God with all our heart, mind, soul and strength. It is obvious that none of us has reached this standard. We have all broken the greatest commandment, and thereby have committed the greatest sin.

God cannot lower his standards to accommodate either Israel's sin or ours. But in his mercy he has made a way by which we can find forgiveness. It is the way of sacrifice. We shall consider that in our next study.

For the classroom

Work with your students and memorize the Ten Commandments. Give more examples from daily life to show how they are necessary to preserve freedom and maximise its enjoyment.

Read to the students how Israel came to be in Egypt and how they were set free (Genesis 37 to Exodus 15) and get them to write an essay on it.

'Spiritual slavery is the worst kind of slavery.' Discuss.

Why do you think nations have sometimes suppressed the worship and service of God as the Egyptians did?

Discuss the similarity between the way God liberated Israel and the way he can save us. Pay particular attention to the fact that:

(a) No one can merit salvation through keeping God's law.

(b) God's law is to be kept as an outworking of salvation. Why do you think this is so?

Trace the allusions to the Passover in the New Testament at John 1:29; 1 Corinthians 5:7; 1 Peter 1:18–19; Revelation 5:6–9.

CHAPTER 9

The Way of Sacrifice and the Value of Life

Please read Leviticus 4:27–35

A basic principle of reconciliation with God

Previously in Chapter 5 we saw that as soon as Adam and Eve sinned they experienced the torment of a bad conscience. They felt naked and unfit to meet God, so they attempted to cover themselves with fig leaves. It was inadequate; and God himself provided them a better covering by slaying animals and making coats for them out of skins. Thus innocent animals died to cover the nakedness of the guilty man and woman before God.

In our last chapter we saw how God saved Israel from his wrath by the sacrifice and blood of the Passover lamb.

These are examples of a basic principle that is constantly repeated in the Bible. There is a way back to God for those who have broken God's law; there is a way of forgiveness and reconciliation with God. That way, however, is the way of substitutionary sacrifice; for sin carries the penalty of death, and that penalty must be paid before God can forgive us. 'Without the shedding of blood', says the Bible (Heb 9:22), 'there is no forgiveness.' That is why the central message of the gospel, for which the Old Testament Scriptures prepare us and which the New Testament explains in detail, is precisely this: 'Christ died for our sins in accordance with the [Old Testament] scriptures' (1 Cor 15:3). But this raises a fundamental question.

Why must sin carry a penalty in addition to consequences?

The difference between the consequences of sin and the penalty of sin. If I give a man a lethal dose of poison, he will die. His death is the consequence of my action, and not the penalty for it. It may be that if I am genuinely sorry, the man's wife and family will eventually forgive me for causing this awful consequence. But the State will not forgive me. For poisoning a citizen is not only an offence against a private individual, it is a crime against the laws of the State; and like all other such crimes, it carries a penalty. If then I am found guilty by the court, the judge will sentence me to the penalty prescribed by the law, and the penalty will be carried out.

The reason why the laws of the State prescribe penalties. It is not a question of revenge: the State itself would forbid the poisoned man's family to take revenge on me. It is because society as a whole has certain values that it regards as being so important that everything possible must be done to uphold them. Society therefore lays down laws to protect those values and inflicts appropriate penalties on those who infringe them. The law against murder, for example, reflects the value that society places on human life. If the State constantly allowed murderers to avoid paying the penalty, the implication would be that human life was no longer regarded as being supremely valuable: it could be destroyed with impunity. Millions of babies have been murdered as a result of 'abortion on demand'. Indeed, when, as has sometimes happened in some countries, the State itself has turned criminal, broken its own laws, and murdered thousands of its innocent citizens, the result is an appalling devaluation of life.

The seriousness of sin against our fellow men and women. The seriousness of not only murder but of any sin against our fellow men and women lies in the value of the individual. Even if human beings do not love and value each other, God loves and places an infinite value on each individual, since they are made in his image. It is precisely because God loves them that his law protects their value by laying down its penalty against those who sin against them.

The seriousness of sin against God. Since God is the source of life and the Creator of all, all sin is ultimately against God. Furthermore, since God himself is the supreme value, sin against him is of awesome significance. God could not possibly take the view that the penalty for sin need not be paid; for that would mean that in the end not only humanity but God himself did not really matter, that God's holiness, justice, truth, beauty and love were not all that valuable after all. People could sin against them with impunity, and easily be forgiven—if, indeed, forgiveness were even necessary.

God's answer to the human predicament. Our predicament is that we have all sinned against our fellow men and women and against God. The penalty for that, according to the Bible, is not only physical death but what the Bible calls the second death, that is, eternal banishment from the presence of God, to dwell for ever under the sense of God's holy displeasure against our sin. If we had to pay that penalty ourselves, we should never finish paying it. Here is the heart of the problem: God's justice demanded that the penalty be paid: God's love longed for our forgiveness. How could the impasse be resolved? God's answer was that he himself in the person of the Son of God, Jesus Christ, should by his death on the cross pay the penalty for us. All God's values would thus be upheld; at the same time forgiveness could be offered to all who would repent and believe: God could remain perfectly just, and yet justify those who believed in Jesus (Rom 3:26).

The function of animal sacrifices in the Old Testament

In Old Testament times, if someone sinned, and then repented and sought forgiveness from God, he had to bring a blemish-free animal, a goat or a lamb, to the altar in the tabernacle or temple, lay his hand on its head and kill it in the presence of God. The priest would smear some of the blood on the horns of the altar. The rest of the blood would be poured out at the base of the altar; and certain parts of the animal would be burned as a sacrifice on the altar. Then the person would be forgiven. Now intelligent ancient Israelites were well aware that the blood of animals could not wipe away human guilt; the death of a goat or a lamb could not pay the penalty of sin. They tell us this themselves (see Ps 40:6). What then was the function of these animal sacrifices?

They taught people that sin is costly. In some countries parents will give their children a toy shop to play with. It has bottles with toy sweets in them; and there is toy money with which the children can buy the sweets. Of course, even the children realize that neither sweets nor money are real. But not only does the toy shop keep them amused: it begins to teach them the value of things. In real life real sweets cost money, and must be paid for. So these animal sacrifices taught the people that sin is a very costly thing; there is always a penalty that must be paid.

They prepared people's minds to understand what the significance of the death and sacrifice of Christ would be, when God sent him into the world to be our Saviour. By using toy money to buy toy sweets the children would begin to learn the function of real money. Animal sacrifices were the 'toy money', so to speak; the suffering, death and blood of Christ would be the 'real money' that would really pay the real penalty and cost of sin.

They prepared people's minds to understand how the death of Christ applies to us men and women. The ancient ceremony made it very clear that when the animal sacrifice died it died not as an example for the sinner to follow, but as a substitute instead of the sinner. The person who sought forgiveness had to place his hand on the head of the animal, thus identifying himself with it, and then kill the animal. The animal died instead of the sinner, who was forgiven and went free. So is it with the death of Christ. We deserved the penalty of sin, which is death. When we accept Christ as Saviour, God counts his death as our death. Christ, talking of himself, explained it like this: 'The Son of Man came . . . to give his life a ransom for many' (Mark 10:45).

But what about those people who lived before Christ came into the world? If the blood of animals could not wipe away guilt, how could these people be forgiven?

An illustration. In some countries in recent history when a man wanted to buy an article, but did not have the money to pay for it there and then, he wrote the words 'I owe you' followed by the cost of the article on a piece of paper. The paper was worth little or nothing in itself. But it was an acknowledgement of the debt and a promise to pay it one day; and on this ground the man was allowed to take the article at once; but of course sometime later he had to pay the price and so redeem the promise of his 'I owe you'.

The ancient animal sacrifices were like those promises. They were an acknowledgement of the debt, and a promise that the debt would one day be paid in full. The person concerned was granted forgiveness there and then; and when Christ came and died as the real sacrifice for sin, Christ redeemed all those promises and paid the full cost of the forgiveness.

The differences between the sacrifice of Christ and the Old Testament animal sacrifices

There are many significant differences between the animal sacrifices offered in Old Testament times and the sacrifice of Christ, and it is immensely important for us to understand them. They are listed in the New Testament at Heb 9:11–10:18. See how many such differences you can spot.

Facing the consequences

What do you mean by the consequences of sin? Give some examples.

Why must sin carry a penalty?

Should parents lay down penalties for disobedience in order to teach their children true values?

John the Baptist announced Christ as 'the Lamb of God who takes away the sin of the world' (John 1:29). How does this bear on our topic?

On what basis can God forgive our sins?

CHAPTER 10

The Way of Personal Experience

Please read 1 Samuel 1:9–27

One of the most attractive features of the Old Testament is that while it is largely the history of a nation, it is full of detailed stories of striking individuals: housewives, army generals, farmers, kings, poets, civil servants, queens, prophets and courting couples. Many of them played a crucial role in the history of their nation; and still appear to us as spiritual heroes and heroines whose example challenges us to emulate them. We shall here have space to study only one of them.

Hannah: The triumph of devotion over corruption and superstition (1 Sam 1:1–2:36)

A heroine in times of national breakdown. Hannah lived at a time (about 1100 BC) when her nation was going through a protracted period of moral, spiritual and political chaos. Some four hundred years had passed since Joshua had led Israel into Canaan (see the book of Joshua). During those centuries Israel had been what is called in political terms a theocracy. That is to say, unlike the surrounding contemporary nations, Israel had no human king. It was their belief that God was their king; and he governed through the Ten Commandments and through a detailed set of criminal, civil, social and ceremonial laws that formed the basis of a solemn covenant Israel had entered into with God. These laws were housed in the one and only temple that the nation had, and the twelve tribes were organised territorially around that central temple. From time to time the priests were responsible to gather the nation together, to rehearse the terms of the covenant, and to teach the people God's laws. Then the local elders in each town and village were in their turn responsible for seeing that God's laws were carried out in their communities. This simple system of government gave to each tribe and each region the maximum of autonomy; and as long as the people's faith in God and respect for his laws remained healthy and vigorous, it worked well. When from time to time two or three tribes compromised with the paganism of the surrounding nations and so fell under their power, God raised up special deliverers who were not only able military leaders, but also moral and spiritual judges and

Timeline 1. Key People in the History of Israel c.1500–930 BC

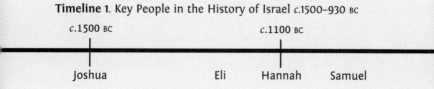

reformers. Time and time again they restored the people to their former freedom under God. The stirring story of their exploits is told in the book of Judges.

But by Hannah's time the nation's system of government was in danger of breaking down completely. A theocracy could only work if the nation as a whole maintained a genuine and vigorous faith in God; and the fact is that the people at large were beginning to lose their faith in God and their respect for his worship in the temple. It was not altogether their fault. The trouble lay with the priests in the temple. The younger, active priests at the time were flagrantly immoral and profane. And when that kind of thing happens religion eventually becomes little more than superstition. It did in this case. There was in the temple a piece of ceremonial furniture called the ark. It was regarded as a symbol of God's throne because it contained the two tables of stone on which were written the Ten Commandments. But when Israel's enemies, the Philistines, attacked Israel in battle, the priests and people brought this ark out of the temple to the army, superstitiously thinking that it possessed magical powers and would be able to save them from their enemies in spite of the fact that they themselves were daily flouting God's law contained in that very ark (1 Sam 4). It didn't, of course. Superstition never does. And Israel suffered a devastating defeat.

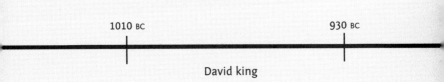

1010 BC   930 BC

David king

69

Hannah saves her nation from disintegration. With immorality in the priesthood, respect for the temple lost, true faith in the living God replaced by superstition, and religion debased into magic, the nation had lost the very centre and heart that kept it together. The danger was that the nation would disintegrate into twelve independent tribes. But there was one man who, by the sheer power of his moral and spiritual authority, averted this danger. He was the prophet Samuel. He brought the people back to repentance, to confession of sin, and to genuine faith and dependence on God, and so to victory over their enemies. He also, under God, guided the people in the creation of a new political institution, a monarchy; and after its initial teething troubles, he saw to the selection of the great and famous King David, who united the nation as none before or after him ever did. By his own example of faith in God, his defence of the nation, his organisation of the building of a new temple, and his extremely popular religious poetry, David brought the nation's worship and service of God to new heights.

If a great deal of the credit for all this goes to the prophet Samuel, even greater credit must go to Hannah. Without her there would have been no Samuel! She was his mother.

Hannah's personal faith and devotion to God. From one point of view Hannah was no different from any other woman of her time, but her early married life was very bitter. In the first place she was only one of her husband's two wives, for polygamy was then a normal practice. Secondly, she was barren in an age when that condition was considered a shame and disgrace. Hannah longed to fill her arms with children and her days with the business of motherhood. Instead, she suffered deep anguish at the hands of her husband's other wife, Peninnah, who taunted and provoked her because of her barrenness. Thus family life, which should have meant love and acceptance, was turned into a battlefield of bitter competition. Her husband loved her; she knew that, but he did not really understand what she was going through. In her distress she turned to the Lord. For eventually Hannah's frustration and anguish led her to reconsider life's values, meaning and purpose.

Why did she so desperately want to be a mother? Instinct cried out for it. But was there nothing more to motherhood than the satisfying of biological urges? Hannah came to believe there was. Was not motherhood's highest purpose to serve the interests of God who had designed and created motherhood? She looked around her and saw the moral and spiritual chaos of her nation. The priests in the temple, who should have taught the people to live for God, were using their high office merely to satisfy their greed and to indulge their biological urges. She watched her husband's other wife proudly boasting as though the credit for her childbearing ability were due to her and not to God her Creator. Thus the atmosphere of the home was polluted with tension and bitterness.

Peninnah's provocation and humiliation of Hannah reached a peak at the annual visit the family made to worship God at Shiloh. Hannah's reaction was not to denounce motherhood and pretend she did not after all want a child. She geared her desire for a child to God's will and interests and to the good of her nation. She thought it out very carefully. If God were to give her a child, then she wanted to give him something in return. What would be the most precious thing she could give? That which the Lord had given her, the child! If the child were to serve the Lord in the temple then it would have to be a boy. So she prayed to God and promised that if he gave her a son, she would devote him at the earliest possible age to the service of God on behalf of the nation.

Eli, the priest, watching and listening, misunderstood her. He thought she was drunk. He should have recognised fervent prayer, but he didn't—another symptom of the sad decline of the priesthood. She did not ask Eli to pray for her; she did not doubt that God had heard her. But she asked him to try to understand. And having poured out her heart to God, she went away and ate, no longer sad.

Hannah believed in a God who listened and cared and who could be trusted. Maybe her years of unhappiness had driven her to talk to God far more than she would otherwise have done. Each time she watched Peninnah go proudly through a pregnancy and then give birth to a healthy baby she must have turned to God in tears with the question, 'Why not me?' Life's deep questions had brought her closer to the only one who could give meaning to her life.

God gave Hannah a son whose very name ('asked from God') was a constant reminder that he was a gift from the God who listens and understands. Hannah, true to her promise, took the little boy she had waited so long for to the temple and said: 'I prayed for this child and the Lord has granted me what I asked of him. So now I give him to the Lord!'

Hannah's example to us. How then as parents and teachers shall we prepare our own children and students for parenthood? What ideals shall we set before them? In many so-called civilized countries, politicians wrestle with rising crime and social unrest, much of it the result of the breakdown in family life and the desacralising of marriage and parenthood. Perhaps the answer to the problem lies not with the politicians but with parents throughout the nation and especially with mothers. What a profound change would come over society if marriage and parenthood recovered their high dignity as being a sacred calling from God! What untold benefits would accrue to society if children were brought up to think that whatever career they followed, their prime motivation should be, like Samuel, selflessly to serve God and the nation!

Children and their parents

Hannah's early married life was not happy. How might you have expected her to react? How did she react?

Hannah saw herself as God's servant (1 Sam 1:11). How did she see God?

Follow the story and note why Hannah was so sure Samuel had been given to her by God.

From evidence in the chapter analyse the characters of Hannah and Peninnah. Which woman do you think would be the better mother? Why?

How did Eli the priest fail his children (read 1 Sam 2)? What effect do you think their bad behaviour had on the way people thought about God?

CHAPTER 11

The Way of the King

Please read 1 Samuel 17

In this chapter and the next we are going to study one of the most famous of all the Old Testament characters, King David. He became king over the tribe of Judah in 1010 BC. Seven years later he was made king over all the tribes of Israel, thus uniting the nation under one crown. In all, he reigned for forty years. Much loved in his own day, he was looked back upon by later generations as Israel's greatest, almost ideal, king. So much so that, when the Old Testament prophets spoke about the future coming of the great messianic king, destined by God to be the Saviour of Israel and of the world, they pointed to two features (among others) that would serve to identify this Messiah–King–Saviour.

Timeline 2. Key People in the History of Israel *c.*1050–930 BC

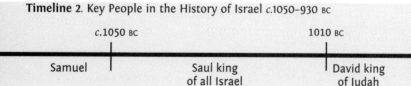

On the one hand he would be a descendant of King David, born in David's ancestral village, Bethlehem. On the other hand, though infinitely greater than King David, he would in many significant respects resemble King David. In other words they held that King David was a prototype of the coming messianic king. Let us now examine, therefore, some of the reasons for this popularity in his own day and for the colossal influence he has wielded ever since.

His military prowess

His defeat of Goliath (1 Sam 17). Judged simply as literature, the story of David's fight with the giant Goliath is worthy to be compared with the epic contest between single-combat heroes, such as that between Hector and Achilles, depicted by Homer, the ancient Greek, in his immortal poem the *Iliad*. But the story of David and Goliath is also history. It occurred at a time when the Sea Peoples, the Philistines, had invaded Palestine and settled along the south-western coastal plain (their settlements have been extensively excavated in recent decades); and they were now beginning to penetrate the interior, in an attempt to subdue the little nation of Israel. During one of the battles, the Philistines, following the military custom of the day, challenged Israel to settle the issues at stake by single combat. None of Israel's leading warriors, least of all the reigning king, Saul,

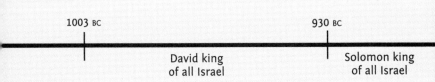

1003 BC — David king of all Israel

930 BC — Solomon king of all Israel

had the courage to face the Philistine hero who was a physical giant and massively armed. So David volunteered. He was only a youth, with little or no military experience. But as a shepherd his faith in God had nerved him to fight with marauding lions and bears to protect his sheep. Now in this national emergency he deliberately armed himself with what seemed the absurdly weak weapons of a shepherd's staff and sling, so that all might see that he relied for victory not on his own strength or skill, but on God. And he triumphed spectacularly. It won him an instant place in his nation's heart (though, in addition, the undying jealousy and persecution of the reigning king, Saul). What is more, the example of his giant-defying faith has fired the imagination and stiffened the resolve of thousands of people since, who in contests of all kinds, both literal and metaphorical, have struggled against overwhelming odds and won.

His international campaigns. David eventually became king at a time when there was a power vacuum in the Middle East between the superpowers based on the Euphrates to the east, and Egypt to the south. David took advantage of this, and eliminated the oppression that the surrounding small nations had exerted over Israel for some centuries (see the book of Judges). He also brought Israel to the point where she might well have developed, if things had turned out differently, into a world power like Egypt, Babylon and Assyria. That is why Israel looked back on David's reign (and that of his successor, Solomon, who made a marriage alliance with the daughter of the reigning Egyptian pharaoh) as the zenith of the nation's history.

His founding of Jerusalem (2 Sam 5)

Practically the first thing David did upon becoming king of all twelve tribes of Israel, was to found Jerusalem and to turn it into the nation's capital city and his own head-quarters, which was therefore called David's city. It was a stroke of genius. If he had done nothing else, this alone would have secured him a place in history.

It united all twelve tribes into a coherent nation; it gave them a city to which each and every Israelite, of whatever tribe, could feel they belonged. It gave the nation a heart. And throughout the centuries of the Jewish dispersion, it has given Jews all around the world a unifying centre.

Just outside its walls Jesus Christ, the man who was God, was eventually crucified, rose from the dead and ascended into heaven. Unforgettably, it was from Jerusalem that the Christian gospel began its worldwide spread.

Today, after a very variegated history, Jerusalem is the holy city of three worldwide religions: Judaism, Christianity and Islam.

According to biblical prophecy, Jerusalem will yet be the centre of concern for all the nations of the earth (Zech 12, 14); and it will be to this city that Jesus Christ will return.

In the vision of eternity that is given us in the last book of the Bible, the eternal heavenly city is called the New Jerusalem (Rev 21).

His political values

The sacredness of power. Ancient Israel believed that royal power was sacred: it was conferred by God through his prophets, and symbolised by the anointing of the king in God's name. Even so, the king was not imposed upon the people against their will, but only by their consent (see 1 Sam 10; 11:14–15; 15:1; 2 Sam 2, 5; 1 Kgs 12). Now when David's predecessor, Saul, became insanely jealous of David's popularity with the people and made many attempts to murder him, David persistently refused to use his military power to assassinate Saul, even though he had many opportunities to do so, and even though the only alternative was exile. Saul had, at the beginning of his reign, been anointed by God and acclaimed by the people. For David, then, to grab power by assassinating Saul would have been a sacrilege (see 1 Sam 24:1–7; 26:1–12). Only when Saul and the crown prince, Jonathan, had been killed in battle by the Philistines, did David (though long since designated and anointed as king-to-be) present himself to the people for them to make him king.

One does not have to go back far into history to see what happens when political power ceases to be regarded as a sacred trust, conferred by God with the consent of the people, and becomes something to be grabbed, and held on-to by endless shootings, murders and assassinations, and in total disregard for the free wishes of the people.

The sanctity of human life (2 Sam 3:17–39). True to the actual conditions prevailing in the ancient world, the Old Testament is full of the records of battles (so, of course, is world news today). But killing enemies on the battlefield is one thing, murdering ambassadors and diplomatic envoys is another. It is interesting to read, therefore, of David's insistence on the sanctity of human life, and his public denunciation of one of his generals for abusing military power, and treacherously 'shed[ding] the blood of war in peace' by assassinating a diplomatic envoy as a revenge killing (1 Kgs 2:5 RV). Modern examples of ambassadors being blown up by government-sponsored terrorism would not be hard to find.

The sanctity of treaties and of the rights of ethnic minorities (2 Sam 21). The Gibeonites were a Gentile minority whose security among the Israelites was guaranteed by a solemn covenant, sworn in the name of God by the responsible leaders in Israel (Josh 9). For some centuries they had lived peaceably in Israel, when for political reasons King Saul and his royal house tried to eliminate them by ethnic cleansing and genocide. David held it to be an outrage both against the Gibeonites and against the sanctity of treaties entered into in the name of God. He therefore allowed the Gibeonites to prescribe such punishment as would restore their security and their faith in Israel's word of honour.

The sanctity of sex and of private property (2 Sam 11:1–12:25). Critics of the Old Testament have often pointed out that King David at one stage committed adultery with the wife of one of his army officers, and then arranged for her husband to be killed. 'Is this', they ask, 'the kind of man that the Bible declares to be "a man after [God's] own heart"?' (1 Sam 13:14). But the critics overlook a most significant thing. If any of the oriental emperors that were David's contemporaries had decided to take the wife of one of his subjects, he would have taken her without compunction. And woe betide her husband if he objected! But in Israel, David's sin was recorded in detail in the state archives and then eventually published in the Old Testament book of Samuel. Published also was the prophet Nathan's denunciation of David's double sin on the ground that it was an outrage against the sacred sanctities of life, sex and marriage, and the citizen's right to a personal, private domain of body, mind and property which must not be violated by any government, however powerful and autocratic. More remarkable still was the publication of David's admission of guilt and confession that it was sin not only against his subjects but also against God. Moreover, not only was David's sin exposed by the biblical historian: David himself wrote about it in his poetry which became part of Israel's public hymn-book, and which we shall discuss in our next chapter.

The use of power

What was the source of David's certainty that he could defeat Goliath?

What was the difference between the attitudes of David and Goliath to God?

Why do you think that David did not simply use his power to get rid of Saul as many other leaders would have done? What does David's behaviour teach us about the right attitude to power?

Why is it important to the individual and society that the sanctities mentioned in this section be respected? What relevance has faith in God to preserving them? Discuss practical ways in which we can build such ethical values into our own lives and promote them in our society today.

CHAPTER

The Poetry and Prophecy of King David

David was not only a warrior and a king, he was a musician, a prolific poet and a prophet. Many of his psalms became part of his nation's liturgy in the public service of the temple at Jerusalem. Thereafter they became part of the Bible and have since been translated into a thousand languages and more, and read and sung by millions. Multitudes have found that the way David pours out his own heart in his poetry strikes profound chords in their own hearts and comforts them in time of suffering and adversity.

Psalms of contrition, repentance and forgiveness. Psalm 32:3–4 reveals that after his double sin of adultery and murder (see 2 Sam 11:1–12:25 and our preceding chapter), David for a while attempted to brazen the whole thing out and to refuse to confess his sin. The result was the torment of a guilt-ridden conscience and agonising psychosomatic effects. Psalm 51 records his plea for forgiveness when he was eventually brought to confess his sin to God. Psalm

32:1–2 captures his intense relief and outburst of joy when he realised that his sins were forgiven. In Psalm 51:12–13 he acknowledges what all people feel when they have discovered the joy of forgiveness: their duty to share this divine blessing with other people and to seek their conversion. And the New Testament (Rom 4:5–8) assures us that whether our sins are great and lurid, or small, mean and ordinary, we too may have the same personal experience as David did, and on the same terms.

The Shepherd Psalm (Ps 23). In the ancient Middle East kings were thought of as shepherds of their people; but David had in addition been a literal shepherd before he became a king. His own feelings of self-sacrificing devotion to both his sheep and then his people brought home to his heart God the Shepherd's infinitely more devoted care for him throughout this life, through its peaceful scenes, dangerous places and on into the eternal home of God in heaven. It has brought real comfort to millions of readers as it has led them to know God not only as some distant, majestic, awe-inspiring figure, but as a personal, loving, caring Saviour.

A song of propaganda (2 Sam 1:17–27). David must have realised that his poems, songs and psalms would be read and sung by the general public, and this particular song, we are told, was written and taught to the people as a deliberate piece of government propaganda. But what unusual propaganda! When King Saul, David's archenemy and would-be murderer, died in battle, and the men of Judah anointed David as their king, he wrote this song in order to shape the Judahites' opinion of King Saul. There is no attempt made to cut Saul's name out of the history books;

no attempt at character assassination; not even one word of criticism, even though David had many good reasons to bear grudges against Saul. There is in fact nothing but an expression of David's affection for Saul and Jonathan in their lives and of his respect for them in their deaths. He exhorted his people to remember all the benefits that King Saul had given to his country. What a positive difference the more frequent inclusion of such poetry would make to history writing! What a breath of fresh air such attitudes would bring into politics!

David's prophecies of the coming Saviour–King–Messiah. Aware as he was of his own faults and short-comings as a king and the intractable problem of human sin, injustice, treachery and cruelty, David had been given a covenant by God that his royal dynasty would last for ever and that eventually one of his descendants would prove to be the God-sent Messiah (*Christos* in Greek) and Saviour of the world (see 2 Sam 7:13 and compare Jer 23:5). This promise was fulfilled by Jesus, who, as the Apostle Paul put it, 'was descended from David according to the flesh' (Rom 1:3). David's Psalm 110:1 is quoted by Christ and his apostles in the New Testament more than any other psalm. David predicted that the Messiah would prove to be more than human, to be God's incarnate Son who, after death by crucifixion (vividly predicted and described in Ps 22), would be raised by God to a position of supreme authority in heaven until the time came for him to return to earth and put all his enemies beneath his feet (see also Pss 16, 118 and Acts 2, 3).

David a prototype of the Messiah. David suffered much in his lifetime. As a young man, though already anointed by God's prophecy as the king-to-be, he was rejected by Saul, hounded and persecuted, until in the end he went into exile with the Gentiles before eventually returning to Israel as their king. Many of his early psalms reflect his sufferings during those years and give us an insight into the sufferings of Jesus the Messiah. He, too, was anointed by God, but rejected and cast out by his own Jewish people, though accepted by millions of Gentiles. Like David, he too will one day return as the Saviour or Judge both of Israel and the world.

In middle life, after he had been long on the throne, David suffered a rebellion, partly through his own fault. The bitterest thing about it was that it was led by his own son, Absalom. It pushed him off his throne and into exile, where Absalom would have had him murdered if he could. David's troops eventually defeated the rebel armies; but that posed David a heart-breaking problem. As Absalom's father he longed to spare Absalom's life, so he gave orders that he should not be executed. But he was not only Absalom's father; he was the nation's king and supreme judge. And justice demanded Absalom's execution. David's subsequent lament over his rebellious son is one of the most moving passages in all literature: 'O my son Absalom, my son, my son Absalom! Would I had died instead of you, O Absalom, my son, my son!' (2 Sam 18:33).

David's sorrow opens for us a window into the heart of God. For he too has suffered a rebellion on the part of us his creatures. As moral governor of the universe, his justice demanded our death. As our Creator, his love longed for our salvation. But he found a solution which David could not: in the person of his Son, he bore the penalty of our sins by dying for us on the cross so that his love may forgive and save all who will repent and be reconciled to him.

The good shepherd

Why do you think people find it so difficult to admit that they have done wrong? What were the terms on which David received forgiveness? You will find it helpful to read Romans 4:1-8. Note that although God forgave David and removed the guilt of his sin, God did not remove the consequences of the sin (2 Sam 12).

Read the Shepherd Psalm (Ps 23). How does it help you to understand what Jesus meant when he said: 'I am the Good Shepherd'? (See John 10:1-21.)

How do you think David was able to keep his attitude to Saul free from bitterness? Where can we learn from his example?

Discuss the use Jesus made of Psalm 110:1 to prove that the Messiah (i.e. he himself) was more than a human descendant of David. (See Matt 22:41-45.)

'The fulfilment of prophecy confirms the reliability of the Bible'—discuss this statement. In this context it is helpful to see that David's prophecies are part of a much wider prophetic dimension in the Bible—unique in all of literature. In Appendix A we give a list of some of the predictions about the coming Messiah (Christ) made in the Old Testament which were fulfilled in the New Testament.

CHAPTER

The Way of Wisdom

Read Proverbs 1:7–19

The Bible is not just one book. It is a fascinating library of books representing many different literary genres. In this series we have already looked briefly at history books like Genesis, and books of law and ritual like Exodus and Leviticus. In our last chapter we enjoyed some of the magnificent poetry of the book of Psalms. Now we consider three books of the Old Testament, examples of what is known as 'Wisdom literature'.[1]

The first is the book of Proverbs. It is concerned with the question: how ought we to order our lives for the best, so as to make the most of them, and not to waste or ruin them? The second is the book of Ecclesiastes. It deals with a deeper question: what is the purpose of life? The third is the book of Job. It asks a still more profound question: why do good people suffer? When people have tried to live their lives as

---

1 The Song of Solomon is also categorized with the books of Wisdom Literature, but we will not have space to consider it here.

best they can, according to God's laws, why does God allow them to suffer, sometimes even more than wicked people?

We will briefly consider the second two, but in this chapter we will mainly think about the book of Proverbs and on its question: What is the wisest way to live?

Proverbs

We face this question at every level—What is the best way to run the country? How shall we bring up the children? What attitude shall I take to my school work? What kind of person shall I choose for my partner? And so forth. Nations have very often summed up their experience in short, pithy, vivid statements, which are easily remembered.

Now no one proverb is meant to say all that could be said about any particular question. It often states vividly one principle among several, all of which will need to be borne in mind, and each applied in the appropriate context. That is why some proverbs sometimes seem to contradict each other.

1. 'Do not answer fools according to their folly, or you will be a fool yourself' (Prov 26:4).

2. 'Answer fools according to their folly or they will be wise in their own eyes' (26:5).

In the book of Proverbs, then, there are long collections of pithy and often unconnected proverbs covering many situations in life. In addition, however, there are some longer passages of connected advice to young people (e.g. 1:8–9:18); and on this we now concentrate.

The fundamental principle of wisdom. The key principle underlying the book of Proverbs is: 'The fear of the LORD is the beginning [that is, the basic, controlling principle] of wisdom' (9:10; cf 1:7).

It is this that distinguishes true wisdom from mere cleverness or shrewdness. In many countries, for instance, it is taken for granted that the smart way to succeed is to use bribery. Proverbs acknowledges that bribery can be effective. See, for example: 'A bribe is like a magic stone in the eyes of those who give it; wherever they turn they prosper' (17:8; see also 18:16). But though bribery can lead to apparent success, the wisdom that is founded on fear of the Lord condemns it as morally evil. See, for example: 'The wicked accept a concealed bribe to pervert the ways of justice' (17:23). Conversely: 'Those who are greedy for unjust gain make trouble for their households, but those who hate bribes will live' (15:27).

Similarly, Proverbs is aware that some people pretend to fear the Lord, but use religion as a cloak for wrongdoing. It warns us: 'the sacrifice of the wicked is an abomination to the Lord' (15:8); 'When one will not listen to the law, even one's prayers are an abomination' (28:9).

True wisdom springs from the recognition that the world is God's world. He created it and organised it in his divine wisdom; and to be wise, we must live according to his laws and ordinances (see 8:22-36). To go against the wisdom of God's laws is folly and will end in disaster: 'all who hate me [God's wisdom] love death' (8:36).

Because it is God's world, we can learn lessons even from the animals and insects that God has made. 'Go to the ant, you lazybones; consider its ways, and be wise' (6:6). The ant does not have to be driven to work. Instinct tells it that if it doesn't work to gather food in summer it will perish in winter. So we too must learn to anticipate our future needs, and work now while we have opportunity to provide for them. That would mean, for example, not wasting our time at school; but rather working hard to be educated and trained, so as to be able to provide for ourselves when we leave school.

Because it is God's world, and God in his wisdom gave all of us work to do, we must not be lazy. Laziness is moral foolishness. Proverbs gives us very vivid descriptions of the lazy man:

- He not only enjoys the drowsy pleasure of lying in bed too long: he is hinged to his bed like a door to its frame (26:14): he turns round, as if to get out; but instead of getting out, turns over onto his other side and goes back to sleep again.
- He makes absurd excuses and exaggerates the difficulties facing him (26:13; 22:13, 'There is a lion outside!').
- Eventually through neglect and missed opportunity, his life comes to irreversible disaster, like a farm which has been allowed to go to ruin (24:30–34).

Because God loves us, he warns young people not to get into the wrong company and in particular not to get involved with gangs and with the Mafia (1:10–19). They will hold out the prospect to a young man of making a lot of money quickly, by robbing people. Such thugs and criminals, says Proverbs, are less intelligent than birds. If a bird sees you lay a trap for it, it will not enter it. But these men 'lie in wait for their own blood; they waylay only themselves' (1:18); that is to say, in ambushing others, they will eventually be arrested, imprisoned, perhaps executed; and in the end have to face God's judgment.

Because it is God's world and he made our bodies, Proverbs warns us not to abuse our bodies and minds with excessive alcohol, or any other drugs. 'Wine is a mocker, strong drink a brawler' (20:1); that is, drunkenness turns a man into a mocking, brawling lout. 'The drunkard and the glutton will come to poverty, and drowsiness will clothe them with rags' (23:21). Drunkenness leads to woe, sorrow, strife, complaints, bruises, bloodshot eyes (23:29-30). Proverbs urges a man, while he is still sober, to visualize what a fool he will make of himself if he gets drunk. It gives a very vivid description of the confused feelings and thoughts of a drunk man: first the fascination and the smoothness of the drink (23:31); but then the sudden bite of a serpent and the poison of a viper. Blurred vision and uncontrollable imagination (23:33). Unsteady legs, like someone at sea trying to sleep lying on the top of the rigging (23:34). Aware of being drunk and defenceless, but with false courage promising himself another drink when he wakes up (23:35).

Because God made our bodies and set up the family as the basic social unit, Proverbs forbids fornication, adultery and promiscuity, and vividly warns of the dangers, and sometimes lethal consequences, of these sins (see, e.g. 7:6-27). In light of the epidemic of AIDS, innocent young people need to hear this gruesome warning.

Proverbs is aware, of course, that often young people resent being told what to do by their parents and teachers. But it points out that behind the moral law stands God, who loves even more than the best parent loves a child. It is, moreover, precisely because he loves us that he will, when necessary, rebuke and discipline us in order to make our lives a delight to him (3:11-12).

God's standards are high. By ourselves and in our own strength we cannot fulfil them. Therefore Proverbs urges us to 'trust in the LORD with all your heart, and do not rely on your own insight. In all your ways acknowledge him, and he will make straight your paths' (3:5-6).

Like many another book in the Old Testament, however, the three Wisdom books raise questions that find their ultimate answers only in Christ.

Big questions from Ecclesiastes and Job

The great and wise King Solomon, the successor to King David, wrote a great deal of the book of Proverbs, but in the end even he became foolish (1 Kgs 11:1-11). He was good at theory, poor at practice. The only perfect wise man was the Lord Jesus Christ. He described himself as 'something greater than Solomon' (Matt 12:42). In him 'are hidden all the treasures of wisdom and knowledge' (Col 2:3). And those who trust him discover that Christ 'became for us wisdom from God, and righteousness and sanctification and redemption' (1 Cor 1:30).

The author of the second wisdom book, Ecclesiastes, looks at life under the sun, that is, life as bounded simply by this earth. He therefore comes frequently to the conclusion that much of life's activities are a mere 'going round in circles', and ends in vanity, emptiness and frustration. But the New Testament has the ultimate answer to his pessimism. Christ has risen from the dead: death is not the end; and because Christ is risen, 'our labour is not in vain in the Lord' (1 Cor 15:51-58).

The third wisdom book, Job, certainly gives us some

answers to the questions: Why does God allow those who trust him to suffer? Is God just? Does he act fairly? Can we trust him even in face of pain, disaster and illness? But the most powerful reason for trusting God through thick and thin is given us in the New Testament: 'We know that all things work together for good for those who love God. . . . He who did not withhold his own Son, but gave him up for all of us, will he not with him also give us everything else?' (Rom 8:28, 32). Just as gold is put through the fire to cleanse it from impurities and increase its value to the maximum, so God's training of his people, and the trials he puts them through are designed, as they were with Job, to purify their faith and develop their character so that they may enjoy the life to come to the full (1 Pet 1:6–9).

For the classroom

Discuss the meaning of 'The fear of the Lord is the beginning of wisdom', and relate this principle to practical situations (see, for example, Prov 1:29; 2:5; 3:7; 8:13; 10:27; 14:26–27; 15:33; 16:6; 19:23; 22:4; 23:17; 24:21).

Get each student to choose a proverb from the book of Proverbs, and discuss with the class what it means to them.

Find other examples in the book of Proverbs where we can learn from the animal world. See, for example, Proverbs 26:11; and compare 2 Peter 2:20–22 in the New Testament.

In what way do you think that God's warnings against bad company, involvement with drugs, and sexual promiscuity show his love for us?

Memorize some of the proverbs, especially Proverbs 3:5–6.

CHAPTER

The Way of the Prophets

Somewhere between a quarter and a third of the whole of the Old Testament is taken up with the writings of a special class of men called the Prophets. To understand why they are so important in the Old Testament and so relevant and important for us today, we must recall (see Chapter 8) the special role which God called the nation of Israel to play. He raised them up to be:

1. A living testimony to the existence of the One True God and a protest against all idolatrous interpretations of the universe.

2. An example of what it means to live in fellowship with the living God, to experience his love, power, salvation, laws and guidance, so that people of all nations might come to see the attractiveness of knowing God personally.

3. The divinely appointed and authenticated channel through whom the Saviour of the world would come into the world, so that all might see that there was real hope for the human race, in spite of

its sins, and be able to recognize the Saviour of the world when he came, and their need for him.

Now so long as Israel remembered God's generosity to them, and gratefully lived according to his laws, all went well. But the Israelites in themselves were no better than anyone else; they were sinful like the rest of us. They increasingly abused their special role, broke God's laws, and sinned just as badly, if not worse, than the surrounding nations. As a result God made them an example to the world of how not to live, so that the rest of us might be taught the holiness of God, his hatred of sin, his standards of righteousness and the inevitable consequences of breaking them.

This is where the prophets come in. They were not simply men who foretold the future—though they did issue remarkable prophecies. They were not priests—though some of them came from priestly families. They did not conduct services in the temple. They were great preachers and reformers who exposed political sins, economic malpractices, social wrongs and religious hypocrisies at all levels of society. They called on the nation as a whole, and individuals in particular, to repent, to change their way of living, to return to God, and prophesied disaster if they did not repent.

All too often, however, the nation mocked, or even persecuted the prophets and continued their sinful way of life. As a result they suffered what God had warned: overwhelming defeat, the loss of their country and mass deportation first to Assyria and then to Babylon. In this they have become a warning to us even today; for if the ancient Jews were no better than us, we are not necessarily better than they. Their experience reminds us of the judgment of God that will overtake us, as individuals and nations, if we do not repent of our sins. The New Testament sums up the lesson that we should learn: 'Now we know that whatever the [Old Testament] law says, it speaks to those who are under the law [i.e. originally the Israelites], so that every mouth may be silenced, and the whole world may be held accountable to God [i.e. for having done the same sins as the Israelites]' (Rom 3:19).

The prophets in the Old Testament are generally referred to as the Minor Prophets (because they wrote only small books) and the Major Prophets (because they wrote large books). We shall here take as examples one of the Minor Prophets and two of the Major Prophets.

The prophecy of Amos

By Amos's time, the nation was politically divided: two tribes in the south, ten in the north. Amos was a southerner, born in Judah, but he preached largely in Samaria among the ten northern tribes of Israel. He lived during the reigns of Uzziah, king of Judah (779–740 BC) and Jeroboam II, king of Samaria (783–743 BC). Amos begins his prophecy by denouncing the war crimes and inhumanities of the surrounding Gentile nations.

Military expansionism conducted with savage cruelty (Amos 1:3-5). The offender here was Damascus, capital of the Aramaean state north of Israel. Under the expansionist policies of its ruler, Hadad, they had invaded Gilead and brutally subjugated the population. They had 'threshed Gilead with threshing sledges of iron'. In the ancient world ears of wheat or barley were threshed by driving a wooden sledge fitted underneath with sharp flints or pieces of metal over the cut stalks. It may be that the phrase 'threshed Gilead with threshing sledges of iron', is simply a metaphor for extreme brutality. But it could be that it is meant literally. Many conquering armies have used, and still use, such hideous tortures to terrorize people.

Slave trade (Amos 1:6–8). The Philistines (Gaza was a Philistine city) sold whole communities into slavery and deported them to a foreign country, Edom. The motivation was to achieve ethnic cleansing, to stop counter-revolution, and to make money.

Profiteering out of war (Amos 1:9–10). This time the culprits were the Tyrians. They were not involved in the war of the Philistines against the Jews. But they made a lot of money by selling whole communities as slaves on behalf of the Philistines; and that, in spite of their early special treaties with the Jews (the 'covenant of kinship', 1:9). Doubtless they would have used the argument that modern nations use today in order to justify their sale of arms to warring states: if we don't sell the slaves for the conquerors (or supply the armaments), someone else will. They therefore made money out of human misery and death.

Ceaseless ethnic hatred (Amos 1:11–12). In past centuries the Edomites doubtless felt that they had been mistreated by the Israelites. But they would not forget the past. They took every occasion to get their revenge on Israel. One can think of many similar situations today.

War crimes (Amos 1:13–15). With the nation of Ammon, territorial expansion had been accompanied by inhuman savagery: they had even killed pregnant women. Of course, there was no Geneva Convention in those days, nor war crimes tribunal. But God had recorded every atrocity and would one day, so Amos said, punish the perpetrators.

Amos not only denounced the sins of the surrounding Gentile nations. He rebuked even more sternly his own nation, Israel and Judah, both for their social and for their religious sins. The state of the nation at the time has been well summed up as follows:

(a) *Political and social conditions.* Over 40 years before Amos's ministry Assyria had crushed Syria, Samaria's neighbour. This permitted Jeroboam II to extend his frontiers (2 Kgs 14:25), and to build up a lucrative trade that created a powerful merchant class in Samaria. Unfortunately the wealth that came to Samaria was not evenly distributed among the people. It remained in the hands of the merchant princes, who spent the new-found riches on improving their own living standards (Amos 3:10, 12, 15; 6:4), and neglected completely the peasant class which had, up to that point, been the backbone of Samaria's economy. The unmistakable symptoms of a morally sick society began to declare themselves in Samaria. In Amos's day oppression of the poor by the rich was common (2:6-7), as was heartless indifference among the wealthy towards the affliction of the hungry (6:3-6). Justice went to the highest bidder (2:6; 8:6). In drought (4:7-9) the poor had recourse only to the moneylender (5:11-12; 8:4-6), to whom they were often compelled to mortgage both their land and themselves.

(b) *The state of religion.* Naturally the social conditions in Samaria affected religious habits. Religion was being not neglected, but perverted. At the national religious shrines (5:5) ritual was being maintained (4:4), but it went hand in hand with godlessness and immorality. Far from pleasing God it invited his judgment (3:14; 7:9; 9:1-4); it did not remove but increased transgression (4:4). God was not to be found at the national shrines (5:4-5) because he could not accept the worship there (5:21-23); the true preoccupations of the people were with other gods (8:14). In addition, this rich ceremonial and the costly sacrifices were being offered at the expense of the poor (2:8; 5:11).[1]

The prophets, then, exposed and denounced the sins both of the Gentiles and—even more so—of the Jews. But they were also commissioned by God to announce his final programme for dealing with the human race's sins and for bringing salvation to the world. In light of this, the very realism of the prophets' stern denunciation of sin has a bright side to it: it shows that the message of hope and salvation which they preached was not some unrealistic utopian dream that had failed to reckon with how ingrained sin is. At the same time the prophets show themselves aware that the salvation of the world must start with the salvation of the individual. All programmes aimed at reformation are bound to fail, unless they can change the heart of the individuals that make up the nations.

Here then in brief are the programmes which two of the Major Prophets announced that God would one day put into operation for the salvation of the human race.

1 *The Illustrated Bible Dictionary*, 44-5.

Isaiah's prophecy of salvation

Against the background of Israel's failure to fulfil their role, Isaiah prophesied that one day God would send into the world his perfect servant. This servant would not only live a life of self-denying service to others, he would suffer and die as a sacrifice for the sins of the world so that men and women might be forgiven and reconciled with God; and then in the joy and peace of being forgiven themselves, be prepared to forgive others, be reconciled to, and love and serve, one another, so making peace. Here is a sample of Isaiah's prophecy:

He was despised and rejected by others;
  a man of suffering and acquainted with infirmity;
and as one from whom others hide their faces
  he was despised, and we held him of no account.

Surely he has borne our infirmities
  and carried our diseases;
yet we accounted him stricken,
  struck down by God, and afflicted.

But he was wounded for our transgressions,
  crushed for our iniquities;
upon him was the punishment that made us whole,
  and by his bruises we are healed.

All we like sheep have gone astray;
  we have all turned to our own way,

and the Lord has laid on him
   the iniquity of us all. (Isa 53:3–6)

This is the prophecy that Jesus Christ claimed to be fulfilled in his own life and death:

'You know that among the Gentiles those whom they recognize as their rulers lord it over them, and their great ones are tyrants over them. But it is not so among you; but whoever wishes to become great among you must be your servant, and whoever wishes to be first among you must be slave of all. For the Son of Man came not to be served but to serve, and to give his life a ransom for many.' (Mark 10:41–45)

Of course, if everyone followed the example of Christ and lived to love and serve others, the world would soon become a paradise. The urgent question is: how do you get people to behave like this? We find the answer in Jeremiah's prophecy.

Jeremiah's prophecy of salvation

The days are surely coming, says the Lord, when I will make a new covenant with the house of Israel and the house of Judah. It will not be like the covenant that I made with their ancestors when I took them by the hand to bring them out of the land of Egypt—a covenant that they broke, though I was their husband, says the Lord. But this is the covenant that I will make with the house of Israel after those days, says the Lord:

> I will put my law within them, and I will write it on
> their hearts; and I will be their God, and they shall be
> my people. No longer shall they teach one another, or
> say to each other, 'Know the LORD,' for they shall all
> know me, from the least of them to the greatest, says
> the LORD; for I will forgive their iniquity, and remember
> their sin no more. (Jer 31:31–34)

Jeremiah is here realistically surveying the long lesson of
history: Israel's persistent failure to live according to God's
law. It would be useless, therefore, simply to command
them once more to try to keep God's law. Experience
had shown that men and women by themselves have
not the moral and spiritual power to keep it. Therefore
Jeremiah announced that one day God would introduce a
new covenant. He would work the miracle of regeneration, and write his laws not on external tablets of stone,
but on hearts and minds. In other words, he would create
a new kind of life, a new nature with new powers. This
is the miracle which, as the New Testament points out,
God does for all who in true repentance receive Christ as
Lord and Saviour (2 Cor 3; Heb 8).

But what if some men and women are just not willing to accept Christ as Saviour and Lord? Will that not in
the end defeat God's programme? No! The prophets assure
us that the Messiah, the Saviour of the world who died
and rose again to bring us forgiveness and salvation, will
one day come again and with divine power and glory set
up his kingdom worldwide. Then the unrepentant will be
excluded from the presence of the Lord to suffer eternally
the fate they have chosen; they shall no longer be allowed

to trouble the earth (see 2 Thess 1:5–10). And here, drawn from another one of the Minor Prophets, is a description of what life will be like under the universal reign of the long-promised Messiah:

In days to come
     the mountain of the Lord's house
shall be established as the highest of the mountains,
     and shall be raised up above the hills.
Peoples shall stream to it,
     and many nations shall come and say:
'Come, let us go up to the mountain of the Lord,
     to the house of the God of Jacob;
that he may teach us his ways
     and that we may walk in his paths.'
For out of Zion shall go forth instruction,
     and the word of the Lord from Jerusalem.
He shall judge between many peoples,
     and shall arbitrate between strong nations far away;
they shall beat their swords into ploughshares,
     and their spears into pruning hooks;
nation shall not lift up sword against nation,
     neither shall they learn war any more;
but they shall all sit under their own vines and under
their own fig trees,
     and no one shall make them afraid;
     for the mouth of the Lord of hosts has spoken.

(Micah 4:1–4)

This is a motto that the United Nations have set up for themselves.[2] It is no empty motto; for though the United Nations will not be able to achieve it, Christ at his second coming will. For just as his birth, life, death, resurrection and ascension fulfilled many of the predictions of the Old Testament prophets, so his second coming will fulfil all the rest.

Hearing the prophets speak

Why do you think people often do not take the prophets seriously? How can we help people to take their message seriously today?

Read Isaiah 53 and discuss how Jesus fulfilled it, using the New Testament. What does this mean to you personally?

2 The parallel passage from Isaiah 2 is partly quoted on a wall outside the UN headquarters in New York City.

CHAPTER 15

The Way from National Religion to Worldwide Faith

This is the last chapter that we shall be able to devote to the Old Testament—in our next chapter we must begin to study the New Testament. Historically there is a gap of some centuries between the two testaments. How, then, did the Jewish nation get from the end of the Old Testament to the beginning of the New? And what moral and spiritual lessons may we learn from this period in their history?

A brief survey of history from the time of David to Christ

David, followed by *Solomon*, reigned over a united Israel, the high point of Israel's prosperity as a nation (1010–930 BC).

Timeline 3. Key People and Events in the History of Israel 1010–4 BC

1010 BC		930 BC
	ISRAEL: United Monarchy	
David	Solomon	

The twelve tribes split into two kingdoms: ten tribes in the north, with their capital, *Samaria*; two tribes in the south, with their capital, *Jerusalem* (930 BC).

The mighty empire of *Assyria* invaded the northern kingdom and deported its citizens to the east (745–721 BC).

The powerful *Babylonian* Empire defeated the southern kingdom and deported the cream of its citizens (among them *Daniel*) to Babylon; its territory became a province of the Babylonian Empire (605–587 BC).

The *Medo-Persian* Empire with *Cyrus* at its head captured Babylon (530 BC) and its empire. Cyrus allowed those Jews who wanted to return to their native land to do so, and ordered them to rebuild their temple (completed in 516 BC). Later, with the help of *Nehemiah*, the Jewish cupbearer to King Artaxerxes I of Persia, who was appointed governor of Jerusalem, they were allowed to rebuild the city of Jerusalem (445 BC). The book of Nehemiah vividly chronicles the rebuilding of the walls of Jerusalem. Many Jews returned; many continued to live in foreign countries. Judaea was now a province of the Persian Empire. It is about this time that the period covered by the Old Testament came to an end, the books of Nehemiah and Malachi being the last written.

Alexander the Great of Macedonia conquered both the *Persian* and the *Egyptian* empires. Judaea passed under his control. Many Jews migrated to Egypt. Alexander went on to conquer most of the then-known world (334–331 BC).

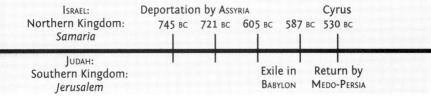

ISRAEL: Northern Kingdom: *Samaria*	Deportation by ASSYRIA				Cyrus
	745 BC	721 BC	605 BC	587 BC	530 BC
JUDAH: Southern Kingdom: *Jerusalem*				Exile in BABYLON	Return by MEDO-PERSIA

Alexander died in 323 BC. His empire was divided among his generals. One of them, named *Ptolemy*, took over Egypt and founded a dynasty which lasted until the Romans took it over in 31 BC. Another of them, named *Seleucus*, took over Asia, and founded a dynasty which lasted until the Romans took it over in 65 BC. At first Jerusalem and Judaea were under the control of the Ptolemaic dynasty in Egypt; but in 198 BC they passed into the control of the Seleucid dynasty.

After some forty years of guerrilla warfare and turbulent politics led by the Jewish family the *Maccabees*, against the Seleucids, Judaea was finally and securely established as a sovereign independent state under the *Hasmonean* dynasty of Jewish kings (128 BC).

The *Roman* general Pompey captured Jerusalem and invaded the temple (63 BC).

Herod, an Edomite by birth, but a Jew by religion, was declared King of the Jews by the Roman Senate (40 BC). He conquered Galilee in 38 BC, and Jerusalem in 37 BC. He was confirmed as a vassal-king by Octavian who later became Caesar Augustus, the first emperor of Rome. It was in the reign of Caesar Augustus, when Herod was King of the Jews, that Jesus Christ was born in Bethlehem in Judaea.

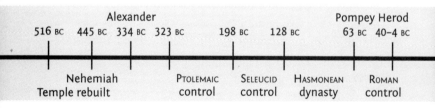

What endures in history?

The great empires of the ancient world, Egypt, Babylon, Assyria, Persia, Greece (under Alexander) and Rome certainly made valuable and permanent contributions to the world's art, architecture, literature, philosophy, science and general civilization; and for these things they are rightly remembered. But the empires themselves have passed away; and the wars and endless bloodshed by which these empires were achieved, are now seen for what they always were: a hideous waste of human lives in the cause of human pride, ambition and power lust.

Compared with these great empires Israel was never more than a tiny nation, and for most of this period of history most of its people were living either as captives or as expatriates in foreign countries. But the old pagan gods whom the great empires worshipped, and who, they thought, gave them victory over the world and over Israel in particular, have largely been abandoned. Very few worship them now. Yet the God of Israel has not only survived: he has become the God of a worldwide faith. Multi-millions, not only of Jews, but of Gentiles, have come to believe on him over the centuries. And, in spite of frequent persecution, more millions now worship this 'God of Abraham, Isaac and Jacob', the God of the nation of Israel, and the God of the Jew, Jesus Christ, than ever before. Here then is something from the ancient world far more lastingly significant and, in our modern world, more widely and permanently influential, than any or all of the great world empires past or present. If only for this reason, this aspect of Old Testament history ought to loom large in the account we give to our students of world affairs. It highlights what has proved to be truly enduring in history.

Some benefits to the world of Israel's exile among the nations

Their exile demonstrated God's impartiality and righteousness (see Chapter 14 for detail). God's choice of Israel to play a special role for him in history certainly gave them many privileges. But privilege was not favouritism. Privilege meant that if they persisted in social and religious sin God would punish them more than he did other nations. He would not spare the nation, nor the royal dynasty of King David, nor God's own temple at Jerusalem, nor the capital city Jerusalem itself from defeat and destruction. God's principle of judgment was this: 'You only have I known of all the families of the earth; therefore I will punish you for all your iniquities' (Amos 3:2). The general lesson is that the more privileged a nation or an individual is, the more strictly God will hold them to account for their misbehaviour (see also Luke 12:47–48).

Israel's continued exile has demonstrated God's faithfulness to his purpose. For two and a half millennia the majority of Jews have lived among the Gentiles, and for most of that time, until recently, have been without a homeland of their own. Yet from before the exile, God promised that he would watch over them, protect them from extinction, and one day restore them to their land (see Ezek 39:22–29). And to this day, in spite of bitter persecution and attempts at genocide, the Jews have never lost their national and ethnic identity or been assimilated or completely destroyed. God has kept his promise so far; and the rest will one day be fulfilled as well.

The synagogue system. From the time of the Babylonian captivity onwards the Jews began to establish synagogues in the Gentile cities, where they could worship God and teach the Old Testament. In the following centuries large numbers of Gentiles, tired of the absurdities and crudities of pagan idolatry, began to attend Jewish synagogues and were brought to faith in the One True God. It was from this group that many of the first Gentile converts to Christianity came (see Acts 13:44–14:1; 17:4, 10–12; Luke 7:2–5).

The translation of the Old Testament into Greek. In the early third century bc the Jews who were then living in Alexandria in Egypt translated the books of the Old Testament from Hebrew into Greek. These translations, which came to be known as the Septuagint, exercised an immense influence in the ancient world. The writers of the New Testament, when they quote the Old Testament, often take their quotations from the Septuagint. The early Christian missionaries subsequently translated the Septuagint into Latin, Egyptian, Ethiopic, Armenian and other languages. The Septuagint was the translation used by the Greek Church Fathers and is still useful today for scholars in establishing the text of the Old Testament.

The contribution of expatriate Jews to world civilization. When God sent the Israelites into exile in Babylon, he commanded them to settle down and to 'seek the welfare of the city where I have sent you into exile, and pray to the Lord on its behalf' (Jer 29:7). They were not to foment trouble but to seek to contribute to the welfare of the state in every way. Not all Jews have always lived up to this ideal. On the other hand, since the Babylonian exile onwards and all down the centuries, expatriate Jews living in Gentile countries have made enormous contributions to world science, medicine, music, art and literature all out of proportion to their numbers.

The author of the *book of Daniel* in the Old Testament is a shining example. Exiled to Babylon, Daniel served loyally in the Babylonian civil service for many years. When the Persians took over the empire, he rose to great heights in the imperial administration. As a Jew who believed the Old Testament prophets, he knew that however much progress the Gentile governments made they would never solve the problem of evil in the world. Only the coming of God's promised Messiah would do that. At the same time Daniel was no religious fanatic or nihilist. He did not run away from life but loyally served the people of the country in which he lived.

On the other hand he relates in his memoirs (Dan 1) how, at the beginning of his studies in Babylon, he refused to eat the food in the university, which had, according to custom, been offered to idols. He was not prepared to compromise with an idolatrous interpretation of the universe which deified the basic forces of nature and human urges, for he saw that this view devalued human beings into slaves of those forces. It was for Daniel a double outrage—against the true Creator God and against the dignity and rationality of the human race.

Daniel relates also (Dan 3) how his friends took a courageous stand for basic human freedom when the state turned totalitarian and oppressive. Nebuchadnezzar demanded on one occasion that all public servants of the state should bow down to an image which the king had set up, and offer to the state that ultimate worship and obedience that should be reserved for God alone. The penalty for not bowing down was to be thrown into a furnace. Three of Daniel's friends dared to defy the king with a magnificently courageous statement and were thrown into the furnace in consequence:

> 'O Nebuchadnezzar, we have no need to present a defence to you in this matter. If our God whom we serve is able to deliver us from the furnace of blazing fire and out of your hand, O king, let him deliver us. But if not, be it known to you, O king, that we will not serve your gods and we will not worship the golden statue that you have set up.' (Dan 3:16–18)

By so doing they demonstrated that their allegiance to the one true Creator God was of higher value than life itself. Their defiance and the dramatic way in which God rescued them led to Nebuchadnezzar's acknowledgement of the existence and glory of the One True God.

It was not so with one of Nebuchadnezzar's successors, the prince regent, Belshazzar. Daniel tells of a famous occasion when Belshazzar at a feast took the golden vessels that had been removed from the temple at Jerusalem by Nebuchadnezzar (and placed in the temple of his gods) and drank from them in full view of his nobles (Dan 5). These vessels had been made of gold to symbolize the fact that God was humanity's chief value and his service our highest duty. By drinking from them Belshazzar was saying with powerful eloquence that he had replaced God as life's supreme value by himself, his satisfaction and his pleasure. At that fateful moment there was a supernatural intervention: the fingers of a man's hand wrote on the palace wall words which Belshazzar could not understand—although the words were common enough terms for weights, measures and money. Daniel was called and had the solemn duty of telling the king their meaning. Belshazzar had made his evaluation of God and rejected him. Now through the writing on the wall God was evaluating Belshazzar. God had set up his balances and they found Belshazzar deficient. Sadly, Belshazzar did not repent and seek the mercy of God, which would have saved him. The golden vessels on his table were a mute witness to the fact that Belshazzar had thrown life's true values away. He had effectively valued himself at zero. That night he lay dead on the streets of Babylon, killed by the invading Medo-Persians who took over his kingdom. What value could be put on him now?

The stories in Daniel make thrilling reading. They are world famous and every child should either read or be told them in full. But in addition they have served as beacons to encourage and nerve moral heroes of all generations to stand for faith in God against the unlawful demands of totalitarian governments. For on such faith in God, true human freedom ultimately depends.

PART 2

······································

The Moral and Ethical Teachings of Jesus Christ

CHAPTER

Jesus the Teacher

Introduction

We come now to the moral and ethical teachings of Jesus Christ. In many ways this is the easiest part of the course to teach, and that for a number of reasons:

The sheer genius of Christ as a teacher. Much of Christ's teaching on how people ought to behave is given through the medium of parables, as we shall presently see. They are marvels of sophisticated simplicity in their penetrating observation of human nature, its strengths and weaknesses, its foibles and perversities. Their story form appeals to the most elementary student, and yet they deliver their message with unforgettable force even to the most learned. As teachers we shall find them an easy and yet satisfying means of communication.

The superficial attractiveness of Christ's teaching. Take the so-called 'golden rule', enunciated by Jesus in his famous 'Sermon on the Mount': 'In everything, do to others what you would have them do to you, for this sums up the Law and the Prophets' (Matt 7:12 NIV). Its utter simplicity coupled with its self-evident rightness gives it an immediate and universal attractiveness. Here is no complicated theory, difficult to understand and open to dispute. Its claim to everybody's obedience is unambiguous and unanswerable. Its implications are limitless. If it were honestly carried out, our world would become a paradise. But, of course, it is not universally carried out; indeed all of us go against it from time to time. And that brings us to our next point.

Why do we all from time to time do wrong? The ancient Greek philosopher Socrates held that no one knowingly does wrong. He meant that when we do wrong, we are not fully aware that what we are doing is wrong. We think, in fact, that it is good. We may well know that what we are doing will harm someone else. But as we do it, we think and feel that it is a good thing to do to harm this other person: it gives us an advantage over him; it satisfies our desire for gain, or power, or revenge. But when we do someone an injustice, Socrates taught, not only do we injure that person, but we also injure ourselves more than we injure them. If only we realised this, said Socrates, we should immediately stop injuring ourselves by wronging other people. But we do not realize it; we are ignorant. Ignorance, according to Socrates, is the cause of our wrongdoing; and it follows that the way to stop people doing wrong is simply to educate them. Only get them to see that in doing wrong to someone else, they are injuring themselves, and they will immediately stop doing wrong.[1]

1 See especially Plato's dialogue of Socrates with Crito.

But is this true? And if it is, would knowing it be enough to get people to stop doing wrong?

For the classroom

Have your students discuss the following questions:

Have you ever done anything wrong, knowing at the time that it was wrong?

Do people ever do things that they know will harm themselves (e.g. like smoking, drug taking or cutting themselves)? Why do they do such things?

If you could steal a lot of money, or murder someone, and be absolutely sure that no one on earth would ever find out, is there any reason why you should not do it?

Is it true that when you do someone an injustice, you actually harm yourself? How would you prove it?

The Apostle Paul once said: 'I have the desire to do what is good, but I cannot carry it out. For the good I would do, that I do not; and the evil I don't want to do, that I keep on doing' (Rom 7:19 own trans). Have any of us ever felt like this?

What are some of the basic requirements of any ethical teaching? If our thinking about ethics and our teaching of ethics is going to be effective, we shall need to be able to give convincing answers to the following questions (among others):

(a) What is good behaviour? And what is bad? How does one define it?

(b) Has anyone the authority to tell us what is good and what is bad? Why can we not decide it individually?

(c) Why don't we always do what is right? Why do we often find it hard to do what is right, and easy to do what is wrong?

(d) What adequate motivation can we have for doing what is right, particularly when other people do wrong? Is there any advantage in doing good? Or ought we always to do good even if we suffer for it?

(e) Where can we find the strength to do what we know to be right and to avoid what is bad?

Now if we are going to be fair to the ethical teaching of Jesus Christ, we must allow him to give us, little by little, his answers to these questions. We begin with his own presentation of himself as teacher and of the nature of his teaching.

Christ's presentation of himself as teacher

At that time Jesus said, 'I thank you, Father, Lord of heaven and earth, because you have hidden these things from the wise and the intelligent and have revealed them to infants; yes, Father, for such was your gracious will. All things have been handed over to me by my Father; and no one knows the Son except the Father, and no one knows the Father except the Son and anyone to whom the Son chooses to reveal him.

'Come to me, all you that are weary and are carrying heavy burdens, and I will give you rest. Take my yoke upon you, and learn from me; for I am gentle and humble in heart, and you will find rest for your souls. For my yoke is easy, and my burden is light.' (Matt 11:25–30)

In this passage Jesus makes *two assertions about himself*:
- he is the almighty Son of God;
- nevertheless, he is gentle and humble in heart.

He gives *two descriptions of his teaching*:
- it is a yoke to which his disciples must submit, and a burden they must carry;
- nevertheless, his yoke is easy and his burden is light.

And then, on the basis of these two assertions and these two descriptions, he issues *two invitations, each accompanied by a promise*:
- come to me all you who are weary and burdened, and I will give you rest;
- take my yoke on you and learn from me . . . and you will find rest for your souls.

The two assertions

Here we find:

1. Christ's answer to the question: what authority has he to tell us what is right and what is wrong?

He is the Son of God, to whom God has given supreme power in the creation, government and salvation of the world ('everything has been committed to me by my Father', Matt. 11:27). In this he is different from the Buddha who taught his disciples how to gain release from their desires, but never claimed to be God, or even a god, and did not know whether there was a God or not. And he is different from Muhammad who claimed to be God's last and greatest prophet but not to be God incarnate. We need, therefore, to understand who Jesus claims to be, because on that depends the authority he claims for his ethical teaching.

2. Strong evidence that Christ's claim is true

It is deranged megalomaniacs who claim to be God, or Napoleon, or Alexander the Great, or a fried egg or something else extraordinary. But Jesus was no deranged megalomaniac; nor was he arrogant or self-assertive. His first claim to be the Son of God was balanced by his next claim, 'I am meek and lowly in heart' (Matt 11:29 RV), and the Gospels give abundant examples to show that this assertion was true. Alexander the Great did get himself proclaimed as the son of the Egyptian god, Ammon; and he did eventually propose, for political reasons, that both his Greek and his oriental subjects should worship him as a god. But Alexander could never have said 'I am meek and lowly in heart'. It is the combination of Christ's claim to deity with his meekness and lowliness of heart that makes his claim both credible and convincing. He has supreme authority, but he is supremely humble. He is God, but he is no tyrant.

The two descriptions

1. Christ's ethical teaching is a yoke

Jesus Christ does not hide the fact that his ethical teaching is a yoke which his disciples must accept and a burden they must carry.

The meaning of the term 'yoke'. In the ancient world a yoke was a specially shaped piece of wood that a farmer would fit onto the neck of his oxen so that he could control them and harness them to plough the fields, thresh the corn or pull the farm carts. Ancient kings, therefore, called their government a 'yoke' because by it they controlled and guided the people. And teachers of morality and religion called their teaching a 'yoke' for the same reason.

There is a vivid story in the Old Testament (1 Kgs 12), which illustrates this meaning of 'yoke'. The people ask the king to make his yoke easier. Instead he makes it harder; and they revolt. Read the story and tell it to the students, or in the group, in full. See also Acts 15:10, where false religious teaching is described as an unbearable yoke.

Christ's teaching, then, is a yoke. He is the Son of God, sent by God to be our rightful king, to govern us and to get us to obey God's rule. This is the authority he claims for telling us what is right and what is wrong; which is why he began his public teaching by proclaiming: 'Repent, for the kingdom of heaven has come near' (Matt 4:17). In submitting to his ethics, we are submitting not simply to some abstract moral principles but to a person to whom we owe personal loyalty.

2. Christ's ethical teaching is an easy yoke

A good farmer would see to it that the yokes that he put on his oxen fitted them well and did not chafe. It made it easier for the oxen to do their work. If someone wants to become a champion tennis player, he or she must submit to a coach. Obeying the coach's instructions may seem hard at first; but it is better than hitting the ball uncontrollably and, in the end, it will make the playing easier, more successful and more enjoyable. It is always better to drive a car according to the maker's instructions. Christ knows how our bodies, minds, emotions and desires were meant to work. He made them! His yoke is designed to fit us and so to make life easier.

The two invitations

The first invitation and promise is addressed to people who are weary and burdened. This is an ever present problem for many. Even young people can be weary and burdened. In many big cities of the world the number of young people who commit suicide is going up. Why? Here are some suggestions:

(a) The seeming pointlessness of life.

(b) The difficulty of finding employment, and the consequent feeling of being useless and unwanted.

(c) The boredom, ill health and worry that arise from alcoholism, drugs, frantic lifestyles.

(d) The psychological wounds and guilt feelings that follow immorality.

(e) The basic insecurity caused by strife in the home, parental divorce, one-parent families.

(f) Constant failure to live up to one's ideals, leading to disgust with oneself.

To those who come to him Christ gives immediate rest, because he gives:

(a) immediate forgiveness and release from guilt: see, e.g. Luke 5:20.

(b) a restored sense of purpose in life: see, e.g. 1 Thessalonians 1:9–10, 'to serve a living and true God'.

(c) an immediate sense of being loved and valued by God, and therefore of being of infinite and permanent significance: see, e.g. Matthew 12:12; Romans 5:5–11.

(d) an assurance of God's care in the practical affairs of life and relief from anxiety: see, e.g. Matthew 6:25–32.

The second invitation and promise is to enter the school of Christ and to be taught and trained by him how to live. His teaching will require standards of behaviour that are very different from the world's standards; and for that reason they may well incur the world's hostility and opposition. But here too Christ promises 'rest to our souls', because he can effect within us a 'new birth' by which we become children of God, and receive new powers with which to carry out his instructions and to live according to his moral standards: see, e.g. 1 John 5:3–4.

CHAPTER 17

The First and Greatest Commandment

Jesus was once asked what in his estimation was the greatest commandment—the basic principle from which all the others are derived? He replied: 'You shall love the Lord your God with all your heart, and with all your soul, and with all your mind. This is the greatest and first commandment' (Matt 22:37-38).

We see at once what, according to Christ, the basic motivation behind all true morality must be: *love*. Not desire for happiness or success, but love. And not love of oneself, nor primarily love for one's neighbour and the community (though, as a later study will show, that comes second), but love for God, the Creator. The world is his world. He made it to serve his pleasure and to run according to his design. It is only rational that our prime duty should be to live according to our Creator's will, and, out of sheer gratitude for our existence, to love him. In this context love for God does not mean some sentimental religious feeling: 'the love of God is this,' says the Bible, 'that we obey his commandments' (1 John 5:3). We are to do so with all our heart, mind, soul and strength.

Humanity's greatest wrong

But here also is Christ's diagnosis of the fundamental trouble both with individuals and with society as a whole. How shall we live as we ought, if we do not love our Maker and live according to his design? How shall we rightly value and treat our fellow men and women, if we deny, or even despise or forget, their Maker? And how would life be anything other than a drudgery, if we served God out of a sullen sense of mere duty, and not out of wholehearted love for him?

In breaking the first and greatest commandment (and we have all done so), we are guilty of the greatest sin— failing to love God. Here we face a fundamental problem. We cannot make ourselves love God. What then can create this love of God within us? The following parable will help us understand.

The parable of the Prodigal Son

> Then Jesus said, 'There was a man who had two sons. The younger of them said to his father, "Father, give me the share of the property that will belong to me." So he divided his property between them. A few days later the younger son gathered all he had and travelled to a distant country, and there he squandered his property in dissolute living. When he had spent

everything, a severe famine took place throughout that country, and he began to be in need. So he went and hired himself out to one of the citizens of that country, who sent him to his fields to feed the pigs. He would gladly have filled himself with the pods that the pigs were eating; and no one gave him anything. But when he came to himself he said, "How many of my father's hired hands have bread enough and to spare, but here I am dying of hunger! I will get up and go to my father, and I will say to him, 'Father, I have sinned against heaven and before you; I am no longer worthy to be called your son; treat me like one of your hired hands.'" So he set off and went to his father. But while he was still far off, his father saw him and was filled with compassion; he ran and put his arms around him and kissed him. Then the son said to him, "Father, I have sinned against heaven and before you; I am no longer worthy to be called your son." But the father said to his slaves, "Quickly, bring out a robe—the best one—and put it on him; put a ring on his finger and sandals on his feet. And get the fatted calf and kill it, and let us eat and celebrate; for this son of mine was dead and is alive again; he was lost and is found!" And they began to celebrate.

'Now his elder son was in the field; and when he came and approached the house, he heard music and dancing. He called one of the slaves and asked what was going on. He replied, "Your brother has come, and your father has killed the fatted calf, because he has got him back safe and sound." Then he became angry and refused to go in. His father came out and began to plead with him. But he answered his father, "Listen! For all these years I have been working like a slave for you, and I have never disobeyed your command; yet you have never given me even a young goat so that I might celebrate with my friends. But when this son of yours came back, who has devoured your property with prostitutes, you killed the fatted calf for him!" Then the father said to him, "Son, you are always with me, and all that is mine is yours. But we had to celebrate and rejoice, because this brother of yours was dead and has come to life; he was lost and has been found." ' (Luke 15:11–32)

This is perhaps the most famous of Christ's parables— a classic of world literature. Dr Kenneth Bailey, who lived for some years among the

Time to shine

Get your group to dramatize the parable.

Palestinians and Bedouin, points out that they have preserved many of the same values as their ancestors who lived in the time of Christ.[1] Their reactions when Dr Bailey told them the parable help us to capture its true meaning.

The prodigal son's outrageous behaviour
His treatment of his father. The prodigal's chief offence was not that 'he squandered his property in dissolute living' (15:13) or that 'he has devoured [his father's] property with prostitutes' (15:30). That was bad enough; but far worse

---

1 *Poet and Peasant.*

was what he did to his father. In ancient Palestine a father would normally make a will specifying how much each son was to receive on his death. For a son to demand his inheritance before his father died would in that society be regarded as an outrage. It was as if the son was saying: 'Father, I wish you were dead! You are stopping me enjoying myself. Hurry up and die and get out of my way. Or else rob yourself and give me my inheritance now.' In a society where family relationships were sacred, such an attitude would be unthinkable; and be felt to be unforgivable.

The application of the parable is obvious. Many people have the same attitude to God as the prodigal to his father. Even if they do not deny the existence of the Creator, they want nothing to do with him. The thought of a Creator and of his laws hampers their enjoyment and restricts their freedom. They wish to live in complete independence from God. They certainly do not love him with all their heart, mind, soul and strength. However they want to go on enjoying all the good things that the Creator has made.

The prodigal's sell-out of the community's capital. Since in pre-industrialised societies, land and cattle were the extended family's basic capital, every effort was normally made to keep the land within the extended family. But the son not only demanded possession of his share of the land before his father died, but on receiving it, sold it and squandered the money in the far country. The point is that when he sold it, no other member of the extended family would have dared to buy it, for that would have been to gain possession of land that belonged to the prodigal's father while he was still living. The prodigal, then, must have sold the land to outsiders and have thus permanently diminished the family's capital. The village would have been outraged, not only when the prodigal went away, but also when he came back, and they discovered that he had wasted every penny of the capital in wild living. The loss was irrecoverable.

The application is again obvious. When an individual rejects or ignores God, and lives simply to gratify himself, he not only damages himself; he diminishes the whole community's moral and spiritual capital. He could also injure the community economically by his alcoholism, absenteeism, laziness, fraud and corruption. And how much more so if a whole nation does similarly?

The father's reaction to the son's demand
When Christ described how the prodigal son devastated his father by making his outrageous request, his hearers would have expected Christ to say that the father flew into a rage and disinherited his son, if not executed him. Such a reaction would have been regarded as totally justified. Instead Christ depicted the father as granting his son's request and letting him depart. Once more the implication is clear. God is no tyrant. He has given men free will and he respects it. When people reject, ignore, despise, insult and deny God, he does not immediately strike them dead, or even withdraw from them life's good things at once. However, he lets them gradually discover the spiritual poverty and moral misery that inevitably ensue when a creature rejects or ignores the Creator.

The prodigal's dawning repentance

At first getting rid of his father's presence and control seemed to the prodigal to have paid off. He had a riotously enjoyable time; or so he thought. But eventually reality caught up with him. He came to poverty, hunger, degradation and loneliness. No one wanted him. This began the process of repentance within him. He decided to go home to his father, and confess his folly. He also planned to put a proposition to his father: 'I am no longer worthy to be called your son; treat me like one of your hired hands' (15:19).

To us, his proposal might seem to indicate genuine repentance, and true reconciliation with his father. But in fact it was not a happy suggestion. On an ancient farm there would be three classes of workers. First there would be the sons of the owner. They would not work for a wage. Being members of the family who would inherit the farm when the father died, they would work for love of the father and of the family and for the good of the family's estate.

Then there would be the serfs, who worked for their keep, and for a minimal wage, but had no independence. They would live on the farm. But there would also be independent workers, who lived in the village and hired themselves out on contract. The prodigal, on his return, wanted to be one of these. He was not going to live and work simply out of love for his father and family. Having foolishly lost all his own share of the estate through his wild lifestyle, he was now proposing to remain independent of his father and to hire out his services to him for money!

Such a proposal could never satisfy the father. It would not heal the estrangement. The prodigal must abandon his foolish independence. He must accept the father as father, and live and work for him out of love for him and the family.

Many people still make the same mistake. They have learned by bitter experience the moral and spiritual poverty that results from living without God; and they vow to change their lifestyle and to serve God. But like the ancient Pharisees their attitude to God remains wrong. Perhaps without thinking, they still assume independence of God and propose now by good behaviour, works and religious observances to earn God's favour, hoping that in the end he will pay them by giving them salvation. But this is false. As creatures of God we can never be independent of him. All that we have that is worth having comes from him and belongs to him. We cannot use what is his to buy anything from him—least of all salvation. The only satisfactory way to live for God is to love him with all our heart, mind, soul and strength, and to serve him freely out of love.

But what can generate such love for God in our hearts?

The father's self-humbling
In normal life, if and when a son, like the one in the parable, came back, all the people of the village would be out to meet him, deriding his rags and filth, pouring their curses on his head for all the damage and shame he had done to the community, and getting ready to stone him, if his father ordered it. But at this point the father did an astounding thing: he ran to meet the prodigal, forgave him, and welcomed him back!

Now in the ancient world, no important man would run for any reason. Running was held to be beneath their dignity. Even the Greek philosopher Aristotle thought that. For the prodigal's father to run at all was to humiliate himself. For him to run to meet his prodigal son, instead of waiting in the house in great dignity and aloofness until the prodigal came to the door and was himself humiliated by being kept waiting—this was astounding behaviour. But it showed the prodigal what his father's heart was really like in a way that he had never realised before. His forgiveness, acceptance and re-instatement of the prodigal in the family as a son, provoked him to love the father with all his heart, and to serve him freely thereafter.

Of course, this part of the parable was meant to point to what God has done for us sinners in Christ. In the ancient world crucifixion was considered the most shameful and humiliating death possible, which is why the Christian message of the cross seemed to the philosophical Greeks crude and foolish, and to the religious Jews a scandal. But for millions it has proved the power of God to salvation. For not only has it made forgiveness and reconciliation with God possible; but the self-humbling of God in allowing his creatures to crucify his Son, in order that by that very suffering he might procure their forgiveness and bestow his love on them, has created in the hearts of those who repent and are forgiven, that responsive love for God which is the only satisfactory motive for serving God, the only adequate motive for sound Christian ethics.

The Christian Apostle John summed it up in two short sentences. 'We love [God], because he first loved us. . . . For

this is the love of God that we keep his commandments'
(1 John 4:19; 5:3 RV).

Love and obedience

'The basis of all true morality is love for God expressed in keeping his commandments.' Discuss.

What was the prodigal's attitude to his father? Where do we see this reflected today in people's attitudes to God?

How does the parable help us to understand how love for God can be generated in our hearts and lives?

CHAPTER

18

The Second Greatest Commandment

According to Jesus Christ the second greatest of all the commandments is: 'You shall love your neighbour as yourself' (Matt 22:39). This was not a commandment that he there and then invented: he quoted it from the Old Testament (Lev 19:18). Its reasonableness is self-evident. If we all carried it out all the time, the world would soon be free of much, if not most, of its pain and suffering. But we don't always do so. Why not?

For the classroom

Get your students to suggest reasons why people do not always love their neighbours as themselves.

One of Jesus' listeners was an expert in the Old Testament, but did not always obey this commandment any more than other people do. So he tried to excuse himself by suggesting that there was a difficulty with its wording which made it virtually impossible to carry it out. 'But who is my neighbour?' he said. What he meant was this: does the term 'neighbour' mean simply those nearest to me, my wife and children, and close relatives? Or is it meant to include my next-door neighbour? Or all the people that live in my block of flats? Or all the people in my town, in my country, and in all the world? Where are we allowed to draw the line? Obviously, if I love my family as myself, and they are hungry, I can share my food equally with them. But if I try to share my food with every hungry person in my city, there won't be enough to keep any of us alive. So who exactly is my neighbour? The term 'neighbour', he maintained, is too vague; and therefore the commandment is unrealistic and unworkable. This, then, was the excuse given by the expert in the Old Testament for why he did not carry out the second greatest commandment (Luke 10:25–29).

The parable of the Good Samaritan

Just then a lawyer stood up to test Jesus. 'Teacher,' he said, 'what must I do to

Making excuses

Was the expert's excuse valid?

If not, how would you answer his objection?

Obviously, there would be no practical sense in our trying to share our small amount of food with every hungry person in the world. But there is enough food in the world to feed everyone. If all governments, all business people, all individuals everywhere loved their neighbours as themselves and shared the world's food fairly, no one would starve. But the world at large does not carry out the second greatest commandment. Does that then give us a valid excuse for not carrying it out ourselves as far as we can?

inherit eternal life?' He said to him, 'What is written in the law? What do you read there?' He answered, 'You shall love the Lord your God with all your heart, and with all your soul, and with all your strength, and with all your mind; and your neighbour as yourself.' And he said to him, 'You have given the right answer; do this, and you will live.'

But wanting to justify himself, he asked Jesus, 'And who is my neighbour?' Jesus replied, 'A man was going down from Jerusalem to Jericho, and fell into the hands of robbers, who stripped him, beat him, and went away, leaving him half dead. Now by chance a priest was going down that road; and when he saw him, he passed by on the other side. So likewise a Levite, when he came to the place and saw him, passed by on the other side. But a Samaritan while travelling came near him; and when he saw him, he was moved with pity. He went to him and bandaged his wounds, having poured oil and wine on them. Then he put him on his own animal, brought him to an inn, and took care of him. The next day he took out two denarii, gave them to the innkeeper, and said, "Take care of him; and

For the classroom

This is one of the most famous of Jesus' parables. So first get your students to read the parable simply as a story—or tell it to them in detail, pointing out how vividly true to life its setting was. The road from Jerusalem to Jericho wound down through high, broken cliffs where bandits could easily lurk and jump out on lonely travellers. Mugging was common then, as it is now. You may wish to get the class to dramatize the parable as well.

when I come back, I will repay you whatever more you spend." Which of these three, do you think, was a neighbour to the man who fell into the hands of the robbers?' He said, 'The one who showed him mercy.' Jesus said to him, 'Go and do likewise.' (Luke 10:25–37)

The first major lesson of the parable
The parable has several lessons to teach. Let us deal first with its last and major point (10:36–37). The expert's excuse for not loving his neighbour as himself was a theoretical difficulty: he did not know exactly to what person or persons the commandment was referring by the term 'neighbour', when it said 'You shall love your neighbour as yourself', so he asked 'Who is my neighbour?' But from a practical point of view his theoretical question was irrelevant and rather silly. Not knowing exactly how many people in the world you may eventually be required to treat as your neighbour does not stop you from acting as a neighbour to someone who at this very moment lies before your very feet in dire need. So when our Lord applied the lesson of his parable, he did not answer the expert's theoretical question. Instead he asked the expert a different, practical question: 'Which of these three [the priest, the Levite and the Samaritan], do you think, was a neighbour to the man who fell into the hands of the robbers?' There was no difficulty in answering that question! Even the expert had to admit that it was the Samaritan who acted like a neighbour and had compassion on the man in need. 'Go and do likewise,' said Christ.

The first major lesson, then, is clear: our duty is to act in a compassionate, loving and practical way to those whom we actually encounter in daily life that are in any need whatever, if we are able to help them. It is right, of course, that we should bear in mind the vast need throughout the world. But we should not allow our personal inability to do much about that need, to paralyse us into doing nothing about the need that we actually meet around us day by day. And certainly we should not use it as an excuse for not acting as a loving neighbour to as many as we can.

This lesson can be reinforced as follows. Another way of expressing the commandment 'You shall love your neighbour as yourself' is to say, as Jesus did on another occasion: 'In everything do to others as you would have them do to you' (Matt 7:12). If you were mugged like the man in the parable, and were lying half dead on the road, would you not want the passers-by to help you? Would you not complain bitterly if they ignored you? Well then, treat anyone who is in any need whatever in the same way as you would wish to be treated if you were in that need.

The second lesson of the parable
The second lesson of the parable is that if our religion does not move us to love our neighbour as ourselves, it is inadequate, if not completely false. Since the story which Christ told was a parable, and not the record of an actual incident, he was free to choose the characters in the story. His choice of a priest and a Levite as the men who passed by without raising a finger to help the wounded man is therefore very significant. Both the priest and the Levite were religious functionaries in the temple of God

at Jerusalem; they ought to have been the very first to love their neighbour as themselves. Why didn't they? Had they been going up to Jerusalem to begin a tour of duty in the temple, they might well have been afraid to touch a nearly dead man, because according to their religious regulations contact with a dead body would have defiled them and temporarily unfitted them for taking part in the temple services (see Num 19). But they were not going up to Jerusalem. Their tour of duty was over and they were going down from Jerusalem back home (Luke 10:31). They had no valid reason, then, for not helping the wounded man. Perhaps they thought that their job was loving God and serving him in the temple; and that they could leave 'loving their neighbour as themselves' to other people to do. If so, they were very mistaken.

It is true that the first commandment is, as we saw in our last chapter, that we should love God with all our heart, mind, soul and strength; and that this must always have priority. But it is not enough by itself. The New Testament comments:

> Those who say, 'I love God', and hate their brothers or sisters, are liars; for those who do not love a brother or sister whom they have seen, cannot love God whom they have not seen. (1 John 4:20)

And again:

> How does God's love abide in anyone who has the world's goods and sees a brother or sister in need and yet refuses help? (1 John 3:17)

The third lesson of the parable
'Loving your neighbour as yourself' means that you must be prepared to act the good and compassionate neighbour not only towards your friends, your fellow countrymen and people whom you like, but also towards people you do not like, and even towards your enemies. We see that from the fact that Christ depicted the man who helped the robbers' victim as a Samaritan.[1]

Now in the parable when the Samaritan saw the wounded man lying by the roadside, he would have immediately recognised him as a Jew. Moreover, he would have known that if this Jew had been uninjured and a Samaritan attempted to touch him, the Jew would have insulted him, if not spat in his face. But in spite of all that the Samaritan went to him, rendered first aid, gave up his seat on the donkey to him, and walked himself; took him to an inn and paid the cost of his stay there until he recovered.

The lesson is clear. 'Loving our neighbour as ourselves' means more than loving just our family and friends, our fellow nationals and people of the same religion or ethnic group. We must love and serve people of all ethnic groups, of all religions, and even those who hate us and are our enemies. Jesus said: 'But I say to you that listen, Love your enemies, do good to those who hate you, bless those who curse you, pray for those who abuse you' (Luke 6:27–28). And certainly no follower of Christ is allowed to persecute people of other religions.

1 The Samaritans had at least part of the same Bible as the Jews had; but they worshipped in a different place from the Jews. The Jews, there-fore, hated the Samaritans, and sometimes persecuted them; and the Samaritans often returned the hostility. See Luke 9:51–56; John 4.

A practical problem

We have now found that in Christian ethics the basic motivation for carrying out both the first and the second greatest commandments is love. But just here there lies a fundamental problem. The reason why we do not behave as we should either towards God or towards our neighbour is precisely because we do not really love them. What is more, try as hard as we can, we often find it difficult if not impossible to love them. It would be useless, therefore, for Jesus simply to tell us that we ought to love God and our neighbour if he could not tell us where we can get the love from to love them with. For without the fuel of love, the engine of Christian ethics will not work. But Christ has seen the problem; and here is one of his answers to it.

The incident of the woman in Simon's house

> One of the Pharisees asked Jesus to eat with him, and he went into the Pharisee's house and took his place at the table. And a woman in the city, who was a sinner, having learned that he was eating in the Pharisee's house, brought an alabaster jar of ointment. She stood behind him at his feet, weeping, and began to bathe his feet with her tears and to dry them with her hair. Then she continued kissing his feet and anointing them with the ointment. Now when the Pharisee who had invited him saw it, he said to himself, 'If this man were a prophet, he would have known who and what kind of woman this is who is touching him—that she is a sinner.' Jesus spoke up and said to him, 'Simon, I have

something to say to you.' 'Teacher,' he replied, 'speak.' 'A certain creditor had two debtors; one owed five hundred denarii, and the other fifty. When they could not pay, he cancelled the debts for both of them. Now which of them will love him more?' Simon answered, 'I suppose the one for whom he cancelled the greater debt.' And Jesus said to him, 'You have judged rightly.' Then turning toward the woman, he said to Simon, 'Do you see this woman? I entered your house; you gave me no water for my feet, but she has bathed my feet with her tears and dried them with her hair. You gave me no kiss, but from the time I came in she has not stopped kissing my feet. You did not anoint my head with oil, but she has anointed my feet with ointment. Therefore, I tell you, her sins, which were many, have been forgiven; hence she has shown great love. But the one to whom little is forgiven, loves little.' Then he said to her, 'Your sins are forgiven.' But those who were at the table with him began to say among themselves, 'Who is this who even forgives sins?' And he said to the woman, 'Your faith has saved you; go in peace.' (Luke 7:36–50)

A vivid contrast. On the one hand, we see a woman who had in the past lived a highly immoral life, but now loved Jesus and showed it in her actions. On the other, we see an outwardly moral and very religious man who was formally polite to Jesus and invited him to dinner, but had no love or affection for him and showed it by his inaction.

The parable of the two debtors. The parable establishes the simple but fundamentally important point that when a man has run up a large debt that he cannot possibly pay; if then his creditor forgives him, he will love his creditor. In other words forgiveness produces love; and the greater the debt, the greater the love when the debt is forgiven.

The application of the parable. Sin is like debt; and we have all sinned. Moreover we cannot pay our debt. No amount of good works in the future can cancel the debt of the past. Since our normal duty is to love God with all our heart, mind, soul and strength, we could never exceed our duty and so have something extra with which to pay for our shortcomings in the past. Moreover if I owe ten billion pounds sterling and I cannot pay, I am bankrupt. But if I owe only one thousand pounds, and I cannot pay, I am still bankrupt. Whether we have sinned much or little we are all spiritually bankrupt.

But Christ can forgive us our sins; and when he does so, and puts the assurance of forgiveness into our hearts, it produces in our hearts a spontaneous love for God, and Christ and for all humanity: a love that was not there before and a love which we could never work up by our own will power.

Christ's explanation of the woman's love. She had been a prostitute. But she had been converted through faith in Jesus. And Jesus had forgiven all her sins, and assured her of God's pardon and acceptance. The result was that there sprang up in her heart a love for Jesus that she could not keep hidden.

The implied diagnosis of Simon's lovelessness. By contrast with the woman, Simon was very religious and, outwardly at least, morally correct. But he had no love for Jesus, nor any sympathy with the woman's demonstration of her love for Jesus. Why so? Because, it would seem, he had never had a conversion experience, had never realised how sinful he was. In fact, he had never come to Jesus for forgiveness and had no assurance of forgiveness in his heart. His religion may have been formally correct and his morals outwardly respectable; but he had no power to love the Lord his God with all his heart or to love his neighbour as himself.

One final lesson

Then Peter came and said to him, 'Lord, if another member of the church sins against me, how often should I forgive? As many as seven times?' Jesus said to him, 'Not seven times, but, I tell you, seventy-seven times.

'For this reason the kingdom of heaven may be compared to a king who wished to settle accounts with his slaves. When he began the reckoning, one who owed him ten thousand talents was brought to him; and, as he could not pay, his lord ordered him to be sold, together with his wife and children and all his possessions, and payment to be made. So the slave fell on his knees before him, saying, "Have patience with me, and I will pay you everything." And out of pity for him, the lord of that slave released him and forgave him the debt. But that same slave, as he went out, came upon one of his fellow-slaves who owed him a hundred denarii; and seizing him by the throat, he said, "Pay what you owe." Then his fellow-slave fell down and pleaded with him, "Have patience with me, and I will pay you." But he refused; then he went and threw him into prison until he should pay the debt. When his fellow-slaves saw what had happened, they were greatly distressed, and they went and reported to their lord all that had taken place. Then his lord summoned him and said to him, "You wicked slave! I forgave you all that debt because you pleaded with me. Should you not have had mercy on your fellow-slave, as I had mercy on you?" And in anger his lord handed him over to be tortured until he should pay his entire debt. So my heavenly Father will also do to every one of you, if you do not forgive your brother or sister from your heart.' (Matt 18:21–35)

This is another parable in which Jesus likens sin to debt. It is another example of Jesus' ability to evoke an intensely vivid scene with the minimum of words. Its relevance to our present study will be obvious. It tells us that a man who claims to have had his sins forgiven by Christ, and who nevertheless is not prepared to forgive someone who has sinned against him, even when that someone repents, is no true Christian. He is an impostor.

CHAPTER

The Christian Attitude to Work

In this chapter we are going to study our daily work. Some people enjoy their work so much that they have little interest in anything else. Other people find work so hard and boring that they wish they did not have to work. Still others, suffering the miseries of unemployment, would be glad to have any kind of work to do, however hard. Why do we have to work? Are there any other rewards and benefits that we get from work besides food, clothes and money? Basic as that question sounds, it might surprise us how people answer it, if they have even thought about it.

Jesus had many things to say about our daily work: but this above all, that it is of the utmost importance, first to control our work by the moral and spiritual principles of God's kingdom, and secondly always to remember that our daily work carries eternal significance and potential for good or ill. Jesus thus:

1. provides us with strong and true motivation for work;
2. teaches us how to get the maximum benefit out of

our work;

3. warns us not to allow daily work to crowd out life's truest, highest and most lasting riches.

For the classroom

Begin your lesson by asking some questions to help your students consider necessary distinctions in relation to work.

Why do we have to work?

Probable answer: in order to produce food, or to earn money in order to buy food, clothes and all the other things that we need and enjoy.

This is a good answer as far as it goes, and the Bible reinforces it (2 Thess 3:7–12). The Creator has designed us with stomachs that get hungry and demand food. The Creator has provided food (though in many parts of the world it is badly distributed); but at the same time he has arranged things so that we have to work in order to get it.

Are there any other rewards and benefits which we get from work besides food, clothes and money?

Some probable answers:

(a) Physical work is good for the body. Lack of exercise weakens the heart and muscles.

(b) It is boring, and psychologically unhealthy, to have nothing to do.

(c) Work itself can be enjoyable. It is hard work to be a professional footballer or ballet dancer. But the work itself is enjoyable, quite apart from the money it earns.

(d) It is psychologically satisfying to feel that one is needed. It is hard work for a mother to look after her children; but she likes to feel that her children need her, and is willing to work hard for them, even though she does not get paid for her work.

The prime motivation and the prime reward for work

Developing a righteous character

According to Christ one of the chief rewards that we should look for from our daily work, whether we are paid for it or not, is that work builds character. What he says is:

> 'Therefore do not worry, saying, "What will we eat?" or "What will we drink?" or "What will we wear?" For it is the Gentiles who strive for all these things; and indeed your heavenly Father knows that you need all these things. But strive first for the kingdom of God and his righteousness, and all these things will be given to you as well.' (Matt 6:31–33)

Christ is not saying that it is wrong to go to work in order to earn a living. God himself knows that we need food and clothes, and work is the normal way of getting these necessities. But these things are not the chief benefit we get from work, nor should they be our prime motivation for going to work. We are to seek first, says Christ, the kingdom of God and his righteousness; that is to say our first aim is to carry out God's kingly rule in all that we do, so that as we constantly obey his rule, we may develop a righteous character.

Suppose boys or girls want to become world-class footballers. How can they do it? They can, of course, begin by reading about football in a book and learning the rules. But reading is not enough. To become good footballers, they must go out onto the football field and practise regularly. In this way they will train themselves to react quickly, to control their passes and their tempers and to keep the rules and not cheat when the referee is not looking. Such training not only helps them to win matches: it does something to each of them as a person. It develops their abilities and builds up their characters as clean players and honest men and women. On the other hand, if they cheat by handling the ball at a crucial moment, they may win the game for their team, but they will have damaged themselves: they will be a less honest, a less good, man or woman, as a result. Their character, their quality as a man or woman, will have been diminished.

And so it is in everyday life. The Bible tells us to be brave, truthful, honest, and not to cheat, tell lies, steal, be immoral, greedy, envious, jealous, spiteful or bad-tempered. But simply reading about them in the Bible will not by itself build all these good qualities into our characters. For that to happen, we shall need constant practice at behaving ourselves as we should, and at resisting temptation. According to Christ, then, it is the chief benefit of daily work that it gives us this practice in obeying God's rules of behaviour, so developing strong, healthy, righteous characters. On the other hand, we shall meet many temptations in the course of our daily work. If we yield to them and are lazy and unreliable, or if we cheat and tell lies, or are greedy and selfish, we may appear to succeed, we may even gain more money and status; but we shall seriously, and perhaps permanently, damage ourselves and our own characters, and eventually suffer great loss.

How serious and permanent could this damage be?
Christ teaches that, though our work may well disappear and be forgotten, its effect on us and on our characters is everlasting. When, therefore, Christ met people who, though they pretended to be religious, were motivated simply by greed for money, and cared neither for God nor for their neighbour, he told them the famous, but solemn story of the Rich Man and Lazarus (Luke 16:19-31). Read the story for yourself and decide why, according to the story, the rich man found himself in torments in the afterlife.

'There was a rich man who was dressed in purple and fine linen and who feasted sumptuously every day. And at his gate lay a poor man named Lazarus, covered with sores, who longed to satisfy his hunger with what fell from the rich man's table; even the dogs would come and lick his sores. The poor man died and was carried away by the angels to be with Abraham. The rich man also died and was buried. In Hades, where he was being tormented, he looked up and saw Abraham far away with Lazarus by his side. He called out, "Father Abraham, have mercy on me, and send Lazarus to dip the tip of his finger in water and cool my tongue; for I am in agony in these flames." But Abraham said, "Child, remember that during your lifetime you received your good things, and Lazarus in like manner evil things; but now he is comforted here, and you are in agony. Besides all this, between you and us a great chasm has been fixed, so that those

who might want to pass from here to you cannot do
so, and no one can cross from there to us." He said,
"Then, father, I beg you to send him to my father's
house—for I have five brothers—that he may warn
them, so that they will not also come into this place
of torment." Abraham replied, "They have Moses and
the prophets; they should listen to them." He said, "No,
father Abraham; but if someone goes to them from
the dead, they will repent." He said to him, "If they do
not listen to Moses and the prophets, neither will they
be convinced even if someone rises from the dead."'
(Luke 16:19–31)

It was not because in this life he was rich; it was
because he had lived simply to make money for his own
selfish enjoyment. The second greatest commandment of
God's law said, as we saw in our last chapter, 'You shall
love your neighbour as yourself.' Now at the rich man's
gate there lay a helpless beggar. But the rich man made
no attempt to help him. It was not that the rich man
did not know the commandments. He was reminded by
Abraham that both he and his brothers had Moses and
the Prophets, that is, the Old Testament. But he simply
thought that it would make no real difference whether he
obeyed the Bible or not, whether he did or did not seek
first the kingdom of God and his righteousness. He found
out, when it was too late to change his way of life, that
the character we form here on earth is of eternal endurance and significance.

On getting the maximum benefit out of work

> Someone in the crowd said to him, 'Teacher, tell my brother to divide the family inheritance with me.' But he said to him, 'Friend, who set me to be a judge or arbitrator over you?' And he said to them, 'Take care! Be on your guard against all kinds of greed; for one's life does not consist in the abundance of possessions.' Then he told them a parable: 'The land of a rich man produced abundantly. And he thought to himself, "What should I do, for I have no place to store my crops?" Then he said, "I will do this: I will pull down my barns and build larger ones, and there I will store all my grain and my goods. And I will say to my soul, Soul, you have ample goods laid up for many years; relax, eat, drink, be merry." But God said to him, "You fool! This very night your life is being demanded of you. And the things you have prepared, whose will they be?" So it is with those who store up treasures for themselves but are not rich towards God.' (Luke 12:13–21)

This parable also deals with the profit that we reap from daily work. Notice that it does not say that it was wrong for the farmer to work hard and make large profits. It is what he did with the profits that it criticised. Nor is he blamed for wanting to enjoy the profits; on the contrary, the complaint is that his false attitude to his profits guaranteed that he would get the minimum, rather than the maximum, enjoyment out of them.

His first mistake: he stored his crops in the wrong

place. His fields had produced far more than his own immediate needs. So he decided to build bigger barns and store his crops here on earth; and then he would be able to say to himself: 'You have ample goods laid up for many years; relax, eat, drink, be merry' (12:19).

But he had forgotten that the length of our lives here on earth is uncertain. He had simply assumed that he was going to live for many years, whereas in fact he died suddenly that very night. And God called him a fool, because it now became evident that he had stored his goods in the wrong place. He must now leave them where he could no longer profit from them. From now on they would all belong to someone else.

But, someone will protest, where else could he have stored his goods? The Bible's answer would be that if he had decided to use his goods for the benefit of others and not simply for himself, in this way he would have laid up for himself treasure in heaven (Matt 6:19–21). The Bible says:

> As for those who in the present age are rich, command them not to be haughty, or to set their hopes on the uncertainty of riches, but rather on God who richly provides us with everything for our enjoyment. They are to do good, to be rich in good works, generous, and ready to share, thus storing up for themselves the treasure of a good foundation for the future, so that they may take hold of the life that really is life. (1 Tim 6:17–19)

But how does using one's profit for other people's good 'store up treasure for us as a good foundation for the future [literally "the world to come"]? Let's use an analogy. Suppose a new manager is appointed over a small engineering works. If he uses the profits wisely to develop the factory, increase the workers' standard of living, and enrich the local community, he will develop his own potential and skills as a manager, and his employer may well promote him eventually to become manager of a much larger factory. He may even find himself being appointed minister of state for engineering. But suppose he yields to temptation and uses the profits to buy himself a palatial house and expensive cars; he will both ruin his character and unfit himself for promotion. Indeed, he may well be prosecuted and imprisoned.

In similar fashion, Christ teaches that a person's attitude to life, and work, and goods and profits here in this life fits—or unfits—that person for responsibilities in the life to come.

The danger of work crowding God out of life

The rich farmer's second mistake: he forgot that, if you would be truly wealthy, you need to become not only rich in material things, but rich spiritually as well. Material riches are small compared with spiritual riches.

A girl who treasured an engagement ring but had no interest in the man who gave it to her would empty the ring itself of its chief significance. The foolish farmer allowed material prosperity to crowd out of his life all thought of God and of fellowship with him and obedience to him. It brought him to spiritual poverty in this life; and he died, unprepared to meet God in the next. 'So it is', said

Christ, 'with those who store up treasures for themselves but are not rich towards God' (Luke 12:21).

If then we are to become rich towards God, we must remember that important as work is there is one overwhelmingly important priority in life: to cultivate friendship and fellowship with God. He is our Creator, and designed us to do our daily work. But he never intended us to be slaves. He wants us to work for him out of love. And if we are going to love him, we must first be reconciled to him, receive the Spirit of Jesus, God's Son, and become ourselves one of God's freeborn sons (Rom 8:14-17). Only so shall we be able to put the principles of God's kingdom into practice in our daily work. How then do we come to know God like this? Jesus tells us: he is the way to the Father (John 14:6).

Martha and Mary

What relevance does the incident described in Luke 10:38-42 have to our present topic?

Now as they went on their way, he entered a certain village, where a woman named Martha welcomed him into her home. She had a sister named Mary, who sat at the Lord's feet and listened to what he was saying. But Martha was distracted by her many tasks; so she came to him and asked, 'Lord, do you not care that my sister has left me to do all the work by myself? Tell her then to help me.' But the Lord answered her, 'Martha, Martha, you are worried and distracted by many things; there is need of only one thing. Mary has chosen the better part, which will not be taken away from her.' (Luke 10:38-42)

CHAPTER 20

The Life to Come and Christian Ethics Now

It is evident from Chapter 19 that Jesus taught that one of the chief frames of reference for Christian ethics is not only a wholehearted belief in the existence of a spiritual dimension to life in this world, but also a similarly rigorous belief in the reality of the life to come, in the existence of heaven and of hell. But many people who admire, and would like to follow, the ethics of Christ find it difficult to accept this frame of reference. Yet to reject it is to cut out of Christian ethics a great part of its motivation; and a system of ethics without an adequate motivation is practically useless. So let us deal here with two of the objections (among many others) that people feel against the very idea of heaven—and of hell.

Objection 1. *Belief in heaven is merely escapism. It encourages people to put up with their miserable social and economic conditions on earth instead of vigorously struggling to improve them, in the vain expectation that they will be compensated for their sufferings here by a paradise in the world to come. It therefore devalues life here on earth, and undermines all serious effort to improve its conditions.*

But the very reverse is true. Christ's teaching about heaven and hell invests life here and all its activities with infinite importance. According to Christ anything less than a loving cooperation with our Creator in the use of our abilities and in the responsible development of earth's resources for the glory of God and the good of our family, nation and world, will have ruinous and eternal consequences for us not only in this short, temporary life, but in the eternal world to come.

A child at school, who believed that life ended when school ended at the age of sixteen and that there was no 'real' grown-up world beyond school, might well be tempted to play around and not take school and its lessons seriously. Indeed the trouble with some school children is precisely that they cannot imagine how serious life beyond school is; and therefore they waste their time at school and enter the adult world unprepared. And so, according to Christ, it will be with people who do not take heaven and hell seriously, for this life is the school that prepares us for the next.

Of course, the logical question to ask here is: what evidence have we that the world to come is real? The Bible's answer to this is to point to the historical evidence for the literal resurrection of Jesus Christ from the dead.[1] It suffices to say here that, according to Paul in 1 Corinthians 15, the resurrection of Jesus Christ in the past is the guarantee that one day in the future all who have trusted him in this life will be raised to live with him in the world to come. And it is the fact that the world to come is real that assures us that our work here on earth is worth doing, and worth doing to please the Lord himself who gave it to us. We are, as the Bible puts it, to be 'always excelling in the work of the Lord, because you know that in the Lord your labour is not in vain' (1 Cor 15:58). Thus belief in the reality of the life to come provides powerful motivation for life here and now.

Objection 2. *If there is a God, then we ought to serve him out of love and not for what we get out of it in the form of some reward in heaven.*

But this objection dissolves when we understand first what the reward for serving God is not, and then what it is.

Contrary to what many people think, the reward for good works is not salvation and acceptance with God, nor forgiveness and eternal life. These things, the Bible explicitly states, are free gifts; they cannot be earned by our good works: 'For by grace [that is, God's unmerited favour] you have been saved through faith, and this is not your own doing; it is the gift of God—not the result of works' (Eph 2:8-9). This fact, that acceptance with God cannot be earned, is something that many people find

1 See Appendix B for some of the key points.

very hard to understand. They are used to paying for what they get and think that human beings have the ability to pay God for his salvation through their good works. This shows that they have underestimated the seriousness of God's diagnosis of human sin. The Bible explains that '"no human being will be justified [i.e. declared righteous] in his [i.e. God's] sight" by deeds prescribed by the law, for through the law comes the knowledge of sin' (Rom 3:20). And that is true. When we try to keep God's law in our human strength we find that we fail, that we 'all have sinned and fall short of the glory of God' (Rom 3:23). If God is going to forgive us, it will have to be on the basis of his love and grace—no human being will ever be able to boast that he has earned forgiveness. This is why the Bible points us away from our own works to what Christ did on the cross when he 'died for our sins'. It is faith in his work, not ours that alone can save.

At this point there is often a protest: 'If you tell me that acceptance with God is not based on my good deeds then you undermine ethics. For are you not in effect saying that I can live as I like and God will still forgive me?' No! In the very place where the Bible tells us that salvation is not a reward for good works it also says of those who believe in Christ: 'For we are what he has made us, created in Christ Jesus for good works, which God prepared beforehand to be our way of life' (Eph 2:10). That is, good works are the outcome and evidence of acceptance by God and not its basis. We shall see two examples of this below.

But what then is the reward for good work? It is the ability and the opportunity to engage in more, and more important, work. Read the famous parable of the Talents[2] or Pounds:

> As they were listening to this, he went on to tell a parable, because he was near Jerusalem, and because they supposed that the kingdom of God was to appear immediately. So he said, 'A nobleman went to a distant country to get royal power for himself and then return. He summoned ten of his slaves, and gave them ten pounds, and said to them, "Do business with these until I come back." But the citizens of his country hated him and sent a delegation after him, saying, "We do not want this man to rule over us." When he returned, having received royal power, he ordered these slaves, to whom he had given the money, to be summoned so that he might find out what they had gained by trading. The first came forward and said, "Lord, your pound has made ten more pounds." He said to him, "Well done, good slave! Because you have been trustworthy in a very small thing, take charge of ten cities." Then the second came, saying, "Lord, your pound has made five pounds." He said to him, "And you, rule over five cities." Then the other came, saying, "Lord, here is your pound. I wrapped it up in a piece of cloth, for I was afraid of you, because you are a harsh man; you take what you did not deposit, and reap what you did not sow." He said to him, "I will judge you by your own words, you wicked slave! You knew, did you, that I was a harsh man, taking what I did not deposit and

2 Older English translations used the term *talents* which referred to a unit of currency.

reaping what I did not sow? Why then did you not put my money into the bank? Then when I returned, I could have collected it with interest." He said to the bystanders, "Take the pound from him and give it to the one who has ten pounds." (And they said to him, "Lord, he has ten pounds!") "I tell you, to all those who have, more will be given; but from those who have nothing, even what they have will be taken away. But as for these enemies of mine who did not want me to be king over them—bring them here and slaughter them in my presence."' (Luke 19:11–27)

Notice that the man who had used his pound well and wisely and had turned it into ten pounds, was rewarded by being given the responsibility of administering ten cities—a hugely greater amount of work than looking after ten pounds. After all it is only reasonable that a person who has worked responsibly and hard at running a small engineering works should eventually be put in charge of a large industrial complex.

The effect of salvation in the Christian work ethic

Consider now Luke's account of Christ's encounters with two different men—one of them poor and the other rich.

As he approached Jericho, a blind man was sitting by the roadside begging. When he heard a crowd going by, he asked what was happening. They told him, 'Jesus of Nazareth is passing by.' Then he shouted, 'Jesus, Son of David, have mercy on me!' Those who were in front sternly ordered him to be quiet; but he shouted even more loudly, 'Son of David, have mercy on me!' Jesus stood still and ordered the man to be brought to him; and when he came near, he asked him, 'What do you want me to do for you?' He said, 'Lord, let me see again.' Jesus said to him, 'Receive your sight; your faith has saved you.' Immediately he regained his sight and followed him, glorifying God; and all the people, when they saw it, praised God.

He entered Jericho and was passing through it. A man was there named Zacchaeus; he was a chief tax-collector and was rich. He was trying to see who Jesus was, but on account of the crowd he could not, because he was short in stature. So he ran ahead and climbed a sycomore tree to see him, because he was going to pass that way. When Jesus came to the place, he looked up and said to him, 'Zacchaeus, hurry and come down; for I must stay at your house today.' So he hurried down and was happy to welcome him. All who saw it began to grumble and said, 'He has gone to be the guest of one who is a sinner.' Zacchaeus stood there and said to the Lord, 'Look, half of my possessions, Lord, I will give to the poor; and if I have defrauded anyone of anything, I will pay back four times as much.' Then Jesus said to him, 'Today salvation has come to this house, because he too is a son of Abraham. For the Son of Man came to seek out and to save the lost.' (Luke 18:35–19:10)

The men in these two stories were in many respects very different. The beggar was very poor, the tax-collector was very rich. But they had this in common: both men had an undesirable and degrading way of making a living. The beggar lived on what he could scrounge out of other people; the tax-collector, in large part, on what he could swindle out of other people. But then Christ saved both of them; and the effect of salvation was that it completely changed the attitude of each man to work and to the way he made his living, and restored both of them to true human dignity.

The blind man
It was not his own fault, of course, that he was forced to beg for a living (though it is an indictment of the society in which he lived, and of many societies still, that disabled people were, and are, heartlessly ignored). But nonetheless it is a demeaning thing when human beings lose their independence and dignity, and instead of being able to maintain themselves and contribute to the good of the community, are obliged to live on what they can scrounge out of others.

Christ saved the man by doing a miracle and restoring his physical sight. But there is more to the story.

The beggar's spiritual perception. The crowd informed him that it was Jesus of Nazareth who was passing by. But the beggar had come to the conviction that this Jesus was no less than the Son of David, the Messiah and King. So he begged the king to use his divine, kingly power to give him his sight. And he was given his request. It proved to be the last time he needed to beg for anything from anybody else.

The beggar's reaction to the gift of sight. The first sight he saw would have been the king himself. What did he expect to see? Someone dressed up in royal robes, served by an army of courtiers and himself serving nobody? What he actually saw was a dusty, travel-stained, simply-dressed figure, a king who had come to be the servant of all, whose self-sacrificing motto was this: 'the Son of Man came not to be served but to serve, and to give his life a ransom for many' (see Mark 10:42–45; Luke 22:24–27). Catching sight of this king, the beggar quit begging and 'followed [Christ] on the way' of self-sacrificing service, as all Christ's true disciples are expected to do.

Here, then, is the great ideal at the heart of Christian ethics: the perception that Jesus is the Son of God, the Son of the owner of the universe, but that he came as the Servant–King to serve and to save us at the cost of his life. Anyone who has the spiritual sight to see that cannot help but follow him, and take the same attitude to life and work as he took.

The tax-collector

Here was a man who was so consumed with greed that he was prepared to work for the hated Roman imperialists and collect their taxes for them from his own nation, thus making money out of his own people's slavery. Not only so, he used his authority to extort from the people far more money than the Romans demanded, pocketing the excess himself. Perhaps he thought that his great wealth would make everybody fear and respect, if not admire, him. Instead they hated him and rejected him from all social intercourse. Understandably so, for here was a man hideously demeaned and distorted by selfish greed and love of money, a lost man destroying by his pursuit of riches the very acceptance, love and friendship he longed for, but could never find in mere money, let alone in tainted wealth. But Christ saw the longing of the impoverished inner heart and soul of this outwardly rich man, and he worked a miracle of transformation within him. He gave the man his (completely undeserved) friendship, accepted him as he was. And suddenly the man found his poverty of heart banished. He no longer felt a consuming compulsion to make money. Christ's unearned and unbought friendship had flooded him with such a sense of spiritual wealth, that he immediately decided to give half of his material fortune away, and to restore fourfold to anyone he had cheated.

Greed and love of money dehumanize a person; mere denunciation of excessive riches very often locks a greedy person inside a self-made prison. The wealth of the love and friendship of Christ opens that prison door and sets the person free to be truly human, to be the master and not the slave of money, to see that people are infinitely more valuable than things and possessions, and to learn, as Jesus taught, that it is more blessed to give than to receive.

These two examples show us clearly how God's salvation actually works. He is prepared to accept people as they are, provided only that they trust Christ; and then their consciousness that they have been accepted and assured of Christ's permanent friendship both in this life and in the life to come motivates them to grateful service to him and others. And this leads us to consider in our next chapter the way in which Christ valued every human being.

Eternal reward

Why is belief in heaven not escapism?

Which of the following marriage situations would you think to be preferable:

(*a*) A man tells his wife-to-be that he is not prepared to assure her of his acceptance of her unless and until she earns it by her good works?

(*b*) A man first unconditionally assures his wife-to-be of his acceptance and then, secure in his love, she loves him and seeks to please him in return?

Most people would regard (*a*) as highly unsatisfactory—an insult to the woman. It would, if she accepted it, turn her into a slave. It is strange, therefore, that millions of people think that their relationship with God must be of type (*a*).

CHAPTER 21

Human Personality and Human Relationships

What is your name? An even more difficult question is, what does your name represent? In the past names carried meanings. 'Andrew', for instance, meant 'brave'; 'Irene' meant 'peace'. But even so, those names did not fully describe the person who bore the name; and nowadays the meanings of names are often lost anyway. But never mind. Even though your name may be a common one, what it represents is something awesomely wonderful: your human personality. There are, and have been, billions of human beings in the world. But your individual personality is utterly unique: there is not another 'you' in all the universe. To start with, you are unique in your genetic make-up.

Christ's concern for damaged personalities

Although each human personality is unique, it is the sad fact that we are all flawed or damaged in some way. It is the purpose of Christ's coming and of his teaching to heal us. The following story is an extreme case; but it makes the point easier to grasp.

What is your name?

That's a fairly simple question. A more difficult one might be: 'What does your name represent?' Consider these further questions:

What is the difference between a number and a name? A soldier is known as Private 105769, say. What does that tell you about him?

What is the difference between a name and a label? The label 'Plum Jam' does not distinguish between pots of plum jam—it only distinguishes them from other kinds of jam. Many girls have the name 'Natasha' which certainly distinguishes them from girls whose name is 'Irene'. But not all Natashas are the same!

What does a human name represent? Read Mark 5:1-20 with your group, and look out for the crucial turning point in the story. Discuss together what the turning point is and what it has to do with the man's personality.

The healing of the demoniac

> They came to the other side of the lake, to the country of the Gerasenes. And when he had stepped out of the boat, immediately a man out of the tombs with an unclean spirit met him. He lived among the tombs; and no one could restrain him any more, even with a chain; for he had often been restrained with shackles and chains, but the chains he wrenched apart, and the shackles he broke in pieces; and no one had the strength to subdue him. Night and day among the

tombs and on the mountains he was always howling and bruising himself with stones. When he saw Jesus from a distance, he ran and bowed down before him; and he shouted at the top of his voice, 'What have you to do with me, Jesus, Son of the Most High God? I adjure you by God, do not torment me.' For he had said to him, 'Come out of the man, you unclean spirit!' Then Jesus asked him, 'What is your name?' He replied, 'My name is Legion; for we are many.' He begged him earnestly not to send them out of the country. Now there on the hillside a great herd of swine was feeding; and the unclean spirits begged him, 'Send us into the swine; let us enter them.' So he gave them permission. And the unclean spirits came out and entered the swine; and the herd, numbering about two thousand, rushed down the steep bank into the lake, and were drowned in the lake.

The swineherds ran off and told it in the city and in the country. Then people came to see what it was that had happened. They came to Jesus and saw the demoniac sitting there, clothed and in his right mind, the very man who had had the legion; and they were afraid. Those who had seen what had happened to the demoniac and to the swine reported it. Then they began to beg Jesus to leave their neighbourhood. As he was getting into the boat, the man who had been possessed by demons begged him that he might be with him. But Jesus refused, and said to him, 'Go home to your friends, and tell them how much the Lord has done for you, and what mercy he has shown you.' And he went away and began to proclaim in the Decapolis how much Jesus had done for him; and everyone was amazed. (Mark 5:1–20)

The disintegration of the demoniac's personality. We do not know what name the man had been given at birth. But apparently, later in life outside powers had invaded him and overmastered his personality. Very likely he tried at first to resist them and retain control over himself; but they were too strong for him. In the end he gave up trying to be himself, and when asked what his name was, he replied 'Legion'.

The cause of the trouble. The symptoms indicate serious mental illness and disintegration of personality; but in this case (not in all cases) the Bible points out that the mental sickness was caused by demon possession.

Alcoholism and drug-taking can have similarly dramatic and easily visible effects. All sin distorts the personality

For the classroom

Take the opportunity to warn the class against experimenting with occult practices, black magic, spiritism or anything of this sort.

According to the Bible—and modern experience in many countries—demon possession is an all too real possibility; and its effect in the end is to overpower, if not destroy, human personality. It is for this reason God solemnly warns in the Old Testament: 'No one shall be found among you . . . who practises divination, or is a soothsayer, or an augur, or a sorcerer, or who casts spells, or who consults ghosts and spirits, or who seeks oracles from the dead. For whoever does these things is abhorrent to the LORD' (Deut 18:9–13).

and, unless forgiven and its power broken, will lead to what the Bible calls 'perishing'; not cessation of existence but irrecoverable distortion, if not disintegration, of the personality, and in the end eternal separation from God.

Effects of the trouble:

(a) *Shamelessness and loss of self-respect.* The parallel account in Luke 8:27 says that 'for a long time he had worn no clothes'. He had lost all sense of shame, and shame should not be ignored. It has a positive role to play in preserving human dignity. Take 'blushing' for example. It is a mechanism which the Creator has built into us: it exposes our feelings of guilt for all to see, and also makes us feel uncomfortable when we have been caught out in some wrong deed or attitude. It also acts as a healthy deterrent and preservative: 'I can't do such and such a thing' we say to ourselves; 'I would blush with shame if I were found out.'

But when people constantly do shameful things, they gradually weaken this shame mechanism in their personalities, if not put it out of action altogether. The result is disastrous. God asks, 'Are they ashamed of their loathsome conduct? No! They have no shame at all; they do not even know how to blush' (Jer 6:15 own paraphrase). One consequence of such behaviour is: 'Therefore God abandoned them to the sinful desires of their hearts, to . . . the degrading of their bodies' (Rom 1:24–27 own paraphrase).

(b) *Morbid fear and anti-social behaviour.* Like some drug addicts and alcoholics he probably felt frightened by other people. At any rate he avoided society, living in lonely places on the mountains and in the tombs. He was an extreme example of what many people, sometimes even young people, feel: they are no good; nobody values

171

them; society demands too much of them and they feel threatened by what people expect of them; they want to escape from life's organised routine; they feel there's no future for them, they might as well be dead.

(c) *Self-loathing and self-destructiveness.* He would constantly cut himself with stones, and violently opposed any attempt to restrain him for his own good. And when Jesus commanded the evil powers that were destroying him to depart, the man at first thought that even Jesus was adding to his torture. So it is with many 'normal' people. They dimly realize that their sins and bad habits are damaging them; but when Jesus commands them to let these things go, they think that Jesus means to make life miserable for them.

The cure of the trouble. But, of course, Jesus had not come to torture him, but to restore his broken personality, his dignity and true freedom. And this is why Jesus asked him: 'What is your name?' The man had virtually given up trying to be himself. Asked his name, he replied, not 'John' or 'Andrew' or whatever his own name was, but 'Legion'. Christ disentangled the man himself from the evil powers that were dominating him, banished the evil powers, and set the man's personality free. And his fellow townsmen found him sitting clothed and in his right mind at the feet of Jesus (Luke 8:35). Now Jesus and not Legion was his lord; and Jesus' lordship means true freedom.

We now turn from this extreme case to think how Jesus sets us free today.

Jesus sets us free
By forgiving our sins. One story tells how, faced with a paralysed man, Jesus first forgave his sins and then gave him

power to get up and walk (Luke 5:17-26). When we sin we feel guilt and a bad conscience. And guilt is like a chain: it binds us and often makes us afraid to look the world in the face. Now one of the words for 'forgiveness' in the New Testament means 'a release'; and it is this that Jesus effects. We can hold our heads high again.

By telling us the truth. 'If you continue in my word,' says Jesus, 'you are truly my disciples; and you will know the truth, and the truth will make you free' (John 8:31-32).

All too often we pride ourselves on the very things that distort our personalities. We think it is clever to lie and cheat. We boast about our aggressiveness. We enjoy being spiteful and cruel and making others feel small. Jesus sets us free by showing us the truth about these false attitudes: they are not our friends, they are our jailers. If we mistake jailers for friends, we shall remain imprisoned and make no attempt to escape. One day these false 'friends' will be our executioners. On the other hand we may feel that it is no good trying to escape: the bad habits and false attitudes are too strong to break. Here too Jesus shows us the truth about the situation: the chains can be broken; as with the demoniac, 'Legion' can be driven out.

By setting us free from fear. Some fear is healthy. Fear of getting burned, for instance, stops us putting our hand into the fire. But some fear is unhealthy. Fear of being laughed at, fear of the gang, fear of violence can compel young people to get drunk, go on drugs, commit crime, whereas, left to themselves, they would not do these things. Jesus teaches us to develop a healthy fear of God, and to let it overcome the false fear.

Do not fear those who kill the body but cannot kill the soul; rather fear him who can destroy both soul and body in hell. Are not two sparrows sold for a penny? Yet not one of them will fall to the ground unperceived by your Father. And even the hairs of your head are all counted. So do not be afraid; you are of more value than many sparrows. (Matt 10:28–31)

The value of human beings

Is it important for us to sense that we are valued? How do you recognize that you are valued? If we are going to treat one another as we should, we must learn to value others and ourselves as God values both them and us. Consider the following passages from the Bible that show how God values human beings.

The value of the unborn child. Psalm 139:13–17 tells us that God watches over and loves the unborn child while it is being formed in the womb. To kill an unborn child is a crime against both the child and its Creator.

The value of a babe-in-arms. When mothers brought their babies to Jesus for him to bless them, the apostles at first rebuked the mothers. They thought that Jesus was too important to trouble himself with babies. But Jesus rebuked the apostles. God values babies as much as he values adults. They too are persons. 'Let the little children

Thinking it through

Each of the brief comments in this section can be used to stimulate group discussion (or to be the subject of a short essay which could then be the basis of a discussion).

to come to me, . . .' said Jesus, 'for it is to such as these that the kingdom of God belongs' (Luke 18:15–16).

The respect and support due to:

(a) *Parents* (Matt 15:1–9). We are to honour them; and, as is clear from this passage, honouring them means not just respecting them and obeying them when we are young, but maintaining them financially when they are old.

(b) *Widows*. Jesus showed a special concern for widows. Some of his strongest denunciations were delivered against those who took advantage of their helplessness and cheated or oppressed them (Luke 7:11–17; 18:1–8; 20:45–21:4).

(c) *The institution of marriage* (Matt 5:27–32). Christ points out with devastating clarity the seriousness of adultery and easy divorce which devalue human relationships and destroy the stability of the family.

The value of the individual. A shepherd may have a hundred sheep that all look alike to a stranger. But if he is a good shepherd, he will know every sheep by name, its character, its strengths and its weaknesses. Christ is just such a shepherd: 'he calls his own sheep by name' (John 10:3). God loves us not simply as humanity in general, but as individuals. And Jesus guarantees that he will never lose so much as one individual that commits himself or herself to him:

'For I have come down from heaven, not to do my own will, but the will of him who sent me. And this is the will of him who sent me, that I should lose nothing of all that he has given me, but raise it up on the last day. This is indeed the will of my Father, that all who

175

see the Son and believe in him may have eternal life; and I will raise them up on the last day.' (John 6:38-40)

'My sheep hear my voice. I know them, and they follow me. I give them eternal life, and they will never perish. No one will snatch them out of my hand. What my Father has given me is greater than all else, and no one can snatch it out of the Father's hand. The Father and I are one.' (John 10:27-30)

CHAPTER 22

Christian Ethics in an Evil World

All those who attempt to teach the ethics of Jesus will sooner or later come up against the objection: 'What's the use of teaching Christian ethics? They have been preached for nearly 2,000 years, and yet the world is still as evil as ever it was.'

At a superficial level we could rightly reply: 'If people don't use soap and water, and as a result remain dirty, it is unfair to blame the soap!'

But many will object: 'Of course it is not the soap's fault! But that does not alter the fact that if people persistently refuse to use soap, you will never make the world a clean place by simply *preaching* the virtues of soap. You will need to find some way of compelling them to use soap. And if you cannot do that, you might as well give up.'

There is, to be honest, a great deal of force in this objection, as we can see if we use another analogy. If you want the two sides in a football match to play the game according to the rules, it is not enough simply to teach the players what the rules are. You will have to have a referee to enforce the rules. If you don't, then one side will begin to cheat. And then the other side will say to themselves: 'It's no good our trying to keep the rules. If we don't cheat like the others, we shall lose the game.' So now both sides will cheat whenever they can.

So what about Jesus? He certainly taught ethics. But did he think it was enough simply to teach ethics? Or did he have something to say about the enforcement of ethics?

Such questions show how important it is to understand exactly what it was that Jesus came to do, and how he proposed to achieve it. The New Testament makes it clear that he came with the prime objective of setting up the kingdom, that is, the government, of God. His very first words were: 'The time is fulfilled, and the kingdom of God has come near; repent, and believe in the good news' (Mark 1:15). The reason for saying that the kingdom of God had now, at this particular point in history, drawn near was that he himself, so he claimed, was God's king whose coming had long been promised in the Old Testament (see, for instance, Zech 9:9 and compare this with John 12:12–15). And now he had come! This was very good news.

Setting up the kingdom of God necessarily involved Jesus in the first place in enunciating the standards of behaviour that would be expected of all who were admitted into his kingdom and the blessedness of those who lived by those standards. This is the purpose of the famous Sermon on the Mount recorded in Matthew 5–7.

The ethical requirements of God's kingdom

They are often contrary to popular,
accepted human standards
One example will be enough to illustrate the point:

> 'You have heard that it was said, "You shall love your
> neighbour and hate your enemy." But I say to you,
> Love your enemies and pray for those who persecute
> you, so that you may be children of your Father in
> heaven; for he makes his sun rise on the evil and on
> the good, and sends rain on the righteous and on the
> unrighteous. For if you love those who love you, what
> reward do you have? Do not even the tax-collectors
> do the same? And if you greet only your brothers and
> sisters, what more are you doing than others? Do not
> even the Gentiles do the same? Be perfect, therefore,
> as your heavenly Father is perfect.' (Matt 5:43–48)

Admittedly, this is so contrary to normal practice that
many people reject it as unworkable. But there is no denying that if everyone behaved in this way there would be no
discrimination against minority groups, no ethnic cleansing, and no aggressive nationalism.

They must be carried out in practice
and not remain mere theory

> 'Not everyone who says to me, "Lord, Lord," will enter
> the kingdom of heaven, but only the one who does

the will of my Father in heaven. On that day many will say to me, "Lord, Lord, did we not prophesy in your name, and cast out demons in your name, and do many deeds of power in your name?" Then I will declare to them, "I never knew you; go away from me, you evildoers."

'Everyone then who hears these words of mine and acts on them will be like a wise man who built his house on rock. The rain fell, the floods came, and the winds blew and beat on that house, but it did not fall, because it had been founded on rock. And everyone who hears these words of mine and does not act on them will be like a foolish man who built his house on sand. The rain fell, and the floods came, and the winds blew and beat against that house, and it fell—and great was its fall!' (Matt 7:21–27)

The famous ancient Roman philosopher Seneca wrote many tracts expounding Stoicism and telling other people how to behave. But he used his position in the state to acquire a vast personal fortune; and when the emperor Nero murdered his own mother, the empress Agrippina, Seneca helped Nero to write a letter to the Roman Senate covering up Nero's crime. But it is not only pagan philosophers that can be guilty of this inconsistency. Christ himself pointed out that some of the Bible teachers of his day were guilty of not practising themselves what they said other people should practise (Matt 23).

*They apply not only to outward acts, but
to inward thoughts and motives*

> 'You have heard that it was said to those of ancient
> times, "You shall not murder"; and "whoever murders
> shall be liable to judgment." But I say to you that if you
> are angry with a brother or sister, you will be liable to
> judgment; and if you insult a brother or sister, you will
> be liable to the council; and if you say, "You fool," you
> will be liable to the hell of fire.' (Matt 5:21–22)

In other words, to fulfil the command of God's law 'You
shall not murder', it is not enough to abstain from actually
murdering someone. If we get violently angry with someone, it is, of course, good to restrain ourselves and refrain
from actual murder. But it is all too possible while refrain-
ing from actual murder, to nurse anger and desire for
revenge in our hearts and secretly to think of all the ways
in which we would enjoy hurting the person concerned
if we could. And that, according to Jesus, is a breaking of
God's law; it is sin against our neighbour and against God,
just as actual murder would be.

Incidentally, we should notice here a very important
distinction between God's law and the laws of any given
country. Human governments can, and should, pass laws
against murder and other crimes; and if people break those
laws by actually committing a crime, they are rightly pun-
ished. But no human government can read our hearts and
know our thoughts (governments that have tried to control
people's thinking have become monstrous tyrannies). But

How far would anger take us?

When Hitler got angry he had the power to put his anger into action; and the result was that he killed millions of people. If when we get very angry we had power like Hitler had, what would happen?

God can, and does, read our hearts and thoughts, and holds us responsible for them.

Humanity's inability to keep God's law

These, then, are a few examples of the ethical requirements of God's kingdom, as Jesus taught them. What, then, did Jesus say about our ability to keep them? Here Jesus shows his profound understanding of human nature and his utter realism: he said it was impossible for us to keep God's commandments well enough to qualify for entry into the kingdom of God.

Consider this example. On one occasion Christ remarked to his disciples: 'how hard it will be for those who have wealth to enter the kingdom of God! . . . It is easier for a camel to go through the eye of a needle.' His disciples were amazed at this and said, 'Then who can be saved?' And Jesus replied, 'For mortals it is impossible'. We can be thankful that he added: 'but not for God; for God all things are possible' (Mark 10:23–27). But his reply underlines the point that we made at the beginning of this chapter: it is no good simply teaching people Christian ethics. The reason is that by themselves people do not have the strength (and often not the desire either) to carry out God's laws to God's satisfaction. Jesus was fully aware of this, of course, and he gave us reasons why this is so. Here are two of them.

182

Humanity is basically evil

'If you then, who are evil, know how to give good gifts to your children, how much more will the heavenly Father give the Holy Spirit to those who ask him!' (Luke 11:13)

Now many people think that this teaching is grotesquely exaggerated. They point out that in spite of much evil in the world, most people are kind and loving, and ready to do all kinds of good deeds. But Jesus does not deny it. Indeed he calls attention to the fact that most human fathers are kind and good to their children. But they are that, he said, in spite of being basically evil.

Naturally we do not like being told this. We prefer to think that we are basically good. So, when we do something good, we readily take the credit for it: 'I did that', we say. But when we do something bad, we often try to excuse ourselves: 'That was not really me,' we say, 'I don't know what made me do it.' But if it wasn't 'really me' who did it, who was it? 'No good tree bears bad fruit,' says Christ, 'nor again does a bad tree bear good fruit; for each tree is known by its own fruit. Figs are not gathered from thorns, nor are grapes picked from a bramble bush' (Luke 6:43–44).

Christ is making two points:

(a) If you have an apple tree that produces forty percent, or even ten percent, rotten apples every year, you say, 'There's something seriously wrong with that tree.' And humanity's behaviour is certainly more than ten percent below God's standards!

(*b*) It is no use a bush saying 'I know I have produced a lot of thorns; but I'm not a thornbush really: I'm a fig tree!' A tree's fruit shows what the nature of the tree is. Similarly our bad deeds are not some superficial phenomenon unrelated to our basic nature. They are the product of that nature and show what that nature is.

Any system of ethics, if it is going to be realistic, must recognize this. History has constantly shown it to be true. There was, for instance, much that was good in Marxist economic theory. It failed because it did not recognize that humanity's trouble was not just alienation from the means of production, but the basic sinfulness of the heart. That was enough to ruin any economic system, however good in theory. Capitalism may, or may not, be a better economic system; but it too suffers endless corruption from the same source.

Humans are rebels against God
This has been demonstrated by what has become the central point of all human history. When God sent his Son into the world, men not only rejected his ethical teaching: they crucified him. And it was not the drug addicts, criminals and Mafia alone who crucified him: it was the religious and political establishment urged on by the demand of the general populace.

But in the week before he was crucified Jesus analysed and expounded the cause and significance of his death by telling the parable of the Wicked Tenants.

> He began to tell the people this parable: 'A man planted a vineyard, and leased it to tenants, and went

to another country for a long time. When the season came, he sent a slave to the tenants in order that they might give him his share of the produce of the vineyard; but the tenants beat him and sent him away empty-handed. Next he sent another slave; that one also they beat and insulted and sent away empty-handed. And he sent yet a third; this one also they wounded and threw out. Then the owner of the vineyard said, "What shall I do? I will send my beloved son; perhaps they will respect him." But when the tenants saw him, they discussed it among themselves and said, "This is the heir; let us kill him so that the inheritance may be ours." So they threw him out of the vineyard and killed him. What then will the owner of the vineyard do to them? He will come and destroy those tenants and give the vineyard to others.' When they heard this, they said, 'Heaven forbid!' But he looked at them and said, 'What then does this text mean:

"The stone that the builders rejected
         has become the cornerstone"?

Everyone who falls on that stone will be broken to pieces; and it will crush anyone on whom it falls.' When the scribes and chief priests realized that he had told this parable against them, they wanted to lay hands on him at that very hour, but they feared the people. (Luke 20:9–19)

Notice that the tenants are not accused of having done their work badly. Their basic fault was this: they wanted to live and work just for themselves; to act as if the vineyard belonged to them and not to the owner and his son. This made them rebels against the owner; and that is why they rejected and killed his son. The parable gives a striking diagnosis and picture of what is the basic trouble with every human heart.

For the classroom

Get your students to read this passage (or read it to them). Make sure they can answer the following questions:

Who does the man who planted the vineyard represent?

Who do the tenants represent? The Jews, or every person, as well, including us?

What does the vineyard represent?

Who does the 'beloved son' represent (Luke 20:13)?

Why is he called 'the heir' (20:14)?

The lesson so far

From this it is clear that it is not enough just to teach ethics: Christ had to do something about humanity's rebellious heart and to make us both willing and able to enter God's kingdom and keep his laws. What was that something? And why did he not force everybody to accept that something, whatever it was? And what did he say he would do to those who persistently refused to accept it?

These and other questions we must answer in our next chapter.

CHAPTER

The Answer to Humanity's Fundamental Flaw

If people misbehave only because they do not know what is right and what is wrong, then clearly it would be sufficient to teach them Christian ethics and they would all begin at once to behave properly. But ignorance of what is right and wrong is not humanity's only—and certainly not the most basic—problem. According to Christ, humanity's basic nature is fundamentally flawed and evil, and lurking in our hearts is a self-centred rebellion against God; so that even when we know quite clearly what God's will is, we find we cannot do it as we should, and do not necessarily want to do it anyway. Simply teaching such people Christian ethics would obviously not be enough. It would be like telling a man with a damaged heart valve that he ought to walk energetically. He would be unable to do it, unless his heart was repaired first.

And so if anyone is going to be admitted into God's kingdom and to be empowered to live according to

Christ's ethical standards, there must first come a revolutionary change of heart. The inborn fear, resentment, independence, enmity against God must be broken down, and replaced by faith and love and dependence on God.

Here is the story of how Jesus effected this miracle of change in the hearts of two very different people. The first man was an outlaw, the second a highly respected religious teacher. Yet both needed this change of heart. As we study their cases we shall find basic principles of entry into Christ's kingdom that are valid for us all.

The conversion of a criminal

> One of the criminals who were hanged there kept deriding him and saying, 'Are you not the Messiah? Save yourself and us!' But the other rebuked him, saying, 'Do you not fear God, since you are under the same sentence of condemnation? And we indeed have been condemned justly, for we are getting what we deserve for our deeds, but this man has done nothing wrong.' Then he said, 'Jesus, remember me when you come into your kingdom.' He replied, 'Truly I tell you, today you will be with me in Paradise.' (Luke 23:39–43)

This man was not simply a petty thief or house burglar. He was a bandit or brigand. The word used to describe him in the New Testament is used by the near-contemporary historian, Josephus, to denote political terrorists. The man may have been a mixture of all these things.

For years, then, he had obeyed nobody, accepted no king, recognised no government. He was an extreme example of rebellion against both God and his fellow men and women.

These facts make his eventual change of heart all the more significant.

From rebel to willing subject

It is worth taking the time to trace the steps that changed this man from being a rebel against God and men, into a willing and obedient subject of Christ's kingdom. Here are a few hints to follow:

(a) He came to see and to admit that compared with Jesus he and his fellow criminal were sinful and deserved the penalty that the human government was imposing on them (Luke 23:40–41).

(b) But Jesus was sinless and innocent; yet he was suffering along with the guilty.

(c) Therefore the government that had condemned Jesus was itself guilty of a deliberate miscarriage of justice.

(d) Jesus claimed to be God's Messiah and King. The government denied it. That is why they were crucifying him, as they indicated by having the charge against him placarded on his cross: 'This is Jesus the King of the Jews.' Who was right? Jesus or the government? Obviously not this unjust government. Then Jesus was. And that meant that Jesus was the Messiah–King sent into the world by God. He was God's Son.

(e) That being so, death would not be the end for Jesus. Jesus would come again to reign and to set up God's kingdom on earth.

(f) But that produced a solemn fear of God in the criminal's heart and conscience. Here was Jesus, the sinless, condemned by the unjust government to suffer along with the guilty. If God cared for justice, then, there would most certainly come a day of judgment when earth's wrongs and injustices would be put right.

(*g*) But if so, what hope was there for the criminal himself? He too—and not just the government!—was sinful and guilty before God. Honestly he confessed it.

(*h*) Then he saw a ray of hope. He heard God's crucified king, Jesus, pray even for those who crucified him: 'Father, forgive them; for they do not know what they are doing' (Luke 23:34). If Christ would pray forgiveness for them, perhaps he would have mercy on him too.

(*i*) But he didn't want only forgiveness. He had long been a rebel. He hated the corrupt human government of his day. But he had never before met a king like Jesus who loved even his enemies and prayed forgiveness for them. Now he found a respect and love for this king welling up in his heart. He wanted above all else to accept him as his own king, to be allowed to enter his eternal kingdom and to obey him forever. 'Jesus, remember me', he said, 'when you come into your kingdom.' His conversion was complete.

(*j*) And the king not only forgave him, but assured him there and then of his immediate acceptance with God and of the guaranteed certainty of entry into God's heaven: 'Truly I tell you, today you will be with me in Paradise' (Luke 23:43).

This story, then, has shown us how Christ can change a person's heart and make him or her willing to obey him. But willingness to obey Christ is one thing; the ability to carry out his ethical commands is another. Christ is quite frank with us: in and of ourselves we do not have the power to carry out his commands. Here then is a story in which Jesus explains what must happen to us if we are to enter God's kingdom and be able to live according to his ethical requirements.

An extreme case?

In some respects this man's case was extreme. But three passages from the Bible will help us to apply its lessons to ourselves. They are Isaiah 53:5-6 and Romans 5:10-11; 8:7-9. Look them up and read them to your group.

The conversion of a professor of theology

Now there was a Pharisee named Nicodemus, a leader of the Jews. He came to Jesus by night and said to him, 'Rabbi, we know that you are a teacher who has come from God; for no one can do these signs that you do apart from the presence of God.' Jesus answered him, 'Very truly, I tell you, no one can see the kingdom of God without being born from above.' Nicodemus said to him, 'How can anyone be born after having grown old? Can one enter a second time into the mother's womb and be born?' Jesus answered, 'Very truly, I tell you, no one can enter the kingdom of God without being born of water and Spirit. What is born of the flesh is flesh, and what is born of the Spirit is spirit. Do not be astonished that I said to you, "You must be born from above." The wind blows where it chooses, and you hear the sound of it, but you do not know where it comes from or where it goes. So it is with everyone who is born of the Spirit.' Nicodemus said to him, 'How can these things be?' Jesus answered him, 'Are you a teacher of Israel, and yet you do not understand these things?

'Very truly, I tell you, we speak of what we know and testify to what we have seen; yet you do not receive our testimony. If I have told you about earthly things and you do not believe, how can you believe if I tell you about heavenly things? No one has ascended into heaven except the one who descended from heaven, the Son of Man. And just as Moses lifted up the serpent

in the wilderness, so must the Son of Man be lifted up,
that whoever believes in him may have eternal life.

'For God so loved the world that he gave his only Son,
so that everyone who believes in him may not perish
but may have eternal life.

'Indeed, God did not send the Son into the world to
condemn the world, but in order that the world might
be saved through him. Those who believe in him are
not condemned; but those who do not believe are condemned already, because they have not believed in the
name of the only Son of God.' (John 3:1-18)

Notice how Jesus underlines the absolute necessity of
being 'born from above' if ever we are to see or enter the
kingdom of God (vv. 3, 5).

Nicodemus believed in God. He had undergone all the
religious rites laid down in the Old Testament. He was
the leading teacher of theology in Jerusalem at that time.
But he had not yet been 'born from above'. He did not even
understand the concept.

What then is this being 'born from above' and why
is it necessary? Jesus answers these questions in verse 6:
'what is born of the flesh is flesh, and what is born of the
Spirit is spirit'.

Take an analogy. In the world around us there are different levels, or kinds, of life. There is vegetable life; above
that, at a higher level, there is animal life; and above that,
human life. A cabbage has vegetable life, a dog has animal life. Now if we feed a cabbage well, it will grow into

a big cabbage. But however well we cultivate it, it will never turn into a dog! To become a dog it would have to receive life from the higher, animal, level. Again, however well you feed and train a dog, it will never turn into a person and be able to play a musical instrument or read a book. To be able to do these human things it would have to receive a different kind of life from that which it already had: it would need to be 'born from above', from the higher level of human life.

So it is with us men and women. At our physical birth we received 'human life', because we were born of human parents—which is what Jesus means when he says 'what is born of the flesh is flesh'. But the kingdom of God is a spiritual kingdom. Its life is a higher kind of life than merely human life. It is the life of the Spirit of God. So if all we have is our merely human life, we would never see (that is, we would never understand) or enter the kingdom of God, any more than a dog could enjoy art or poetry, if all it had was animal life. It would never be able to play a piano—unless somehow it could be infused with human life. In the same way, to be able to enter the kingdom of God and to have the power to live according to its ethical requirements we must first receive the life of God's Spirit.

How then, and by what process, do we get this life of God's Spirit? The vital point to grasp is that it is a gift. We cannot earn it, or produce it ourselves. In that sense, it is like our physical life: none of us earned, merited or deserved our physical life. It was a gift, given us by God through our parents. Similarly when it comes to spiritual life: Jesus gives us spiritual life as a gift.

But what do we have to do to receive it? The simple answer is that we have to 'believe on the Lord Jesus' (Acts 16:31), or, as the Bible puts it elsewhere, to receive him (John 1:12).

But what does it mean to believe on the Lord Jesus? Here it would be worth pausing to study the analogy that Jesus himself used to help Nicodemus in John 3:14-16. One helpful way to do this is by reading the story of Moses and the serpent in the wilderness in Numbers 21:4-9, noticing its main facts and then observing how it compares with our situation. When we do we can see the following:

(a) The Israelites had sinned against God.

(b) They were bitten by poisonous snakes.

(c) They were dying, and were unable to save themselves.

(d) God in his mercy had Moses erect a serpent made of bronze on a pole.

(e) But that by itself would have saved nobody. If the Israelites wished to be saved from dying and to receive new life, they had to believe what God said and, as their only hope, to look away from themselves to the serpent on the pole. When they so looked, God did the miracle and saved them: they lived.

Now apply the analogy to us and our situation:

(a) We have sinned against God.

(b) The poison of sin is destroying us; unless we are born from above and given new spiritual life, we shall ultimately perish.

(c) We cannot save ourselves.

(d) But God has sent his Son into the world to bear the

penalty of our sins. He has been lifted up on the cross.

(e) We must admit that we deserve God's judgment on our sin; and that Jesus is our only hope. And when we look away from ourselves to Jesus who died on the cross for us, and we put our faith solely in him, God does his great work of regeneration in our hearts and gives us the gift of eternal life.

Thus both the criminal on the cross, and religious and upright Nicodemus, entered the kingdom of God through faith in Jesus. It is also in this way that we enter the kingdom of God here and now, by becoming the spiritual children of God. And though at the beginning we are only spiritual babies we now have what we did not have before—a new life with the potential to develop and to learn to carry out God's ethical requirements and to be loyal subjects of his kingdom. Nicodemus, who at first came to Jesus by night, later developed the courage to profess his allegiance to Christ publicly by asking the Roman governor Pilate for the body of Jesus after the crucifixion (John 19:38).

CHAPTER 24

The Very Heart of Christian Ethics

In our last chapter we studied two key elements in the teaching of Jesus:

1. None of us has the power to carry out the ethical teaching of Jesus as it should be carried out unless we first receive the Spirit of God and are 'born from above'.

2. Jesus is able and willing to give us the Spirit of God as a free gift and so to effect within us this 'birth from above'.

But this brings us back to the question of the enforcement of ethics which we raised in Chapter 23: If Jesus can give people the power which they need to live according to his ethical standards, why does he not compel everyone to receive that power and so make the world a better place to live in? After all, according to the Bible, Jesus is the almighty Son of God. Can he not do anything he likes?

The answer is, first, that God can certainly do anything he likes, but there are some things that he does not like to do. And one of those things is turning human beings into machines that automatically carry out his commands without having any real choice. God has given his human creatures free will. At the physical level he has given us eyes; but also eyelids! We don't have to look at the beauties of creation if we don't want to.

Similarly at the moral and spiritual level. God commands us to love him with all our hearts; but he will never force us to love him against our will, since forced love is not love at all. In the same way, being 'born from above' depends, as we saw in our last chapter, on our trusting in Jesus and entering by faith into a heart-to-heart relationship with him. Such faith cannot be forced: it must be voluntary.

Granted then, somebody will say, that God cannot force people to believe in him, and love him. But surely he could use his almighty power to stop bad people from doing evil to others? He could, of course, if he wanted to. When he saw a man about to tell a lie, he could strike him dumb. But that would virtually remove the man's free will: he could not disobey God even if he wanted to. Then again, if we all knew that the moment we told a lie we would immediately be struck dumb, few of us would actually tell a lie: we would be afraid of the penalty. But that would not necessarily change our hearts. Some footballers would happily commit a foul if they thought it would help them win the game. But they fear the referee would see them and immediately impose a penalty.

So they refrain from committing a foul, but not because they have realised that cheating, even in a game, is wrong, and have repented of it. They are still cheats at heart.

Christ could, of course, strike people dead the moment they did wrong. If he did, the whole human race would have been wiped out long ago and we should not be here today. But he doesn't; and the Bible explains the reason: 'The Lord . . . is patient with you, not wanting any to perish, but all to come to repentance' (2 Pet 3:9). 'God our Saviour . . . desires everyone to be saved and to come to the knowledge of the truth' (1 Tim 2:3-4).

And so when Jesus came the first time to set up the kingdom of God, the Bible makes it very plain that he did not come to condemn the world, but that through him the world might be saved (John 3:17). He therefore made no attempt to eliminate or destroy the wicked, as many people—even some of his disciples—had hoped he would. What he did is explained in the following parable.

The parable of the Sower

And he told them many things in parables, saying: 'Listen! A sower went out to sow. And as he sowed, some seeds fell on the path, and the birds came and ate them up. Other seeds fell on rocky ground, where they did not have much soil, and they sprang up quickly, since they had no depth of soil. But when the sun rose, they were scorched; and since they had no root, they withered away. Other seeds fell among thorns, and the thorns grew up and choked them. Other seeds fell on good soil and brought forth grain, some a hundredfold, some sixty, some thirty. Let anyone with ears listen!' . . .

'Hear then the parable of the sower. When anyone hears the word of the kingdom and does not understand it, the evil one comes and snatches away what is sown in the heart; this is what was sown on the path. As for what was sown on rocky ground, this is the one who hears the word and immediately receives it with joy; yet such a person has no root, but endures only for a while, and when trouble or persecution arises on account of the word, that person immediately falls away. As for what was sown among thorns, this is the one who hears the word, but the cares of the world and the lure of wealth choke the word, and it yields nothing. But as for what was sown on good soil, this is the one who hears the word and understands it, who indeed bears fruit and yields, in one case a hundredfold, in another sixty, and in another thirty.' (Matt 13:3–9, 18–23)

For the classroom

Read both the parable and its explanation and then make sure that your students can answer the following questions:

What process in real life answers to the sowing of the seed in the parable?

How many different reactions to the sowing were there? How are they different? What do they represent?

What, according to Jesus, are the chief things that keep people from truly receiving God's word?

Now we are ready to learn some further, very important lessons from this parable:

The life and all the potential for growth and fruit is in the seed.

(a) This is true at the physical level. Soil can produce nothing until the life-carrying seed is put into it.

(b) It is true at the spiritual level also. It is the Word of God that carries within it the life-creating, fruit-producing power.

(c) Jesus said: 'The words that I have spoken to you are spirit and life' (John 6:63).

(d) The Christian Apostle Peter says of his fellow Christians 'you have been born anew, not of perishable but of imperishable seed, through the living and enduring word of God' (1 Pet 1:23).

We should

(a) *let the seed sink down into our hearts* and not remain simply on the surface of our minds where it can easily be snatched away.

(b) *ensure that nothing chokes the word* so that it is never able to produce fruit.

Evidence should be visible in the lives of those who claim to have received Jesus' word that it has begun to produce in their lives the fruit of God's Spirit which is 'love, joy, peace, patience, kindness, generosity, faithfulness, gentleness, and self-control' (Gal 5:22–23). An apple tree does not become an apple tree by bearing apples. But an apple tree that never bore any apples would be no use. A baby does not get life by crying; but if it really has life it will cry.

Finally, *those who genuinely believe in Jesus* and receive his word *may expect on times to suffer distress and persecution*

(Mark 4:17); and they must be prepared to endure it.

Now this last point is so important that we must think it through. First of all, it is true to experience. Believers in Jesus are not exempt from illness. More than that: they often suffer persecution which non-believers escape. But why does God allow it? Why does he not cure believers of all illnesses, protect them from all persecution, and give them total prosperity?

Because faith and love must be tested and allowed to demonstrate that they are genuine. Let's take some analogies.

Suppose you are well-off, and whenever a certain man comes to see you, you are generous to him. The man, therefore, visits you frequently, says that he loves you and calls you his friend. Then suppose you lose all your wealth. You can no longer give the man anything. So he stops coming. Obviously he does not love you now. But the question is: did he ever really love you yourself for your own sake? And the answer is, No! He never did love you: he simply loved the gifts you gave.

Or suppose a businesswoman claims that she believes in acting justly. And suppose she does act justly as long as she does not suffer for it. But then she realises that if she acts justly she will lose a million pounds. So she acts unjustly and keeps her money. Does this woman really love and believe in justice? No!

The great Greek philosopher Plato held that no man could consider himself truly just unless he was prepared not only to receive no reward for acting justly, but to be persecuted for acting justly when he could, by acting unjustly, avoid persecution and receive reward.

Similarly, the Christian Apostle Peter explains to his fellow Christians why God allows them to suffer: 'now for a little while you may have had to suffer grief in all kinds of trials. These have come so that the proven genuineness of your faith—of greater worth than gold, which perishes even though refined by fire—may result in praise' (1 Pet 1:6–7 NIV).

But someone may object: 'Is it not unjust for evil men to persecute people simply because they believe in God and Jesus?' Yes, it is horribly unjust! And God will one day punish them for it, if they do not repent (2 Thess 1:3–10). 'But why does not God stop their persecution now at once? What right has he to call on Christians to endure it?'

Let the Apostle Peter explain:

> If you endure when you are beaten for doing wrong, where is the credit in that? But if you endure when you do right and suffer for it, you have God's approval. For to this you have been called, because Christ also suffered for you, leaving you an example, so that you should follow in his steps.
>
> 'He committed no sin,
>   and no deceit was found in his mouth.'
>
> When he was abused, he did not return abuse; when he suffered, he did not threaten; but he entrusted himself to the one who judges justly. He himself bore our sins in his body on the cross, so that, free from sins, we might live for righteousness; by his wounds you have been healed. For you were going astray like

sheep, but now you have returned to the shepherd and
guardian of your souls. (1 Pet 2:20–25)

Here we reach the very heart of Christian ethics:
Christians owe their salvation, forgiveness, eternal life
and ultimate heaven to the fact that while they were
still unrepentant and hostile to God, Christ was willing
to suffer and die for them that they might be brought
to repentance, forgiven and reconciled to God. Thus
Christians are called upon to put up with the suffering
inflicted on them by evil people, rather than cut off from
them all chance of repentance by calling down on their
heads God's immediate judgment.

Jesus, of course, was no masochist perversely enjoying
ill-treatment and suffering. He was no weakling either. He
could have summoned twelve legions of angels to destroy
his persecutors (Matt 27:52–54). Nor did he believe in a
God who was so sentimental that he would never punish
anyone. He, more frequently than anyone else in the Bible,
warned people of the penalty and consequences that God
must eventually inflict on them if they persisted in sin
and did not repent. It was Jesus Christ who said: 'And if
your eye causes you to stumble, tear it out; it is better
for you to enter the kingdom of God with one eye than
to have two eyes and to be thrown into hell, where their
worm never dies, and the fire is never quenched' (Mark
9:47–48). It was Jesus Christ who described the impen-
itent as being thrown 'into the outer darkness, where
there will be weeping and gnashing of teeth' (Matt 25:30).
Moreover Jesus claimed that he will be the judge at the

final judgment (Matt 25:31-46). Harvest time will come (see the parable of the Tares and the Wheat, Matt 13:24-43).

Jesus was therefore not interested in simply teaching people ethics and telling them that they should be good. He was concerned to redeem, if possible, even the worst of sinners, and by his death to provide a way of salvation for them. True Christians will follow his example. They cannot, of course, die for the sins of men in the way that Christ did. Only Christ could offer an atoning sacrifice for sins. But true Christians will feel impelled by the love and example of Christ to take the gospel of Christ to the world, and even to their persecutors, and to exemplify it by their behaviour, cost what suffering it may. Like Christ himself, they will not be content to preach ethics.

The words of Christ

Look up the passages from Matthew and Mark referred to here and discuss with your group the things that Christ himself says about coming judgment.

CHAPTER

The Teacher's Claims about Himself

A popular way of studying the ethical teaching of Jesus is to take his famous maxims and parables and concentrate on them without paying much attention to Jesus himself. After all, if one is teaching geometry, there is no need to begin by asking who invented or discovered its basic theorems. Knowing about the famous geometer Euclid's life and character adds nothing to the cogency of the theorems that he enunciated. They stand, or fall, simply on the strength of their inherent logic. Why, people ask, should it not be the same with Jesus' ethical teaching?

And then one is naturally attracted at first to Jesus' maxims because not only are they self-evidently true to life, but they are phrased in direct, pithy, sometimes humorous, always vivid and often unforgettable language. Some of them were stunning reversals of the generally accepted norms of behaviour of the time: 'love your *enemies*', for instance (instead of the normal 'love your friends and *hate* your enemies'), and 'the *meek* shall inherit the earth' (whereas everybody thought it was the aggressive and the violent who were more likely to get power). Some of them, again, were lightning-flash exposures of moral inconsistency and hypocrisy: 'you strain out [of your drink] a gnat but swallow a camel!' (Matt 23:24). This was said of people who go to great lengths to avoid break-ing some petty regulation and then without compunction flout the great fundamental principles of the moral law. Or consider the deliciously grotesque but effective exag-geration of: 'Why do you look at the speck of sawdust in your brother's eye and pay no attention to the plank in your own eye? How can you say to your brother, "Let me take the speck out of your eye," when all the time there is a plank in your own eye? You hypocrite, first take the plank out of your own eye and then you will see clearly to remove the speck from your brother's eye' (Matt 7:3-5 own trans.). Or ponder the devastatingly obvious truth of this unanswerable reply to religious critics who complained that Jesus was mixing with and befriending morally unclean and sinful people: 'The healthy do not need a doctor, but the sick do. . . . I have not come to call the righteous, but sinners' (Matt 9:12-13 own trans.).

Such memorable sayings certainly provide an under-standably attractive introduction to Christian ethics. But when we proceed to study the ethics of Jesus as a coher-ent system we soon make a far-reaching discovery: one cannot isolate Jesus' ethical teaching and study it sim-ply as an ethical system without considering the person of Jesus himself. For everywhere one finds that Jesus is himself the kingpin of his whole ethical system, in the sense that if what he said about himself is not true, his ethical system is invalidated and falls to pieces. Thus we are inevitably confronted with the deeper question: 'Who, then, is this Jesus?'

So let us first list some examples of this feature of his ethics and then assess their implications.

Jesus makes loyalty to himself the ultimate criterion of true morality

Here are some sample statements:

(a) 'Blessed are you when people revile you and perse-cute you . . . on my account . . . your reward is great in heaven, for in the same way they persecuted the prophets who were before you' (Matt 5:11–12).

Particularly significant here is the comparison which Jesus draws between his disciples and the Old Testament prophets. The prophets were persecuted by their contemporaries for faithfully proclaiming the words of God. Christians are warned that they may be persecuted for faithfulness to Jesus. In this equation, then, the Christians are the counterparts of the prophets, Jesus is the counterpart of God!

(b) 'Whoever loves father or mother . . . son or daugh-ter more than me is not worthy of me' (Matt 10:37). In other words a disciple's supreme loyalty must be given to Jesus.

(c) 'If you love me, you will keep my commandments' (John 14:15).

The motive for keeping Jesus' commandments is love to Jesus personally.

(*d*) 'Do you love me? . . . Tend my sheep' (John 21:16).
A disciple's motivating power for caring for his fellow disciples is primarily love for Jesus.

(*e*) 'Everyone therefore who acknowledges me before others, I also will acknowledge before my Father in heaven; but whoever denies me before others, I also will deny before my Father in heaven' (Matt 10:32–33).

In other words, people's loyalty or disloyalty to Jesus in this life will determine what kind of reception they get in the next.

Jesus declares that he himself will be the judge at the final judgment

Any serious ethical system must be prepared to state what, if any, is the ultimate penalty for wrongdoing. Atheistic systems deny that there is any penalty beyond what a person may (or may not) suffer in this life. Millions, therefore, they admit, will never get justice either in this life or in any life to come. Jesus, as is to be expected, believed and taught that there will be a final judgment, when ultimate justice will be done to the living and the dead. But what is not always realised is that Jesus claimed that he will be the judge who tries each case, pronounces sentence, and imposes the penalties at that final judgment.

(*a*) 'The Father judges no one but has given all judgment to the Son, so that all may honour the Son just as they honour the Father. . . . and he [the Father] has given him authority to execute judgment, because he is the Son of Man' (John 5:22–23, 27).

This announcement, incidentally, carries an important

implication for the nature of the final judgment, namely that human beings will be judged by one who is, and forever remains, human himself; who knows what it is to be human; who during his life on earth was tempted as humans are tempted (Heb 4:15); whose merciful kindness, truth, justice and sinlessness have been demonstrated, not merely in some remote heaven, but in our broken and sinful world. We cannot stay to explore this point further here: our present task is simply to notice that Jesus made this claim. But just in case it might be thought that this quotation from John 5:22-23, 27 is an isolated text untypical of the rest of the New Testament, let us notice in passing that this claim that Jesus will be the final judge subsequently forms a central part of the apostles' preaching. Peter, for instance, announces to a Gentile centurion, Cornelius: 'And he [God] commanded us to preach to the people and to testify that he [Jesus] is the one whom God appointed as judge of the living and the dead' (Acts 10:42 own trans.). And Paul elsewhere declares to the philosophers of Athens that 'God has set a day when he will judge the world with justice by the man he has appointed' (Acts 17:31 own trans.)—and Paul, of course, means Jesus.

(b) 'Not everyone who says to me "Lord, Lord," will enter the kingdom of heaven, but only one who does the will of my Father in heaven. On that day many will say to me, "Lord, Lord, did we not prophesy in your name . . . and do many deeds of power in your name?" Then I will declare to them, "I never knew you; go away from me, you evildoers"' (Matt 7:21-23).

Here two things stand out. First, that religious activity, even when carried out in the name of Jesus, will not necessarily gain his approval at the judgment. And secondly, according to Jesus, the decisive consideration will be whether he 'knows' the person concerned or not. In contexts like this the verb 'to know' clearly does not mean 'to know that someone exists or not'. It is a relational term, as for instance in the statement 'I am the good shepherd. I know my own and my own know me' (John 10:14). When at the last Jesus says to someone 'I never knew you', he is saying that he never had any personal relationship with that someone, or that someone with him. He never recognised him or her as one of his own. Thus, according to Jesus, the verdict at the judgment will turn on the question of the individual's relationship with him.

Four surprising claims that Jesus made

Any serious system of ethics which regards people as responsible for their actions (and not as predetermined biological machines who cannot rightly be blamed for defects in their machinery nor for their resultant bad behaviour) must have some way of coming to terms with the fact that all people from time to time break the moral code and harm other people—and then wish they hadn't. What can be done about it? Saying 'sorry' is good, but hardly enough by itself. If reparations are possible, they can be insisted on. But reparations are not always possible. Some way must, therefore, be provided of making forgiveness possible without implying that the breaking of the moral code does not, in the end, matter, and that sin can be conveniently ignored. Naturally, in a system of ethics that holds that the ultimate authority behind the moral law is God, this need for forgiveness becomes paramount.

It is not surprising, therefore, that the possibility of forgiveness looms large in Jesus' ethical teaching. The first surprising thing is what he actually claimed.

Jesus claimed to have personal authority to
forgive humanity's sins even against God

To see the full significance of this claim, we must study the startling effect it had on his contemporaries when they first heard it.

Consider Luke's account of Jesus healing a paralysed man.

> One day, while he was teaching, Pharisees and teach-
> ers of the law were sitting nearby (they had come
> from every village of Galilee and Judea and from
> Jerusalem); and the power of the Lord was with him
> to heal. Just then some men came, carrying a para-
> lyzed man on a bed. They were trying to bring him in
> and lay him before Jesus; but finding no way to bring
> him in because of the crowd, they went up on the roof
> and let him down with his bed through the tiles into
> the middle of the crowd in front of Jesus. When he
> saw their faith, he said, 'Friend, your sins are forgiven
> you.' Then the scribes and the Pharisees began to ques-
> tion, 'Who is this who is speaking blasphemies? Who
> can forgive sins but God alone?' When Jesus perceived
> their questionings, he answered them, 'Why do you
> raise such questions in your hearts? Which is easier,
> to say, "Your sins are forgiven you," or to say, "Stand

up and walk"? But so that you may know that the Son of Man has authority on earth to forgive sins'—he said to the one who was paralyzed—'I say to you, stand up and take your bed and go to your home.' Immediately he stood up before them, took what he had been lying on, and went to his home, glorifying God. Amazement seized all of them, and they glorified God and were filled with awe, saying, 'We have seen strange things today.' (Luke 5:17–26)

Notice: (1) that there were present a number of Jewish experts in the Old Testament, who would have been familiar with its doctrine of forgiveness; (2) that when Jesus said to the paralysed man, 'Your sins are forgiven', these experts accused Jesus of what to them was the most serious sin a person can commit—blasphemy against God; (3) that this shows what they understood Jesus to be saying. He was not saying: 'God forgives all who truly repent, and therefore we should all forgive one another, and I personally forgive you for any wrong thing you may have done against me.' No, Jesus was claiming divine authority. 'Who can forgive sins but God alone?' said the experts; and they meant it as a rhetorical question, carrying the unspoken answer, No one! And they were right: none but God has the authority to forgive sins against God. And therefore it raised with them, as it raises with us, the question: Who is this Jesus who claims for himself God's own prerogative to forgive sins? (See also Luke 7:49.)

Moreover, Jesus would have clearly understood why the experts were accusing him of blasphemy. But he made no attempt to withdraw or modify his claim. Rather he did a miracle to demonstrate that he, the Son of Man, did have, even while he was still here on earth, divine authority to forgive humanity's sins (John 5:24).

The second surprising claim that Jesus made with regard to forgiveness is perhaps even more startling.

*Jesus claimed that his own death would lay the
necessary legal basis for the just and honourable
forgiveness of humanity's sins against God*

    (*a*) 'And he took a cup, and after giving thanks he gave it to them, saying, "Drink from it, all of you; for this is my blood of the covenant, which is poured out for many for the forgiveness of sins"' (Matt 26:27–28).

    (*b*) 'For the Son of Man came not to be served but to serve, and to give his life a ransom for many' (Mark 10:45).

To these stupendous claims Jesus added two more:

*Jesus claimed that after his crucifixion,
he would rise from the dead*

> Then he began to teach them that the Son of Man must undergo great suffering, and be rejected by the elders, the chief priests, and the scribes, and be killed, and after three days rise again. (Mark 8:31)

*Jesus claimed that after his resurrection
and ascension he would come again*

    (*a*) 'In my Father's house are many dwelling places. I go to prepare a place for you . . . I will come again and will receive you unto myself that where I am you may be also' (John 14:2–3 own trans.).

(b) 'Then shall they see the Son of Man coming in a cloud with power and great glory' (Luke 21:27 own trans.).

Like all the other claims, these last two form an integral part of Jesus' ethical system. As the Christian Apostle Paul was later to admit, if Jesus did not rise from the dead, his death cannot be regarded as the basis of humanity's forgiveness (1 Cor 15:17); and without forgiveness Jesus' ethical system is fatally flawed. And if Jesus' prophecy of his second coming is false, so is the declaration that at his second coming he will be humanity's judge. And without that judgment Jesus' ethical teaching loses its ultimate authority and credibility.

CHAPTER

Why Jesus was Crucified

Here is how Matthew and John record the crucifixion of Jesus:

> While he was still speaking, Judas, one of the twelve, arrived; with him was a large crowd with swords and clubs, from the chief priests and the elders of the people. Now the betrayer had given them a sign, saying, 'The one I will kiss is the man; arrest him.' At once he came up to Jesus and said, 'Greetings, Rabbi!' and kissed him. Jesus said to him, 'Friend, do what you are here to do.' Then they came and laid hands on Jesus and arrested him. Suddenly, one of those with Jesus put his hand on his sword, drew it, and struck the slave of the high priest, cutting off his ear. Then Jesus said to him, 'Put your sword back into its place; for all who take the sword will perish by the sword. Do you think that I cannot appeal to my Father, and he will at once send me more than twelve legions of

angels? But how then would the scriptures be fulfilled, which say it must happen in this way?' At that hour Jesus said to the crowds, 'Have you come out with swords and clubs to arrest me as though I were a bandit? Day after day I sat in the temple teaching, and you did not arrest me. But all this has taken place, so that the scriptures of the prophets may be fulfilled.' Then all the disciples deserted him and fled.

Those who had arrested Jesus took him to Caiaphas the high priest, in whose house the scribes and the elders had gathered. But Peter was following him at a distance, as far as the courtyard of the high priest; and going inside, he sat with the guards in order to see how this would end. Now the chief priests and the whole council were looking for false testimony against Jesus so that they might put him to death, but they found none, though many false witnesses came forward. At last two came forward and said, 'This fellow said, "I am able to destroy the temple of God and to build it in three days."' The high priest stood up and said, 'Have you no answer? What is it that they testify against you?' But Jesus was silent. Then the high priest said to him, 'I put you under oath before the living God, tell us if you are the Messiah, the Son of God.' Jesus said to him, 'You have said so. But I tell you,

> "From now on you will see the Son of Man
> seated at the right hand of Power
> and coming on the clouds of heaven."'

Then the high priest tore his clothes and said, 'He has blasphemed! Why do we still need witnesses? You have now heard his blasphemy. What is your verdict?' They answered, 'He deserves death.' Then they spat in his face and struck him; and some slapped him, saying, 'Prophesy to us, you Messiah! Who is it that struck you?' (Matt 26:47–68)

Then Pilate took Jesus and had him flogged. And the soldiers wove a crown of thorns and put it on his head, and they dressed him in a purple robe. They kept coming up to him, saying, 'Hail, King of the Jews!' and striking him on the face. Pilate went out again and said to them, 'Look, I am bringing him out to you to let you know that I find no case against him.' So Jesus came out, wearing the crown of thorns and the purple robe. Pilate said to them, 'Here is the man!' When the chief priests and the police saw him, they shouted, 'Crucify him! Crucify him!' Pilate said to them, 'Take him yourselves and crucify him; I find no case against him.' The Jews answered him, 'We have a law, and according to that law he ought to die because he has claimed to be the Son of God.'

Now when Pilate heard this, he was more afraid than ever. He entered his headquarters again and asked Jesus, 'Where are you from?' But Jesus gave him no answer. Pilate therefore said to him, 'Do you refuse to speak to me? Do you not know that I have power to release you, and power to crucify you?' Jesus answered him, 'You would have no power over me unless it had been given you from above; therefore the one who handed me over to you is guilty of a greater sin.' From then on Pilate tried to release him, but the Jews cried out, 'If you release this man, you are no friend of the emperor. Everyone who claims to be a king sets himself against the emperor.'

When Pilate heard these words, he brought Jesus outside and sat on the judge's bench at a place called The Stone Pavement, or in Hebrew Gabbatha. Now it was the day of Preparation for the Passover; and it was about noon. He said to the Jews, 'Here is your King!' They cried out, 'Away with him! Away with him! Crucify him!' Pilate asked them, 'Shall I crucify your King?' The chief priests answered, 'We have no king but the emperor.' Then he handed him over to them to be crucified. (John 19:1–16)

In our last chapter we saw that it is impossible to study the ethical teaching of Jesus seriously as a coherent whole without coming face to face with the stupendous claims that Jesus made about himself. We listed, therefore, some of those claims and promised ourselves that in this and the following chapters we would attempt to assess them.

A good place to begin that assessment is Jesus' death, since there is no question about the historical fact that he was crucified by the Roman procurator, Pontius Pilate, in the reign of the Emperor Tiberius. It is attested not only by the Christian New Testament but also by the very anti-Christian Roman historian, Tacitus (*Annals* xv.44). The question is: *Why* was he crucified? As we study the answers that the New Testament gives to this question, we shall find that they involve most of the claims of Jesus which presently concern us; and simultaneously they present powerful evidence that those claims are true.

Why was Jesus crucified?

The New Testament gives two distinct, yet inter-related, sets of answers:

(*a*) For reasons which we shall consider below, the leaders of the Jews in Jerusalem engineered his death and persuaded the Roman procurator, Pilate, to carry it out. (Note: not all Jews in Palestine were involved, and certainly not the majority of the Jewish nation, most of whom lived abroad and did not hear about the death of Jesus until afterwards.)

(*b*) Jesus died of his own volition in obedience to God's will, as he explained beforehand to his disciples: 'No one takes my life from me, but I lay it down of myself. I have authority to lay it down and I have authority to take it again. This command I received from my Father' (John 10:18 own trans.).

The Jewish leaders' case against Jesus
The case was, in essence, that Jesus was guilty of blasphemy in claiming to be equal with God, and therefore was rightly put to death according to the Old Testament law of Leviticus 24:16. Here are some leading instances.

Jesus claimed equality with the Creator:

> Therefore the Jews started persecuting Jesus, because
> he was doing such things on the sabbath. But Jesus
> answered them, 'My Father is still working, and I also
> am working.' For this reason the Jews were seeking all
> the more to kill him, because he was not only breaking
> the sabbath, but was also calling God his own Father,
> thereby making himself equal to God. (John 5:16–18)

One Sabbath (the day that God commanded the Jews
to take as a rest day [Exod 20:8–11]) Jesus found a man
who had been paralysed for thirty-eight years and used
his divine power to heal the man completely. The Jewish
leaders accused Jesus of breaking the Sabbath by engaging
in the work of healing. But Jesus pointed out that, while
according to the Genesis story God rested from his work
of creation on the seventh day, God still is constantly at
work upholding, developing and restoring his creation. We
can see that ourselves. The healing mechanisms which
God has placed in the human body, for instance, are not
designed to switch off one day in seven! But Jesus' claim
was more than that: 'My Father is still working, and I also
am working', he said, bracketing himself with the Creator,
and his work with the Creator's work.

That, at least, is what the Jewish leaders understood
him to be claiming, as we see from the narrative. Far from
saying that they had misunderstood the implications of
his claim, Jesus went on to make its details more explicit:
he does everything which God does (John 5:19); he is the
source of all life, as God is (vv. 21, 26); he will be the final
judge (vv. 22–27); he will raise the dead (vv. 28–29).

To the Jewish leaders this was extreme blasphemy and

they tried to stone him, as indeed they had a duty to do according to the Old Testament law (Lev 24:16)—if, that is, what he claimed was not true.

Jesus claimed pre-existence: 'Then the Jews said to him, "You are not yet fifty years old, and have you seen Abraham?" Jesus said to them, "Very truly, I tell you, before Abraham was, I am." So they picked up stones to throw at him' (John 8:57-59).

It is important to notice that Jesus was not speaking as a reincarnationist. Such a person would have said: 'Before Abraham was born, I was', that is, 'I lived on this earth once before, in the time before Abraham; I subsequently died, but now I have been re-incarnated.' Jesus did not say that. He said, 'Before Abraham was, I am.' That is to say he was claiming the same timelessly eternal existence as God has. Once more the Jews attempted to stone him; for to them what he said was not only nonsense but blasphemy.

Jesus claimed oneness with God: '"My sheep hear my voice. I know them, and they follow me. I give them eternal life, and they will never perish. No one will snatch them out of my hand. What my Father has given me is greater than all else, and no one can snatch it out of the Father's hand. The Father and I are one." The Jews took up stones again to stone him' (John 10:27-31).

Here Jesus is claiming to have the same power as God. No one can pluck the sheep out of his hand any more than they could out of God's hand. To have the same power as God, Jesus must be God, one in essence with God, though not in identity. Once more the Jews pick up stones to stone him, the appropriate punishment for what they regarded as sheer blasphemy.

The Jews' ways of accounting for Jesus' claims
Some said he was mad: 'Again the Jews were divided because of these words. Many of them were saying, "He has a demon and is out of his mind"' (John 10:19–20).

Theoretically, of course, this is one way of accounting for Jesus' claims (that is, if they were not true); for when people are basically unstable emotionally and mentally, then they can develop bizarre ideas in religion, as in any other subject. But other Jews gave the obvious answer: 'these are not the sayings of one who has a demon'. For the words of Jesus have brought freedom from guilt and from fear, and peace, joy, love and hope to millions, and still do. All over the world many violent people who have received them have become peaceful, and many criminals have turned into law-abiding citizens. It is impossible to think that the one whose words have had such an effect was himself an unstable and dangerous madman.

Other Jews said he was a doctrinally wild schismatic and heretic, a rebel against the orthodox Jewish faith: 'The Jews answered him, "Are we not right in saying that you are a Samaritan [to the Jews Samaritans were heretical] and have a demon?"' (John 8:48).

Jesus' reply was: 'I do not have a demon; but I honour my Father'; and we today, after 2,000 years of history, are in a position to assess this claim that he honoured his Father. The Jew, Jesus, has brought multi-millions of Gentiles to believe, not in just any God, but in the God of Abraham, Isaac and Jacob, that is in the God of the Jews. No other Jew has ever done anything like it. True Christians assert with equal fervour as the Jews do, that 'there is one God' (1 Tim 2:5). Christians believe that God is a tri-unity; but they do not believe in three gods any more than Jews do. What sense would it make to say that Jesus was a dangerous Jewish heretic?

Still other Jews said that Jesus was in league with the devil himself: 'the Pharisees ... said, "It is only by Beelzebul, the ruler of the demons, that this fellow casts out the demons"' (Matt 12:24).

From this it is clear that Jesus performed miracles of healing, that the Pharisees admitted that he did, and that the power by which he performed these miracles was supernatural. But they were unwilling to admit that this supernatural power was God's power; for if it were, all Jesus' claims about himself would be true. This drove them therefore to the only alternative explanation: his supernatural power must be satanic; Jesus was in league with the devil!

But the conclusion was, as Jesus pointed out, logically absurd: 'if Satan drives out Satan, he is divided against himself; how then will his kingdom stand?' (Matt 12:26). Satan is scarcely in the business of destroying himself.

And then there is the moral argument, which the crowd raised on another occasion: 'Can a demon [that is, a morally evil spirit] open the eyes of the blind?' (John 10:21). If we are faced with a choice between God and Satan, and must distinguish between the two, we cannot decide by simply asking which power is superhuman: for both are. We must ask which superhuman power is good and which is bad. That brings home to us the seriousness of the moral choice that Jesus confronts us with. If his claims are not true, his superhuman power must be satanic and evil. But any attempt to class Jesus' miracles as satanically evil, is self-evidently morally perverse. We recognize modern medicine's achievements in curing, where possible, diseases like blindness, paralysis and leprosy, as undeniably good. To say that when Jesus did these things they were satanically evil is to call white, black and to turn all moral judgment upside down. 'If I cast out demons by Beelzebul [i.e. by Satan's power],' said Jesus, 'by whom do your own exorcists cast them out?' (Matt 12:27).

The culmination of all this came at the trial of Jesus. At the preliminary investigation before the high priest, Caiaphas, Jesus remained silent in the face of many false accusations. Finally the exasperated high priest put him on oath: 'I put you under oath before the living God, tell us if you are the Messiah, the Son of God.' 'You have said so,' Jesus replied. Upon this the high priest tore his robes, and said, 'He has blasphemed! Why do we still need witnesses? You have now heard his blasphemy. What is your verdict?' They answered, 'He deserves death' (Matt 26:63–66). When the Jewish leaders subsequently brought Jesus to be tried by the Roman procurator Pontius Pilate they first advanced as their prime charge against Jesus that he was involved in political treason against the Roman emperor (and we shall consider this in the next chapter). But Pilate's considered verdict was: 'As for me, I find no basis for a charge against him.' Thwarted at this level, the Jewish leaders then substituted this other charge: 'We have a law, and according to that law he must die, because he claimed to be the Son of God' (John 19:6–7 NIV).

The Jews' reaction: a lesson for us

The Jews are to be commended that they at least took the claims of Jesus seriously. In this they are a lesson for us. Nowadays it is possible to hear people say: 'I can't and don't believe that Jesus was the Son of God; but I do believe that he was a very good man and an excellent teacher of ethics.' But to talk like that is silly! If Jesus deliberately claimed to be the Son of God when he wasn't, then the last thing you can say about him is that he was a good man. He was in that case, as the Jews maintained, a deliberate blasphemer and worthy of death. And his teaching of ethics would aggravate his crime, not lessen it. Deliberately to deceive people into believing that he was equal with God, while all the time pretending to urge on them the absolute importance of telling the truth, would have been the mark of a most despicable charlatan. If Jesus was not God incarnate, he was the worst possible of all ethical teachers.

Christ's claim in the courtroom

Try to imagine the courtroom scene and ask members of the class or group to think why the court condemned Jesus for blasphemy.

Discuss the proposition: 'It is impossible to take the ethics of Jesus seriously without considering his claim to be the Son of God.'

Discuss the proposition: 'There is strong moral evidence to support Jesus' claim to be the Son of God.'

CHAPTER 27

The Death of Jesus and the Salvation of the World

Please read John 19:12–15

In the previous chapter we began to investigate the answers given in the New Testament to the question: Why was Jesus crucified? We saw that the principal charge made against him by the Jewish leaders was that of blasphemy because he claimed to be the Son of God. In this chapter we shall consider the other major charge they made against Jesus, then some details of Jesus' trial before the Roman procurator Pontius Pilate, and finally the reaction of the early disciples to Jesus' death.

The second major charge had to do with another claim that Jesus made.

Jesus' claim to be the Messiah

The background to this charge was the fact that in the Old Testament God, through the prophets, promised that one day he would send a great deliverer to liberate the Jewish nation from all their troubles and enemies and bring them complete salvation. This great deliverer came to be called the Messiah (derived from the Hebrew *mashiach* which means 'anointed'; Christ is the Greek translation of this name).

At the time of Jesus, some sections of the people thought of this promised Messiah as a political figure who would call the nation to arms and with God's help drive out the hated Roman imperialists. From time to time, indeed, men had arisen claiming to be the Messiah and had led their followers in disastrous rebellions against the Romans. Two such people, Theudas and Judas the Galilean, are mentioned in Acts 5:36-37 (see also Acts 21:38 for another example of a similar thing at a later date).

Now, Jesus certainly claimed to be the Messiah, and, when challenged at his trial by the Jewish authorities, he openly confessed his claim (see Matt 26:63-64 and Luke 22:66-67). But never once did Jesus represent himself as a political leader. On one occasion, seeing the crowd about to try to make him king by force, he deliberately withdrew (John 6:15). Challenged publicly as to whether it was right for Jews to pay taxes to Caesar, he unhesitatingly told the people that they must pay the taxes (Luke 20:19-26). Many times he had forewarned his disciples that God's will for him was that he should be crucified (as, for instance, Matt 16:21-23). And when the troops came to arrest him in the Garden of Gethsemane, and one of his disciples drew a sword in order to defend him, he rebuked that disciple and forbade him to use it (Matt 26:47-56).

Nevertheless, the Jewish high priest, sincerely or otherwise, persuaded himself and his colleagues that Jesus was another of these false political messiahs, who would, if left alone, raise a nationwide insurrection against the Romans that would result in the nation's complete destruction (see John 11:47–53). So they accused him before Pilate of claiming to be the King of the Jews in a political sense, and of fomenting rebellion against the Roman government. On these grounds they demanded his crucifixion.

Some details from Jesus' trial before Pilate

> Pilate replied, 'I am not a Jew, am I? Your own nation and the chief priests have handed you over to me. What have you done?' Jesus answered, 'My kingdom is not from this world. If my kingdom were from this world, my followers would be fighting to keep me from being handed over to the Jews. But as it is, my kingdom is not from here.' Pilate asked him, 'So you are a king?' Jesus answered, 'You say that I am a king. For this I was born, and for this I came into the world, to testify to the truth. Everyone who belongs to the truth listens to my voice.' Pilate asked him, 'What is truth?'

> After he had said this, he went out to the Jews again and told them, 'I find no case against him. But you have a custom that I release someone for you at the Passover. Do you want me to release for you the King of the Jews?' They shouted in reply, 'Not this man, but Barabbas!' Now Barabbas was a bandit. (John 18:35–40)

> Then the assembly rose as a body and brought Jesus before Pilate. They began to accuse him, saying, 'We

found this man perverting our nation, forbidding us to pay taxes to the emperor, and saying that he himself is the Messiah, a king.' Then Pilate asked him, 'Are you the king of the Jews?' He answered, 'You say so.' Then Pilate said to the chief priests and the crowds, 'I find no basis for an accusation against this man.' But they were insistent and said, 'He stirs up the people by teaching throughout all Judaea, from Galilee where he began even to this place.'

When Pilate heard this, he asked whether the man was a Galilean. And when he learned that he was under Herod's jurisdiction, he sent him off to Herod, who was himself in Jerusalem at that time. When Herod saw Jesus, he was very glad, for he had been wanting to see him for a long time, because he had heard about him and was hoping to see him perform some sign. He questioned him at some length, but Jesus gave him no answer. The chief priests and the scribes stood by, vehemently accusing him. Even Herod with his soldiers treated him with contempt and mocked him; then he put an elegant robe on him, and sent him back to Pilate. That same day Herod and Pilate became friends with each other; before this they had been enemies.

Pilate then called together the chief priests, the leaders, and the people, and said to them, 'You brought me this man as one who was perverting the people; and here I have examined him in your presence and have not found this man guilty of any of your charges against him. Neither has Herod, for he sent him back to us. Indeed, he has done nothing to deserve death. I will therefore have him flogged and release him.'

Then they all shouted out together, 'Away with this fellow! Release Barabbas for us!' (This was a man who had been put in prison for an insurrection that had taken place in the city, and for murder.) Pilate, wanting to release Jesus, addressed them again; but they kept shouting, 'Crucify, crucify him!' A third time he said to them, 'Why, what evil has he done? I have found in him no ground for the sentence of death; I will therefore have him flogged and then release him.' But they kept urgently demanding with loud shouts that he should be crucified; and their voices prevailed. So Pilate gave his verdict that their demand should be granted. He released the man they asked for, the one who had been put in prison for insurrection and murder, and he handed Jesus over as they wished. (Luke 23:1–25)

From then on Pilate tried to release him, but the Jews cried out, 'If you release this man, you are no friend of the emperor. Everyone who claims to be a king sets himself against the emperor.'

When Pilate heard these words, he brought Jesus outside and sat on the judge's bench at a place called The Stone Pavement, or in Hebrew Gabbatha. Now it was the day of Preparation for the Passover; and it was about noon. He said to the Jews, 'Here is your King!' They cried out, 'Away with him! Away with him! Crucify him!' Pilate asked them, 'Shall I crucify your

King?' The chief priests answered, 'We have no king but the emperor.' (John 19:12–15)

The verdict about Jesus

Study John 18:28–40, Luke 23:1–25, John 19:12–15 in detail and then answer the following questions:

How did Jesus prove to Pilate that he was not an earthly political king?

What kind of a king did Jesus say he was and what kind of a kingdom had he come to set up?

Left to themselves what verdict did Herod and Pilate come to about Jesus?

By what arguments and means did the Jewish leaders force Pilate to crucify Jesus?

Read John 18:38–40 and Luke 23:18–25 again. Do you see any significance in the fact that having accused Jesus of stirring up insurrection, the priests chose Barabbas rather than Jesus?

Comment on the suggestion: 'all of us from time to time in life are faced with the choice, Jesus or Barabbas. To reject Jesus the Prince of Truth and Life is to choose Barabbas the murderer.'

A detail from the crucifixion

Then two bandits were crucified with him, one on his right and one on his left. Those who passed by derided him, shaking their heads and saying, 'You who would destroy the temple and build it in three days, save yourself! If you are the Son of God, come down from the cross.' In the same way the chief priests also, along with the scribes and elders, were mocking him, saying, 'He saved others; he cannot save himself. He is the King of Israel; let him come down from the cross now, and we will believe in him. He trusts in God; let God deliver him now, if he wants to; for he said, "I am God's Son."' (Matt 27:38-43)

So the Jewish leaders managed to get Pilate to crucify Jesus; and, as we see from the passage just quoted, they thought that his death finally proved that all his claims were false. How could he be the Messiah and save Israel if he could not save himself from arrest, crucifixion and death? If he really was God's Son, surely God would not allow him to die such an excruciating and ignominious death. But Jesus did die. The Jewish leaders felt that at last they had triumphed and had put an end to Jesus and his influence forever.

But three days after his burial a report went round Jerusalem that Jesus' tomb had been discovered to be empty (Matt 27:62-28:15). Within less than eight weeks more than three thousand people had come to believe that Jesus had risen from the dead (Acts 2:41) and they became his disciples—which is more than had ever believed on him before he died. And since then, of course, the number has multiplied into millions.

The early Christians' attitude to Jesus' death

Now, some of the historical evidence that Jesus did actually rise from the dead will be dealt with in Appendix B. What interests us here is what these thousands of new converts thought of Jesus' death. They did not regard it as a disaster, nor even as an unfortunate happening that had been remedied by the resurrection. For them it was the most important and significant thing that Jesus ever did. What is more, they immediately began the custom of meeting together regularly at least once a week (generally on the first day of the week, the day Christ rose from the dead) on purpose to remember and celebrate Jesus' death. The simple ceremony by which they did this was called 'the breaking of bread' (Acts 2:42; 20:7) or 'the Lord's Supper'. Here is a description of it given by the Christian Apostle Paul.

> For I received from the Lord what I also handed on to you, that the Lord Jesus on the night when he was betrayed took a loaf of bread, and when he had given thanks, he broke it and said, 'This is my body that is for you. Do this in remembrance of me.' In the same way he took the cup also, after supper, saying, 'This cup is the new covenant in my blood. Do this, as often as you drink it, in remembrance of me.' For as often as you eat this bread and drink the cup, you proclaim the Lord's death until he comes. (1 Cor 11:23–26)

This ceremony, Paul reminds us, was instituted by Jesus himself the night before he died. It is, then, Jesus' own chosen way of being remembered.

Remember me

It is obvious that in instituting this ceremony, Jesus foresaw that its constant repetition all down the centuries would emphasize what he regarded as the most important feature of his work here on earth. He could, of course, have directed that once a week, when his disciples met together, one of them should publicly recite Jesus' Sermon on the Mount. The effect of this would have been to stress Jesus' role as a teacher of ethics. But he did not choose this way of being remembered. He could, alternatively, have directed that someone should stand up and publicly read an account of his outstanding miracles. This would have suggested that Jesus' chief function was that of a miracle worker. He did not choose this way either. He chose a ceremony that by its very form would recall his death. And not merely the fact of his death, but the purpose of it: the giving of his body to the sufferings and death of the cross and the pouring out of his blood for the forgiveness of sins (Matt 26:28).

If this, then, was the purpose of his death, it is understandable that he should insist on placing his death at the centre of his people's memory, and indeed, of the world's attention. His ethical teaching could not have procured forgiveness for humanity, nor could his miracles. Indeed the effect (healthy enough in itself) of his ethical teaching would be to make people more aware of their sins, and therefore of their guilt, than ever before. Only his death as a divinely-appointed sacrifice for sin could procure the necessary forgiveness and reconciliation with God.

Moreover, Jesus carefully laid down the details for this remembrance ceremony in order to make clear whose death and whose sacrifice it was that would procure forgiveness. When he handed his disciples the bread as a symbol of his body, he did not tell *them* to offer this symbol to God as a way of obtaining forgiveness: he told *them* to eat it. Similarly when he handed them the cup of wine as a symbol of his blood, he did not tell *them* to pour it out as a sacrifice for sin. *They* were to drink it (Matt 26:26–27). There was no salvation in the symbols: they were to be simply the means of remembering and proclaiming Jesus' death, as the centre-point of history, to all successive generations. It was to be clearly seen and understood, then, that the salvation of the world depended on nothing that the human race could do, or suffer, or sacrifice, but solely on the sacrifice that Jesus made when he died on the cross.

That is a stupendous claim, which we must now turn to assess.

CHAPTER

Jesus' Claim to be the Saviour of the World

In the last chapter we saw how Jesus, before he died, made it clear that the salvation of the world depended solely on the sacrifice he was to make through his death on the cross. This claim is so stupendous that we naturally ask what kind of evidence there is that it is true. Let us call first then on Christ's forerunner.

The testimony of John the Baptist

John the Baptist identified himself as the divinely appointed forerunner of the Messiah whose task it was officially and publicly to introduce the Messiah to his nation and to the world (see Isa 40:3-5; John 1:23). Accordingly, when he introduced Jesus at the beginning of Jesus' ministry, John naturally declared who Jesus was: the Son of God (John 1:30-34). But in addition he declared what Jesus had come to do: 'Here is the Lamb of God', said John, 'who takes away the sin of the world!' (John 1:29).

The significant thing is that this announcement was first made, not after Jesus had died, nor even at the end of his life on earth; it was made at the very beginning of his ministry. Right from the start it was announced that Jesus had come to die for the sins of the world. And Jesus himself subsequently repeated the claim: 'For the Son of Man came not to be served but to serve, and to give his life a ransom for many' (Mark 10:45), and 'I am the good shepherd. The good shepherd lays down his life for the sheep. . . . I lay down my life for the sheep' (John 10:11, 15). In this, of course, Jesus is unique. No other world teacher, not the Buddha, not Mohammed, not Socrates or Plato, not Napoleon, not Marx, nor any other philosopher, politician or founder of religion has ever announced at the start of his career that his main purpose in life was to die for the sins of the world.

And there are good reasons for this. If the claim were not true, then only a mentally deranged megalomaniac would make it. Only someone who was infinitely more than a finite human being could possibly offer himself as an adequate sacrifice for the sin of the whole world. And only a man who was himself sinless, and therefore not worthy of death himself, could offer his own death as a substitute for the death of sinners. It is understandable, therefore, that no other religious leader has ever made any such claim.

Yet Jesus made it. Then, was he mad? Perhaps the only appropriate answer to such a question is to say that if Jesus of Nazareth was mad, then by that standard no one in the whole course of world history has ever been sane.

The witness of the Old Testament

According to the New Testament, the Christian gospel is not simply that 'Christ died for our sins', but rather that 'Christ died for our sins in accordance with the scriptures [that is, the Old Testament]' (1 Cor 15:3). In other words, the New Testament claims that Jesus' death was the fulfilment of the promises and prophecies which God had made centuries before. In those prophecies God had indicated that he would send his great servant, the Messiah, into the world to pay the penalty of sin and die in order that sinners might be forgiven and reconciled to God. This is, of course, what Jesus himself claimed both before his death and after his resurrection:

> Then he [Jesus] said to them, 'These are my words that I spoke to you while I was still with you—that everything written about me in the law of Moses, the prophets, and the psalms must be fulfilled.' Then he opened their minds to understand the scriptures . . . 'Thus it is written, that the Messiah is to suffer and to rise from the dead on the third day, and that repentance and forgiveness of sins is to be proclaimed in his name to all nations . . .' (Luke 24:44–47)

So the idea that God's great servant, the Messiah, would suffer and die for the sins of the world was no new idea, unheard-of until Jesus suddenly sprang it on his contemporaries. Centuries earlier God had had it clearly announced and written down in the Old Testament. The only question for Jesus' contemporaries was: did Jesus' life, death, and resurrection match these Old Testament prophecies? The Jewish leaders were so sure that he was not the Messiah, that seemingly forgetting what their prophets had said, they put him to death—which is the last thing they ought to have done if they were trying to prove that he was *not* the Messiah.

But the same question remains for us as we make up our minds about the claims of Jesus.

The Servant of the Lord

Isaiah 52:13-53:12 is one of the most famous passages in the Old Testament (written, according to biblical scholars, more than 600 years before the time of Christ) that predicted what would happen to God's servant, the Messiah, when God sent him into the world.

See, my servant shall prosper;
   he shall be exalted and lifted up,
   and shall be very high.
Just as there were many who were astonished at him
   —so marred was his appearance, beyond human semblance,
   and his form beyond that of mortals—
so he shall startle many nations;
   kings shall shut their mouths because of him;
for that which had not been told them they shall see,
   and that which they had not heard they shall contemplate.

239

Who has believed what we have heard?
  And to whom has the arm of the Lord been revealed?
For he grew up before him like a young plant,
  and like a root out of dry ground;
he had no form or majesty that we should look at him,
  nothing in his appearance that we should desire him.
He was despised and rejected by others;
  a man of suffering and acquainted with infirmity;
and as one from whom others hide their faces
  he was despised, and we held him of no account.
Surely he has borne our infirmities
  and carried our diseases;
yet we accounted him stricken,
  struck down by God, and afflicted.
But he was wounded for our transgressions,
  crushed for our iniquities;
upon him was the punishment that made us whole,
  and by his bruises we are healed.
All we like sheep have gone astray;
  we have all turned to our own way,
and the Lord has laid on him
  the iniquity of us all.

He was oppressed, and he was afflicted,
  yet he did not open his mouth;
like a lamb that is led to the slaughter,
  and like a sheep that before its shearers is silent,
  so he did not open his mouth.
By a perversion of justice he was taken away.

Who could have imagined his future?
For he was cut off from the land of the living,
    stricken for the transgression of my people.
They made his grave with the wicked
    and his tomb with the rich,
although he had done no violence,
    and there was no deceit in his mouth.

Yet it was the will of the LORD to crush him with pain.
When you make his life an offering for sin,
    he shall see his offspring, and shall prolong his days;
through him the will of the LORD shall prosper.
    Out of his anguish he shall see light;
he shall find satisfaction through his knowledge.
    The righteous one, my servant, shall make many
    righteous,
    and he shall bear their iniquities.
Therefore I will allot him a portion with the great,
    and he shall divide the spoil with the strong;
because he poured out himself to death,
    and was numbered with the transgressors;
yet he bore the sin of many,
    and made intercession for the transgressors.

                                        (Isa 52:13–53:12)

A possible objection. Now someone may be tempted to argue: Since this prophecy was written long before Jesus was born and he would have known all about it, would it not have been easy for him to provoke the Jewish authorities to put him to death, and to make a martyr of himself, and so persuade his followers that he was the fulfilment of this prophecy? Such an argument may sound superficially attractive but it meets an insuperable objection: if Jesus set himself to fulfil this prophecy, he had to be sure that, after he was executed, he would rise from the dead. If he did not rise, his claim would be shown to be bogus. Which is why, of course, no one else but Jesus ever announced that he was going to fulfil the prophecy. That then brings us back to the question of the evidence for Jesus' resurrection. We have compiled some of the main evidence, and you will find it in Appendix B of this book, along with further suggested reading.

The testimony of personal experience

Let us begin with an analogy. The world is so made that we all find ourselves with stomachs that get hungry and drive us to look for food. It would be odd indeed if the world nowhere contained any food to satisfy that hunger. But how do we know that a loaf of bread, say, is good and genuine food and not a cheat? We know it by eating it and finding that it perfectly satisfies our hunger.

In the same way we all find ourselves with a conscience. We did not invent it. It witnesses to us that we have sinned against God and our fellow men and women, and deserve to suffer the penalty of our sin. We inwardly crave forgiveness. But where can we find forgiveness consistent with universal justice? It is just here that Jesus offers himself to us. He says he is our Maker and our judge: he must and does uphold God's law and condemn

For the classroom

Read and study Isaiah 52:13–53:12, noting its detail very carefully.

Take a New Testament and read its four accounts of the death of Jesus. They can be found at the end of the four biographies of Jesus (called 'Gospels') by the Apostles Matthew, Mark, Luke and John, with which the New Testament begins.

Compare what happened to Jesus with the predictions of Isaiah 53.

Then decide for yourselves how strong the evidence is that when Jesus died for our sins, he died for our sins, 'according to the Scriptures' (1 Cor 15:3).

Re-read Isaiah's prophecy and make sure the class has understood the two most important points it makes.

(a) God's servant was not only to suffer rejection, torture, and death at the hands of his fellow men, and to do so without retaliation. He was to suffer at God's hands as well. The Lord was to lay on him 'the iniquity of us all' (v. 6), and thus make him answerable for it. The Lord would then 'make his life an offering for sin' (v. 10). That would mean that God would treat him as our substitute. He would be wounded for our transgressions and crushed for our iniquities (v. 5). The Lord himself would crush him with pain (v. 10) and punish him (v. 5), so that he might suffer the penalty of God's law against sin instead of us. He was to 'be numbered with the transgressors' and so 'make intercession for the transgressors' (v. 12). The result would be that we could be 'justified' (NIV), that is, 'be accounted righteous' (ESV), be forgiven and acquitted before God's judgment bar (v. 11), and be made whole, have peace with God (v. 5).

(b) God's servant would die (v. 8) and be buried (v. 9). But after that he would prolong his days (v. 10). God's will would then prosper in his hand (v. 10) and he would triumph and be greatly exalted and universally acknowledged (53:10–11 and 52:13–15). The only way this could happen would be by the resurrection of God's servant from the dead.

our sins. Their penalty must be paid. But he is not only our judge. Because he is our Creator, he loves us, his creatures, as only a Creator could. And because he loves us, he was prepared to die for us to pay our penalty and to give us in its place his peace and eternal life. But how do we know that it, or rather he, is true? By believing and receiving him, and discovering that he meets, as no one else can, the need of our conscience.

Ultimately it comes down to the question: if there is a Creator God, how would I recognize him? The Bible's answer is: you would recognize your Creator by the fact that, though you are a sinner, he would do anything, consistent with righteousness, however extreme, rather than let you perish. To put it in the Bible's own words: 'God commends his love to us in this, that while we were still sinners, Christ died for us' (Rom 5:8 own trans.). 'For God so loved the world that he gave his one and only Son, that whoever believes in him shall not perish but have eternal life' (John 3:16 NIV).

PART 3
· ·
Christian Ethics

CHAPTER

The Spread of Christian Ethics in the World

In this chapter we return to what is the major topic of this book, namely the question of ethics. Now, the most detailed and extensive passages of ethical instruction in the New Testament are to be found in the so-called Epistles. These are letters written by apostles and other Christian leaders to churches, several of which had been but recently founded. They contain detailed ethical instruction on personal morality, family life and relationships, attitudes to one's neighbour, to the State, to daily work, to one's employer or employees, and so forth; and in many cases this ethical instruction occupies from a quarter to a third of the letter. The instruction had to be both basic and detailed because most of these new Christian churches were composed of a mixture of people. There were, to start with, Jews, who even before their conversion to Christ had been well taught in the ethics of the Old Testament. But there were also Gentiles whose pagan background and ethical standards were very different from those of the Jews, often luridly so. And then there were in different parts of the Roman Empire very big national, cultural and social differences. The new Christians in Philippi, for instance, lived in a city that, though in Greece, was a Roman colony. Its citizens were proud of it: they tended to wear Roman dress and often spoke Latin. Their city was very well-ordered. The new Christians in Crete, on the other hand, belonged to an ethnic group of which one of their own poets had written: 'The Cretans are always liars, evil beasts, lazy gluttons' (Titus 1:12 ESV). Cities like Athens and Corinth were marvels of polished sophistication, Athens a university city with brilliant architecture and a world reputation for intellectual excellence, and Corinth a wealthy commercial centre. When the Athenians first heard the Apostle Paul preach, their comment was typically cynical: 'What does this babbler want to say?' (Acts 17:18). At the other extreme the citizens of Lystra in Lycaonia (a district of Pisidia, north of the Taurus mountains) thought that Paul and Barnabas, his fellow missionary, were the pagan gods Zeus and Hermes come down to earth in human form! They would have offered them sacrifice, had Paul not prevented it (Acts 14:8–17).

It would be a formidable challenge to apply Christian ethics to such diverse groups of people in these different regions. And in great cosmopolitan cities like Rome, the capital of the empire, or Ephesus, the chief city in Asia Minor, the challenge would be doubly difficult. For Christianity is not a philosophy that can be adequately practised by an individual who in that situation keeps to himself or to his own ethnic or cultural group. Christianity is a life that demands to be lived in active fellowship with other believers. Whether originally Jews or Gentiles, Asiatics or Europeans, educated or uneducated, slaves or free, members of the Roman ruling classes or of some small nation subdued by the Romans and incorporated into their empire—all these, if they became Christians, were expected to accept, respect and positively love one another, and to take willing, active part in the fellowship of their local cosmopolitan Christian church. Christianity certainly made great demands.

Questions obviously arise; and the first of them is the down-to-earth historical and geographical question of how, when and where such groups of Christian converts came into existence. And that question can be answered by examining maps of the Mediterranean world that deal with the spread of the gospel in the first century (see related suggestions in *For the classroom*).

But there is another question that goes deeper and comes to the heart of the problem of ethics in which we are interested.

What was it about the Christian message that so affected people of such diverse backgrounds that many were willing to abandon their old lifestyle and adopt the Christian ethic?

To illustrate the question let us take two extreme cases.

1. The Corinthians (for Paul's visit see Acts 18)
Corinth was a large and wealthy city with a population (including slaves) of some 650,000 people. It was also a port. As to morals, consider the following summary of its reputation:

Like any large commercial city, Corinth was a centre for open and unbridled immorality. The worship of Aphrodite fostered prostitution in the name of religion. At one time 1 000 sacred [priestess] prostitutes served her temple. So widely known did the immorality of Corinth become that the Greek verb 'to Corinthianize' came to mean 'to practice sexual immorality.' In a setting like this it is no wonder that the Corinthian church was plagued with numerous problems.[1]

For the classroom

Here is an opportunity to work on a project together.

Get, or draw, a large map of the Mediterranean countries as they were in the first century AD. Mark also the extent of the Roman Empire.

Using the information supplied by the Acts of the Apostles, trace on your map the journeys of the early Christian missionaries, and how the Christian gospel spread from the Upper Room in Jerusalem where Christ commissioned his apostles and disciples (Luke 24:33–49; Acts 2:5–28:30).

Using both Acts and the Epistles, plot on your map the cities where Christian churches had been established, both in Asia and in Europe, by AD 70.

Here are a few approximate dates to help your students perceive that we are not dealing with legends but with datable historical events. Churches were founded: at Jerusalem, AD 30; at Antioch in Syria in the early 40s; at Philippi, Thessalonica, Beroea and Corinth between AD 50–52; at Ephesus, Colossae and Laodicea between AD 53–57; and in the island of Crete between AD 62–67.

1 'Introduction to 1 Corinthians', *NIV Study Bible*.

The Apostle Paul, writing to his subsequent converts in this city, understandably protests:

> Neither the sexually immoral nor idolaters nor adulterers nor male prostitutes nor homosexual offenders nor thieves nor the greedy nor drunkards nor slanderers nor swindlers will inherit the kingdom of God. (1 Cor 6:9–10 own trans.)

But then he adds: 'And that is what some of you used to be' (v. 11)—that is, they were that before their conversion to Christ.

Then, what made them willing to abandon their old lifestyle? We know from our own experience of the world that people of this kind are not normally attracted to, still less changed by, a course of lectures on ethics. What was it about the Christian message that changed them?

2. The Apostle Paul, himself

This is his own description of his lifestyle before he became a Christian, when he was still known as Saul of Tarsus:

> even though I, too, have reason for confidence in the flesh. If anyone else has reason to be confident in the flesh, I have more: circumcised on the eighth day, a member of the people of Israel, of the tribe of Benjamin, a Hebrew born of Hebrews; as to the law, a Pharisee; as to zeal, a persecutor of the church; as to righteousness under the law, blameless.

Yet whatever gains I had, these I have come to
regard as loss because of Christ. More than that,
I regard everything as loss because of the surpassing
value of knowing Christ Jesus my Lord. For his sake
I have suffered the loss of all things, and I regard them
as rubbish, in order that I may gain Christ. (Phil 3:4–8)

Here was a man meticulous in carrying out the religious rituals of his faith. By our standards, of course,
he was a fanatic, bitterly persecuting those whom he
regarded as heretics. But that is not how he would have
seen himself at the time. He did what he did out of
what he genuinely thought was love and devotion to God
whose honour these 'heretics' had grievously blasphemed.
In addition, he could honestly say that he had made a
determined effort to keep the moral law of God. While
he was not perfect, none could fault him or accuse him
of moral laxity.

Then what was it about the Christian message that
made him eventually think that his lifestyle needed to be
changed or that his own ethic was so hopelessly inadequate that he must abandon it like so much rubbish?
And in what ways was the Christian ethic superior to that
which he had followed up to this point?

Four major factors in the effectiveness
of the Christian gospel

The natural place to look first for answers to the questions
raised above is the Acts of the Apostles. In the course of his
history, Luke has included a whole series of sermons and

speeches delivered by various Christian leaders before different audiences (see box 'Sermons and Speeches in Acts').

Now these speeches and sermons, as Luke has given them to us, are, of course, only extended summaries of what was said on each occasion.[2] But they show clearly the main structure of each speech and its major supporting arguments. And they lead us to this profoundly important discovery: except for number 10 which was given to people who had long since become Christians, and number 13 where Paul is defending himself against charges of illegal behaviour, there is scarcely one sentence of ethical teaching to be found in all of these sermons and speeches put together. Historically this is highly significant. There is no denying that Christianity rapidly established itself in the ancient world. What we want to know is: how did it manage to do it? And the answer we find in the Acts of the Apostles is that the preaching that induced people to abandon their old lifestyles and adopt the Christian ethic was not itself instruction in ethics. Ethics only came later after people had been converted.

What message was it, then, that converted people?

We suggest that it would be well worth your time to read the sermons and speeches listed below, and, where appropriate, the records of the conversions that follow. As you do so, note any of the following themes that occur in any of the speeches or sermons and their contexts:

2 For further discussion on this point, see Gooding *True to the Faith*, 289 f., 395 f.

- The death of Jesus and the offer of forgiveness
- The resurrection of Jesus and its implications
- The offer of the gift of the Holy Spirit
- The promise of the second coming of Jesus, and the warning of the Day of the Lord and judgment.

These we suggest are the four major elements in the preaching of the early Christians that produced in people a change of heart, faith in the Lord Jesus and a willingness to abandon sinful living and to follow Christ's ethical teaching whatever that might be.

And not only so. In our next chapters we shall study how these four major elements of Christian faith form the basis of the ethical teaching that is subsequently built upon them, provide the ideals which Christian people are expected to aim at, and impart the motivation and the power to attain ever more closely to those ideals.

Sermons and speeches in Acts

1.	Peter, before the Jerusalem crowd	2:14–36
2.	Peter, before the Jerusalem crowd	3:12–26
3.	Peter, before the Jewish Council	4:5–12
4.	Peter, before the Jewish Council	5:29–42
5.	Stephen, before the Jewish Council	7:2–53
6.	Peter, to some Gentiles	10:34–43
7.	Paul, in a synagogue in Pisidian Antioch	13:16–41
8.	Paul, before the townsfolk of Lystra	14:14–18
9.	Paul, at the Athenian Areopagus	17:22–31
10.	Paul, to the church elders of Ephesus	20:18–35
11.	Paul, to the Jerusalem mob	22:1–21
12.	Paul, before a Jewish religious court	23:1–10
13.	Paul, before a Roman civil court	24:10–21
14.	Paul, before King Agrippa	26:2–29

CHAPTER

The Impact of the
Death of Christ
Part 1: A New Life

Fully to understand Christian ethics we should notice:
1.   Those many particulars in which the New Testament repeats and maintains the ethical instruction of the Old Testament.
2.   Those many features in which New Testament ethics are distinctive.

So, for instance, the Old Testament has said: 'Honour your father and your mother' (Exod 20:12). The New Testament repeats it and reinforces it by noting that this commandment is the first one among the Ten Commandments which carries a promise with it: 'so that it may be well with you and you may live long on the earth' (Eph 6:2-3).

'You shall love your neighbour as yourself', said the Old Testament (Lev 19:18). The New Testament not only repeats it, but lays it down as a basic principle of its own system of ethics: 'Owe no one anything, except to love one another; for the one who loves another has fulfilled the law. The commandments, "You shall not commit adultery; You shall not murder; You shall not steal; You shall not covet"; and any other commandment, are summed up in this word, "Love your neighbour as yourself." Love does no wrong to a neighbour; therefore, love is the fulfilling of the law' (Rom 13:8–10).

On the other hand, when Christ commanded his disciples to love one another, he did not simply repeat the Old Testament command that they should love their neighbours as themselves. What he said was: 'I give you a new commandment, that you love one another. Just as I have loved you, you also should love one another' (John 13:34). What was new about it? Why, the standard of loving which he set for them, when he added the words 'just as I have loved you'. He had loved them while he lived; but after he died, the early Christians came to see his death as the supreme expression of his love for them. And if this was the standard expected of them in their love for one another, then the Christian ethic was demanding indeed. 'We know love by this,' writes the Apostle John, 'that he laid down his life for us—and we ought to lay down our lives for one another' (1 John 3:16).

What this means in practical terms we shall consider later on. The immediate point is that here is a simple and obvious example of one of the major distinctives of Christian ethics: the impact on those ethics of the death of Christ. This is the topic that we are now going to explore.

In the first place, the death of Christ made it possible for people to have a completely new start in life.

A new start

Here is how the early Christians talk:

> So if anyone is in Christ, there is a new creation: every-
> thing old has passed away; see, everything has become
> new! All this is from God, who reconciled us to himself
> through Christ, and has given us the ministry of rec-
> onciliation; that is, in Christ God was reconciling the
> world to himself, not counting their trespasses against
> them, and entrusting the message of reconciliation to
> us. So we are ambassadors for Christ, since God is mak-
> ing his appeal through us; we entreat you on behalf of
> Christ, be reconciled to God. For our sake he made him
> to be sin who knew no sin, so that in him we might
> become the righteousness of God. (2 Cor 5:17–21)

When they say 'everything old has passed away', they are not indulging in fanciful exaggeration. They are refer-ring to the fact that the death of Christ has broken the chains of guilt which bound them to their past and stulti-fied all their attempts to adopt a reformed lifestyle.

Let us use an analogy. Suppose a man has betrayed his country and in his attempt to escape justice has robbed, forged bank notes and committed violence. He may wish to be done with this way of life and make a completely new start. But unless and until he has paid the penalty for his past misdeeds and been reconciled to the government and society in general, he has no realistic hope of leading a normal and healthy life. And if the penalty for his crimes is death, he has no future at all!

Now we may not think of ourselves as having been guilty of such lurid crimes as this man; but we have all broken God's law, trespassed against his commands and, as the Bible puts it, 'we have all turned to our own way' (Isa 53:6). We could have no valid future, however hard we tried to reform ourselves, unless and until God could forgive our trespasses, release us from our past, and reconcile us to himself. And this is what the death of Christ has made it possible for God to do. 'In Christ God was reconciling the world to himself, not counting their trespasses against them' (2 Cor 5:19). 'We were reconciled to God through the death of his Son', says Scripture (Rom 5:10). 'Through him [Christ] God was pleased to reconcile to himself all things, whether on earth or in heaven, by making peace through the blood of his [Christ's] cross' (Col 1:20).

In Old Testament times when a man had committed some heinous crime, he was first executed, and then his body was hung on a tree until sundown. The purpose was publicly to exhibit God's curse, that is, God's profound disapproval of the criminal's sin (Deut 21:22–23). Similarly, God's law pronounced God's curse on anyone who broke it (Deut 27:26). So God's Son not only died to pay the penalty of our sin: he was also publicly hung upon a cross of wood, to display before the universe God's uncompromising disapproval of human sin. 'Christ', says the Bible, 'redeemed us from the curse of the law by becoming a curse for us—for it is written, "Cursed is everyone who hangs on a tree"' (Gal 3:13). God can, therefore, freely pardon all who own their guilt, repent, and accept God's Son as their substitute. But at the same time he has clearly demonstrated before the universe that in pardoning them, he has not gone soft on sin!

In addition, the death of Christ has provided his disciples with new terms and conditions for living.

A new covenant

These are the terms of the new covenant, as the Bible calls it, which:

> (a) Christ announced and symbolised, when on the night before he died he gave a cup of wine to his disciples, saying, 'This cup is the new covenant in my blood, which is poured out for you' (Luke 22:20 NIV).
>
> (b) Christ actually made, enacted and guaranteed, when he died on the cross.

Here are those terms:

'This is the covenant that I will make with them
  after those days, says the Lord:
I will put my laws in their hearts,
  and I will write them on their minds,'

he also adds,

'I will remember their sins and their lawless deeds no
more.'

Where there is forgiveness of these, there is no longer
any offering for sin. (Heb 10:16–18)

This new covenant, then, sets the terms and conditions according to which Christ's disciples are enabled to live and develop a truly Christian lifestyle. First, Christ puts his laws into his disciples' minds and hearts so that these laws cease to be merely an external code of rules and regulations, and become part and parcel of the disciples' way of thinking and feeling, their second nature, so to speak.

On the other hand this does not mean that Christ's disciples are able forthwith to lead a perfectly sinless life.

Let us use an analogy that will help to explain why that is. If you want a computer to control the flight of an aeroplane, you must put into the computer a program designed for that purpose. Without such a program, the computer, however good it was, would not be able to fly the aeroplane at all. So, unless Christ puts God's laws into our hearts and minds, we cannot control our lives as true Christians should.

But suppose the computer into which you put the program has certain limitations on what it can do, and certain defects here and there. It may well be able to control the aeroplane's flight 70 per cent of the time; but it will also make mistakes some of the time; and the human pilot will have constantly to monitor it and be ready to correct its mistakes. So it is with Christian disciples. At birth they inherited imperfect genes, defective bodies, minds and emotions. Now Christ has put God's laws into their hearts and minds; and they are determined to carry them out. Increasingly they will succeed. But sometimes they will fail; and Christ, their 'pilot', will have to correct them.

Does it matter, then, when Christian disciples fail and sin? Of course, it matters. Well, then, what happens? Do they lose their salvation and have to start all over again? No! It is here that the final clauses of the new covenant come into play. God has foreseen the failure, and Christ's death has already paid the penalty for it in advance. And so God can assure Christ's disciples, 'their sins and iniquities I will remember no more'. The disciples must, of course, confess their failure to God; but God's own guarantee is that 'if we confess our sins, he is faithful and righteous to forgive us our sins and to cleanse us from all unrighteousness' (1 John 1:9 own trans.). And the Holy Spirit assures us that no further offering of the sacrifice of Christ, or of anything else is needed (Heb 10:18, see above). Christ has paid in advance the full cost of the disciples' training in holiness.

Here is an illustration. You cannot learn chemistry without conducting experiments. But when students do experiments, they are liable from time to time to make mistakes; and mistakes can be dangerous and do a lot of expensive damage. At the school I attended as a boy, parents had to deposit a sum of money in advance with the school, to pay for any damage that might be caused by the mistakes of their children as they learned chemistry. If Christian disciples are to learn to use the new powers that Christ has given them to live a holy life, they will need a lot of practice; and inevitably they will make mistakes and fail from time to time. But serious as that is, it does not cancel their salvation. Christ's death has already paid the penalty of failure; and the disciple is free to continue the training process in fellowship with God.

'If that were so,' says someone, 'would it not undermine ethics and morality and encourage disciples to be careless and lax in their behaviour?' No, not at least if they are true disciples; because, as we shall see in our next chapter, the death of Christ establishes a new ethic of love, gratitude and moral consistency. For example, Paul writes:

> The love of Christ constrains us; because we thus judge, that one died for all, therefore all died; and he died for all, that those who live should no longer live unto themselves, but unto him who for their sakes died and rose again. (2 Cor 5:14–15 own trans.)

What difference does it make?

Find and discuss examples of ethical injunctions from the Old Testament which are repeated in the New Testament. What difference would it make to society today if they were practised?

What is the relevance of the death of Christ to Christian ethics and behaviour?

Before you read the next chapter, try to think of reasons, based on 2 Corinthians 5:14–15, why the fact that there is forgiveness for sins through the death of Christ on the cross does not undermine ethics and morality.

For the classroom

Ask your students to write an essay on the commandment 'You shall love your neighbour as yourself', paying special attention to the reasons why it is called a 'new commandment' in the New Testament. Suggest that the students try to find practical examples of carrying out this commandment both in the Bible and in everyday experience.

CHAPTER

The Impact of the
Death of Christ
Part 2: A New Ethical Motivation

The Bible tells us that when a person places his or her life in Christ's hands, Christ puts God's laws into their heart and mind and gives them the resources to live a holy life (Heb 10:16–17). But the development of true holiness is not an automatic process. Because of human weakness, followers of Christ still fail and still sin. But, knowing their weakness, God has foreseen their failure and has graciously provided forgiveness. In the midst of life's challenges, trials and joys, a follower of Christ participates in God's training process knowing that, even though sin is serious, it does not cancel his or her salvation.

But, says someone, would this not tend to undermine ethics and morality by encouraging disciples to be careless and lax in their behaviour? The answer is no, not at least if they are genuine disciples of Christ; because the death of

Christ establishes a new ethic of love and gratitude.

A new ethic

In our natural state we do not really love God and Christ. We may fear God as our judge. We may even try to keep God's laws; though often those laws provoke resentment, if not rebellion, in our hearts. But we do not really love God. Yet when a man or woman comes to realize that the Son of God loved me personally and gave himself to die for me, to suffer the penalty that my sins deserved, and to gain for me pardon and peace with God, and the gift of eternal life—then it produces a profound love and gratitude to Christ in that person's heart. And if we love him, says Christ, we shall keep his commandments (John 14:23). Listen again to how the early Christians talk in the Bible:

> Herein is love, not that we loved God, but that he loved us, and sent his Son to be the propitiation for our sins. . . . We love him, because he first loved us. (1 John 4:10, 19 KJV)

> I have been crucified with Christ; yet I live; and yet no longer I, but Christ lives in me. And that life which I now live in the flesh I live by faith in the Son of God, who loved me and gave himself up for me. (Gal 2:20 own trans.)

Of course, it is not only love and gratitude that motivate a believer to desire above all else to live to please Christ. It is logic as well. As we see from the above quotations, a true believer very soon comes to reason things out like this: 'If Christ had not died for me, I should have perished eternally under the penalty of my sins. It is Christ who has bought for me the gift of pardon and eternal life. I therefore owe my life to Christ. I must therefore live that life to please him.'

This in turn leads on to the ethic of moral consistency.

A new normal

The Christian Apostle Paul tells us that when people heard him preach that salvation is not by our works and that we receive it as a free undeserved gift altogether and totally by God's grace, many of them thought he meant that once you are saved, you can live just as sinfully as you please, because your salvation does not depend on your works, but on God's grace. That was not, of course, what Paul meant. Far from it. But listen now to the way he rebuts their false understanding.

> What shall we say then? Shall we continue in sin, that grace may abound? God forbid. We who died to sin, how shall we any longer live therein? Or are ye ignorant that all we who were baptised into Christ Jesus were baptised into his death? (Rom 6:1–3 RV)

What does Paul mean when he says 'we died to sin'? He means this:

1. A true Christian disciple believes that his sin was so serious that it deserved the penalty imposed by God's holy wrath against sin.

2. He further believes that Jesus died to suffer this penalty as his substitute, and that God has been graciously willing to count Jesus' death as his death. In that sense, when Jesus died, he died.

3. The believer, therefore, loves Jesus for dying for him.

4. How then can the believer, after all that, deliberately or even carelessly and without repenting, continue committing the sins that caused Christ's death? If he does so, his acts contradict what he says he believes; and this inconsistency is so great that it questions whether he is a true believer at all.

Sometimes even true believers can so far forget themselves as temporarily to behave in this inconsistent way. If they do, then Christ will not withdraw their salvation; but he will correct them, if need be by severe discipline, as we shall see in the final section of this chapter.

A Christian is guided by two systems of ethics. In the first place he is bound, as all other people are, whether they acknowledge it or not, by the ethics of creation. The Bible, to quote one of many instances, forbids murder. Why? Because every human being, Christian or non-Christian, religious or irreligious, believing or atheist, is a creature of God, made in the image of God. To murder someone who is made by God in God's own image is a dire insult to, and crime against, the Creator, and merits appropriate punishment (Gen 9:6). Christians are not exempt from this law; and if Christians were to make their religion an excuse for executing, murdering or warring against other people 'because they do not belong to our religion', it would be a denial not only of the Christianity they profess to believe, but of the fundamental ethics of creation as well.

But in addition to the ethics of creation, Christian disciples are also bound by the ethics of redemption.

The ethics of redemption

The early Christians constantly refer to the Lord Jesus as their Saviour; and they speak of his salvation as having delivered them from dangers and slaveries of various kinds. And the Bible itself calls on Christians not to surrender the freedoms which Christ has achieved for them (Gal 5:1).

Christ offers deliverance

from the power of darkness (Col 1:13)

from the fear of death (Heb 2:14–15)

from the coming wrath of God (1 Thess 1:10)

from the law of sin and death (Rom 8:2)

from the guilt of sin (Eph 1:7)

from temptation (2 Pet 2:9)

from the slavery of continuing to sin (John 8:31–36)

from the slavery of immorality (2 Pet 2:18–19)

But there is another side to Christ's salvation. The early Christians speak of having been bought by Christ at the cost of his own life (1 Cor 6:20), and as a consequence they confess that they are no longer their own, they belong body, soul and spirit to Christ. At first sight it might seem that there is a glaring contradiction between 'being set free from slavery' and 'being no longer your own, but belonging to Christ'. In actual fact there isn't.

Take an analogy. Suppose that against the advice and warnings of the local mountain guides, I decide to climb a steep and dangerous mountain in winter. Foolishly I take the wrong route and presently I get stuck. Paralysed by fear I can go neither up nor down; and I am in danger of starving and freezing to death. At the risk of his life a mountain rescue expert climbs up and rescues me from the tiny ledge on which I have been stranded. So now I am physically free to move. In that sense the guide has given me my freedom. But having risked his life to do so, he will not allow me to carry on as I did before, foolishly going my own way and getting myself into further life-threatening positions; for that would be to waste all the costly effort he put into rescuing me in the first place. And it would not be giving me true freedom, if he allowed me to go off and accidentally fall to my death. No, he will demand that I commit myself entirely to him. Roping me to himself he will tell me what route I have to take, where to place my feet, all the way down the mountain until he finally gets me to complete safety.

And so Christ. Having delivered us, not at the risk, but at the actual cost, of his own life, he regards himself as having bought us by his blood. He tells us bluntly that we are no longer our own. He ropes us to himself for the rest of life's journey (and for all eternity, for that matter) and expects us to follow and obey him every step of the way.

Sometimes, of course, Christian disciples forget this. The Apostle Paul's converts at Corinth seemed to forget that following Christ demands high standards of ethical behaviour. They began to indulge in sexual immorality as they had done before their conversion. Paul had to remind them that as Christians they were not free to behave like that, for 'you are not your own', said he, 'for you were bought with a price. So glorify God in your body' (1 Cor 6:19-20 ESV).

These Christians in Corinth were also behaving very badly towards one another in their church meetings and Paul wrote to explain the implications of ignoring their Christian profession:

> For I received from the Lord what I also handed on to you, that the Lord Jesus on the night when he was betrayed took a loaf of bread, and when he had given thanks, he broke it and said, 'This is my body that is for you. Do this in remembrance of me.' In the same way he took the cup also, after supper, saying, 'This cup is the new covenant in my blood. Do this, as often as you drink it, in remembrance of me.' For as often as you eat this bread and drink the cup, you proclaim the Lord's death until he comes.
>
> Whoever, therefore, eats the bread or drinks the cup of the Lord in an unworthy manner will be answerable for the body and blood of the Lord. Examine yourselves, and only then eat of the bread and drink of the cup. For all who eat and drink without discerning the body, eat and drink judgment against themselves. For this reason many of you are weak and ill, and some have died. But if we judged ourselves, we would not be judged. But when we are judged by the Lord, we are disciplined so that we may not be condemned along with the world. (1 Cor 11:23-32)

True Christians are linked by a covenant relationship with Jesus Christ who died for their sins (Heb 10:12–16). The Bible shows us in the above passage that the reality and significance of this covenant is affirmed every time Christ's followers participate in the 'cup of the Lord'. Christians who live inconsistent and openly sinful lives will be disciplined and corrected by the Lord. Christ's death has far-reaching implications for Christian ethics.

Remember me

What was it that the Corinthians were doing that led to Paul describing them as drinking 'the cup of the Lord [communion] unworthily'? See 1 Corinthians 11:17–22 and also 3:18; 5:1; 6:1; 10:14.

What would the Lord do to these people if they did not repent?

People who reject Christ will be condemned at the final judgment. On what basis can Paul say that believers are disciplined so that they are not condemned with the world? See John 5:24 and Romans 8:1.

What ethical impact is the Lord's Supper (or Communion) meant to have on the life of a disciple of Christ?

Discuss with your class or group the statement: 'certainty of salvation does not undermine ethics'.

CHAPTER

The Impact of the Death of Christ
Part 3: A New System of Values

For the early Christians the death of Christ was not simply a matter of history. It was, rather, an historical event that forever altered their basic values and therefore had a profound practical effect on their ethics. The fact was that Christ had died for them—had therefore valued them more than his own life's blood. It was an awesome truth to grasp, as the Apostle Peter pointed out in a letter to some Christians in the first century who were facing real pressure of persecution for their faith.

> Therefore prepare your minds for action; discipline yourselves; set all your hope on the grace that Jesus Christ will bring you when he is revealed. Like obedient children, do not be conformed to the desires that you formerly had in ignorance. Instead, as he who

called you is holy, be holy yourselves in all your conduct; for it is written, 'You shall be holy, for I am holy.'

If you invoke as Father the one who judges all people impartially according to their deeds, live in reverent fear during the time of your exile. You know that you were ransomed from the futile ways inherited from your ancestors, not with perishable things like silver or gold, but with the precious blood of Christ, like that of a lamb without defect or blemish. (1 Pet 1:13-19)

Let us then think about this new system of values.

The redeeming death of Christ shapes new values

Placing a new value on our use of time

Peter's phrase 'the time of your exile' reminds Christian disciples that they are now resident aliens on earth. Heaven has become their home country and capital city. Their 'citizenship is in heaven' (Phil 3:20). Like an ambassador in a foreign country they are here on earth to represent heaven's government (2 Cor 5:20). Like a businessperson abroad, he or she is here on earth to do business for his or her heavenly king, to serve him and his interests in all the duties and tasks of daily life. They are no longer to fritter away their lives in aimless, fruitless, irresponsible activity. Each day and all of life's powers are to be used to the full, and that for two reasons. First, their time on earth is limited. Once finished it does not come again: its opportunities must be seized while they last. And secondly, their lives and time have been bought at the incalculable cost of the precious blood of Christ. God is understandably concerned to see that the Christian spends such expensively-bought time properly. Not a minute is to be wasted.

Consider this analogy. A father who has sacrificed and saved up to buy his son a bicycle will not be pleased to see his son misusing the bicycle, neglecting it and allowing it to rust to pieces.

Placing a new value on people

> But take care that this liberty of yours does not somehow become a stumbling-block to the weak. For if others see you, who possess knowledge, eating in the temple of an idol, might they not, since their conscience is weak, be encouraged to the point of eating food sacrificed to idols? So by your knowledge those weak believers for whom Christ died are destroyed. But when you thus sin against members of your family, and wound their conscience when it is weak, you sin against Christ. (1 Cor 8:9–12)

The fact that my fellow disciple is a brother or sister for whom Christ died means that I must treat him or her with great respect. I must not do them any physical damage. But, more important even than that, I must not damage them psychologically or spiritually. I must never put pressure on anyone to make them go against their conscience. It may be that they have a conscience against doing something that seems to me quite harmless or trivial. I am at liberty to reason with them and to show them that their conscience is unjustified. But so long as they have this conscience against doing something, I must not force them to go against it. Why not? Because conscience is a very important mechanism that regulates their relationship with Christ. To force anyone to do something which they feel would displease Christ is to make them sin against Christ, and to rob Christ of that person's loving obedience which Christ died to win. And it also damages an important mechanism in the brain and personality.

A matter of conscience

Discuss the idea that conscience is like a watch.

> (a) The watch could be working perfectly well, running 60 minutes to the hour, and yet be telling the wrong time because it is not adjusted according to the local time zone. So our consciences need to be adjusted according to God's word, the Bible.

> (b) When an expensive analogue watch needs to be adjusted, you must use the mechanism in the watch that has been designed for that purpose. If instead of that, you simply force the hands of the watch with your finger round to where you want them to be, you will upset or even break the watch's own mechanisms.

Get your group to relate any experience they may have had when fellow students, members of their family, or employers have put pressure on them to go against their conscience.

The death of Christ fosters in each believer a sense of direct individual responsibility to Christ.

For to this end Christ died, and lived again, that he might be Lord of both the dead and the living. . . . for

> we shall all stand before the judgment-seat of God. . . .
> So then each one of us shall give account of himself to
> God. (Rom 14:9, 10, 12 RV)

The Christian believes that Christ died for her personally and individually, and not merely for the undifferentiated mass of humankind. She cannot, therefore, hide behind her group, or family or nation. She is aware that one day she must give account of herself personally and directly to the Lord who loved her and died to redeem her. It means, therefore, that she must daily live and make all her decisions with constant reference to the Lord; and this constant answerability to the Christ who loves her builds a strong sense of responsibility into her character.

The ethics of obligation and indebtedness

We should begin by discussing the basic differences between these two terms. In our society there are certain things we do because the government passes a law and thus compels us to do them, whether we want to or not; and if we don't do it we have to pay a fine or go to prison. That's one simple example of *obligation*.

But consider a scenario in which a friend is in need and asks you to lend her some money. Maybe you have not got much money yourself; but a year or so ago, you were seriously in debt, and she paid your debt for you. Now you feel you must help by lending her the money she needs. In other words, you feel *indebted* to her. Why do you feel like that?

Or, if one day you were asleep in your house when it caught fire. A friend of yours, at the risk of his life, braved the flames, rushed in and rescued you, and in the process got badly burned himself. Now he writes to you and says that his elderly mother, who lives near you, needs someone to do her shopping for her every week, and asks you to do it. Would you write back and say: 'She is your mother, not mine—you must do the shopping for her; I will not do it'? Or would you feel that you must do it, even though it would be a burden every week; and if you didn't do it, no one would put you in prison? If the latter, why would you feel like that?

Now consider the following parable:

> Then Peter came and said to him, 'Lord, if another member of the church sins against me, how often should I forgive? As many as seven times?' Jesus said to him, 'Not seven times, but, I tell you, seventy-seven times.

> 'For this reason the kingdom of heaven may be compared to a king who wished to settle accounts with his slaves. When he began the reckoning, one who owed him ten thousand talents was brought to him; and, as he could not pay, his lord ordered him to be sold, together with his wife and children and all his possessions, and payment to be made. So the slave fell on his knees before him, saying, "Have patience with me, and I will pay you everything." And out of pity for him, the lord of that slave released him and forgave him the debt. But that same slave, as he went

out, came upon one of his fellow-slaves who owed him a hundred denarii; and seizing him by the throat, he said, "Pay what you owe." Then his fellow slave fell down and pleaded with him, "Have patience with me, and I will pay you." But he refused; then he went and threw him into prison until he should pay the debt. When his fellow-slaves saw what had happened, they were greatly distressed, and they went and reported to their lord all that had taken place. Then his lord summoned him and said to him, "You wicked slave! I forgave you all that debt because you pleaded with me. Should you not have had mercy on your fellow-slave, as I had mercy on you?" And in anger his lord handed him over to be tortured until he should pay his entire debt. So my heavenly Father will also do to every one of you, if you do not forgive your brother or sister from your heart.' (Matt 18:21–35)

Notice that Jesus is using debt as a picture of our sins, which made us liable to God's judgment (the prison and punishment of the parable).

The first man owed his master a huge debt. This is a picture of the size of the debt we all owe God. The second man owed his fellow servant a comparatively small debt. Since the master had mercy on the first servant and forgave him his great debt, he was morally indebted or obliged to forgive his master's other servant a relatively tiny debt.

A woman who professes to be a Christian thereby admits that she is eternally indebted to Christ for having forgiven her sins and the eternal punishment due to those sins. But if she refuses to forgive her fellow servant she is denying that she has this indebtedness or obligation to Christ. And to deny this is to deny that she has herself been forgiven. She will thus have to suffer the penalty of her own sins.

A true Christian will obey the exhortation:

> Put away from you all bitterness and wrath and anger and wrangling and slander, together with all malice, and be kind to one another, tender-hearted, forgiving one another, as God in Christ has forgiven you. (Eph 4:31-32)

But the ethics of indebtedness do not simply concern the matter of being forgiving. They concern our positive willingness to help others.

> We know love by this, that he laid down his life for us— and we ought to lay down our lives for one another. (1 John 3:16)

'Laying down one's life for someone' may mean physically dying for that person; like a person who dives into a river to save a child from drowning, saves the child, but has a heart attack and drowns. But it can also mean doing things which are much less heroic, and which are therefore more difficult to do, as John goes on to say:

> How does God's love abide in anyone who has the world's goods and sees a brother or sister in need and yet refuses help? (1 John 3:17)

From all this it will become readily apparent that the Christian ethic is certainly not a minimalist ethic. It does not merely forbid us to do wrong, nor simply exhort us to do the minimal amount required by sheer justice. It requires us to go the extra mile, to be generous and unstinting in our kindness (Luke 6:38). Its exhortation to the former thief is typical: 'Thieves must give up stealing; rather let them labour and work honestly with their own hands, so as to have something to share with the needy' (Eph 4:28).

CHAPTER

The Impact of the Resurrection of Christ

One cannot read the early chapters of the Acts of the Apostles without becoming aware of a tremendous eruption of new spiritual energy breaking forth upon the world. The result was the emergence of the Christian church. We rightly ask two basic historical questions: what was the source of this spiritual energy, and what set it loose on the world at this particular time in history? The answer which the early Christians themselves give is: the resurrection of Christ three days after he was buried, and the coming of the Holy Spirit fifty days after the resurrection, on the day of Pentecost (Acts 1 and 2).

It was these twin events, they tell us, that transformed them from a bunch of frightened, bewildered men cowering behind locked doors (John 20:19) and thrust them out, bold as lions, to confront the murderers of Jesus, publicly charge them with his death, and inform them of his resurrection. It was these twin events that impelled them and

Is the resurrection important?

If Christ's resurrection did not happen, if the New Testament's records of it could be proved untrue, then the whole of Christianity would collapse. Nothing worthwhile could be salvaged from it. We can see that ourselves, if we read the New Testament and observe how central the resurrection is to its preaching and teaching. But what is more significant is that the early Christians themselves were aware that if the resurrection of Christ was not a fact, then there was nothing in Christianity worth having. Take, for example, the Apostle Paul. Writing to his converts in Corinth he says: 'If Christ has not been raised, your faith is futile and you are still in your sins' (1 Cor 15:17). For a summary of the evidence for the resurrection, see Appendix B.

their successors in the face of bitter opposition and persecution to establish the gospel of Christ throughout the world.

But the resurrection of Christ and the coming of the Holy Spirit were not only the motive power that impelled them to proclaim the Christian message: they were also the message itself—it was this message of the resurrection of Christ and the offer of the gift of the Holy Spirit that called forth faith in people's hearts, gave them new hope, faced them with the guilt and futility of their lives, brought them to repentance, and gave them joy and peace in believing in Jesus. And with that, new energy, new powers, new goals and new ethical standards. It gave them in the first place a completely new worldview.

A completely new worldview

The resurrection of Christ demonstrated unmistakably that death is not the end. It was not the end for Christ himself; and so, death would not be the end for his followers either. Jesus' resurrection did not merely mean that his soul had survived the death of his body and gone off into heaven. It meant that his body had physically risen from the dead. Death itself had been undone.

The implications were immense. Since Jesus' body was a perfectly human body, his resurrection carried implications for every man, woman, boy and girl that ever lived or would ever live. Since God had intervened in this part of Nature that was the physical body of Christ in order to reverse the process of death, then God could and would one day restore the whole of Nature. He had, indeed, promised in the Old Testament that he would do this; now the resurrection of Jesus was the firstfruits that confirmed the coming of the promised harvest. This is how the early Christians talked about it:

> Repent therefore, and turn to God so that your sins may be wiped out, so that times of refreshing may come from the presence of the Lord, and that he may send the Messiah appointed for you, that is, Jesus, who must remain in heaven until the time of universal restoration that God announced long ago through his holy prophets. (Acts 3:19–21)

> For the creation waits with eager longing for the revealing of the children of God; for the creation was subjected to futility, not of its own will but by the will of the one who subjected it, in hope that the creation itself will be set free from its bondage to decay and will obtain the freedom of the glory of the children of God. (Rom 8:19–21)

But in fact Christ has been raised from the dead, the
first fruits of those who have died. (1 Cor 15:20)

*The resurrection also demonstrated unequivocally that evil
will not be allowed to have the last word in our world.* The
judicial murder of Jesus had been brought about by a
combination of human pride, envy, fear, ignorance, cruelty and cowardice, swept on by mob hysteria, political
blackmail and government incompetence, with the devil
himself instigating and stage-managing the whole affair.
But the resurrection of Christ nullified this travesty of
justice. It not only vindicated him as innocent of the
charges on which he had been crucified: it declared him
to be Lord and Christ, son of the owner of the universe.
At the same time the resurrection was God's advance
warning and guarantee that he has appointed the day in
which he will judge this world righteously, and see to it
that evil is put down, and earth's wrongs righted. Jesus
Christ will be the appointed judge (Acts 17:30–34); and he
will conduct the universe, thus purged of evil, on to the
next stage of its glorious development.

*The resurrection also declared that matter is essentially
good.* Ancient philosophers like Socrates and Plato had
held that matter was ultimately undesirable if not positively bad; that the body was the sepulchre of the soul
and tended to contaminate it. Various forms of Hindu philosophy still hold this view: the matter of the universe is
like the rim of a wheel endlessly circling round the centre
(and getting nowhere). We must, they teach, try to escape
from the material world around us and from our material
bodies, into eternal, undifferentiated spirit.

But the resurrection of Christ teaches us the very opposite, for it restored Jesus to a physical, material, though changed and glorified, human body. It thus affirmed that matter in general and the human body in particular is essentially good (though our human bodies are spoiled by sin and disease) and will one day be changed. Human bodies are not to be despised and certainly not maltreated as a means to supposed spiritual excellence.

The effect of this new worldview

The effects of this new worldview on the disciples of Christ were both immediate and long-term. Here we give three examples.

1. *The resurrection of Christ has implications for attitudes towards property and possessions.* We shall look at this in a later chapter.

2. *The resurrection of Christ released his followers from the tyranny of the fear of death.* The early Christians speak of it like this:

> Since, therefore, the children share flesh and blood, he himself likewise shared the same things, so that through death he might destroy the one who has the power of death, that is, the devil, and free those who all their lives were held in slavery by the fear of death. (Heb 2:14–15)

This gave them peace and assurance as to what lay beyond death (whether the process of dying was instantaneous and painless, or torturously painful). But in addition it gave them the courage not to compromise with evil. If death were the end of everything, with no life beyond, and no final judgment to put wrongs right, then compromise with evil might often be the sensible course to take, on the principle that half a loaf is better than no bread. But death is not the end. To die, like Christ himself therefore, in the stand for God and truth, is no disaster, whereas to compromise God and truth for the sake of a few more years' life on earth would be (see Luke 12:4–9).

3. *The resurrection of Christ made the early Christians feel it was worthwhile positively and aggressively to attack the forces of spiritual evil that lie behind earth's troubles.*

They did not raise armies or resort to violence. They did not try to subvert any government. They did not grapple with human flesh and blood. It was not people they were fighting, but the spiritual darkness, untruth, superstition, corruption and oppression that distort people's lives and personalities. They were under orders from Jesus himself not to fight with physical weapons, nor retaliate when they were persecuted, beaten, stoned, imprisoned. They were to use the same tactics and weapons as Jesus used. The Apostle Paul put it like this: 'for the weapons of our warfare are not merely human, but they have divine power to destroy strongholds' (2 Cor 10:4); and again, 'For our struggle is not against enemies of blood and flesh, but against the rulers, against the authorities, against the cosmic powers of this present darkness, against the spiritual forces of evil in the heavenly places.' (Eph 6:12). And their aim was, as Paul expressed it to King Agrippa: 'to open their eyes so that they may turn from darkness to light and from the power of Satan to God, so that they may receive forgiveness of sins and a place among those who are sanctified by faith in me [Jesus]' (Acts 26:18).

Now you might think that the message which the early Christians proclaimed was inoffensive enough. But that would be to ignore the vested interests and darker powers that move people to oppose the Christian gospel. The Acts of the Apostles shows that it soon became apparent that Christians would constantly encounter such bitter opposition that only an unshakeable conviction of the resurrection of Christ, and of their own eventual resurrection, would be enough to carry them through.

Apostolic ethical situations

We now look briefly at several important passages from the Acts of the Apostles that illustrate some early ethical issues. Notice on each occasion (a) the question of ethical principle that faced the Christian apostles; and (b) what happened when they refused to compromise:

1. *Acts 4:1–22; 5:17–42*. The situation here was that the apostles had miraculously healed a lame man in the name of Jesus. The crowd was delighted. But the authorities were not: for they had been involved in the crucifixion of Jesus. Public preaching that Jesus had risen from the dead challenged their authority. They therefore forbade the apostles to preach any more in the name of Jesus, and threatened dire consequences if they disobeyed. What would you or I have done? At stake was:

(a) A question of truth.

(b) The right of free speech.

(c) The principle: we ought to obey God rather than man.

(d) The gospel, which, if preached, could bring forgiveness and peace with God to multitudes.

The apostles refused to obey the authorities' ban on preaching; and they suffered a severe beating, and subsequently persecution (8:1; 12:1).

2. *Acts 14:8–19*. The situation here was that Paul and Barnabas had performed a miracle of healing. The local populace were delighted. But in their pagan superstition they thought that the apostles were two of their pagan gods come down to earth; and the local priests of the pagan god Jupiter started to put on a great public ceremony and sacrifice oxen to Paul and Barnabas. Now, for human beings to bow down before fellow human beings and offer sacrifice to them degrades the offerers; and it also dishonours the true God. Yet if Paul and Barnabas forbade them, it would be regarded as an affront to their local religion; and this could cause great trouble. What would you have done? The apostles protested and stopped the sacrifice; and as a result, both Jews and pagans joined in stoning Paul, dragged him out of the city and left him for dead.

3. *Acts 24:1–27*. Unjustly accused and imprisoned, Paul had proved his innocence in court. But because of local political pressure the Roman governor Felix kept Paul still in prison. He made Paul aware, however, that if Paul was prepared to pay him a bribe, he would be allowed to escape. What would you have done? Paul, as a Christian, had a conscience against using corrupt methods to undermine the government's system. He refused to use bribery, and as a result was left in prison.

4. *Acts 25:6–12; 2 Timothy 4:6–8; 4:16–17*. To avoid death by assassination gangs in Palestine, Paul appealed to the

court of the emperor Nero at Rome. At his first trial he was acquitted and went off on further missionary journeys. A few years later, however, he was arrested again, condemned to death by Nero and executed.

To sum up so far, then.

(a) The resurrection of Christ was the power that impelled the Christian missionaries out into the world to preach.

(b) The resurrection of Christ was the main subject of the message they preached.

(c) And when in the course of their fight against evil they had to face the ethical question either to stand with the truth, act justly, and suffer for it, or to escape suffering by keeping silent, denying the truth, and acting corruptly, it was faith in the resurrection that nerved them to stand for truth and right, even at the cost of life itself.

On this issue, Paul's letters show clearly the secret of his strength.

> In the presence of God, who gives life to all things, and of Christ Jesus, who in his testimony before Pontius Pilate made the good confession, I charge you to keep the commandment without spot or blame until the manifestation of our Lord Jesus Christ. (1 Tim 6:13–14)

> Remember Jesus Christ, raised from the dead, a descendant of David—that is my gospel, for which I suffer hardship, even to the point of being chained like a criminal. But the word of God is not chained. Therefore I endure everything for the sake of the elect, so that

they may also obtain the salvation that is in Christ Jesus, with eternal glory. The saying is sure:

If we have died with him, we will also live with him;
if we endure, we will also reign with him;
if we deny him, he will also deny us;
if we are faithless, he remains faithful—
for he cannot deny himself. (2 Tim 2:8–13)

CHAPTER

The Impact of the Coming of the Holy Spirit
Part 1: A New Relationship

When we listen to the early Christians talking in the New Testament, it is at once clear that they have undergone some profound and radical change. They speak about its cause both objectively and subjectively.

Objectively, they trace its beginning to an historical event that was as precisely timed as the death and resurrection of Jesus. It was the coming of the Holy Spirit on the day of Pentecost (that is, the fiftieth day after Jesus rose from the dead, Acts 2:1-4). Indeed, the first striking thing about this event is the matter of its timing. We might have expected, for instance, that the disciples would report that the Holy Spirit came upon them the first time they saw Jesus risen from the dead. And if they did, we might well think that this was simply their way of describing the tremendous subjective, psychological impact made on them by the sight of the risen Christ. But this is not what they say. They do record that the first time the risen Jesus met with the eleven disciples in the Upper Room, he performed the symbolic gesture of breathing on them to indicate that it was he who would, after he had gone back to heaven, send the Holy Spirit to them (John 20:21–22). But they simultaneously report that the Lord Jesus insisted that they were to continue to wait in the city of Jerusalem, because the Holy Spirit would not come at once but only at an unspecified time some days later (Acts 1:4–8). This certainly created an expectancy that something was going to happen; however they were still not told what form the coming of the Holy Spirit would take, except that they would then be endued with power. And when it happened, the decision as to whether the coming had taken place or not, was not left to the private impression of individuals at different times and in different places and circumstances. When the Holy Spirit came it was an objective event simultaneously witnessed and experienced by a group of some 120 believers, an event which proceeded forthwith so to impact the crowd in Jerusalem as to produce a crop of 3,000 conversions that very same day (Acts 2:1–13, 41). It was, as we shall later see, a great turning point in history.

The next interesting thing is one of the words that they use to describe this historic happening: they talk of the Holy Spirit 'coming'. The language goes back to Jesus Christ himself who told his disciples:

> 'Nevertheless, I tell you the truth: it is to your advan-
> tage that I go away, for if I do not go away, the Advocate

will not come to you; but if I go, I will send him to you. And when he comes, he will prove the world wrong about sin and righteousness and judgment: about sin, because they do not believe in me; about righteousness, because I am going to the Father and you will see me no longer; about judgment, because the ruler of this world has been condemned.

'I still have many things to say to you, but you cannot bear them now. When the Spirit of truth comes, he will guide you into all the truth; for he will not speak on his own, but will speak whatever he hears, and he will declare to you the things that are to come. He will glorify me, because he will take what is mine and declare it to you.' (John 16:7–14)

Now the disciples, we remember, were all of them Jews, and they were used to reading in their Hebrew Scriptures how their ancient heroes and spiritual leaders had been empowered by the Holy Spirit. And, indeed, Christ himself, while he was here on earth, claimed to perform his miracles by the power of the Holy Spirit (Matt 12:28). But, as we see from the passage cited above, when Christ spoke of the 'coming' of the Holy Spirit, he was speaking of something that would not, could not, and did not happen until he himself had gone away. The Holy Spirit was going to be 'another Advocate' (John 14:16). Christ himself had been an advocate to his disciples while he was on earth. Now the Holy Spirit was to come to take his place, to carry on the work that Christ left unfinished. And just as Christ, when he came, remained here on earth in a human body for 33 years, so when the Holy Spirit came, he would come to stay until the second coming of Christ. He would not dwell in a human body of his own as Jesus had done, but in the worldwide community of Jesus' disciples and in the individual body of each and every believer. His task would be two-fold:

1. to vindicate Jesus worldwide, to demonstrate his claims to be true, to bring home to people the significance of his death, resurrection and ascension, to offer salvation, to warn of the inevitable day of judgment.

2. to lead believers into ever-deepening understanding of who Jesus is, his wealth, glory and power.

A new life

So much, then, for the Christians' account of the objective coming of the Holy Spirit. But when they talk of their subjective, personal experience of receiving the Holy Spirit, it becomes evident that it has not only caused them to change their lifestyle: it has given them literally a new life. Let's look again at a passage we considered in Chapter 30:

> So if anyone is in Christ, there is a new creation: everything old has passed away; see, everything has become new! (2 Cor 5:17)

The phrase 'there is a new creation' is not intended as hyperbole: the Christians mean us to understand it literally, as we see from the string of expressions they use elsewhere to describe what has happened to them. They talk of having been 'created in Christ Jesus for good works' (Eph 2:10); of having undergone 'regeneration' (Titus 3:5 ESV); of 'having been spiritually dead and then brought to life' (Eph 2:5 own trans.); of 'walk[ing] in newness of life' (Rom 6:4) by having been united with the living, risen Christ. And what interests us particularly at this point is the effect it had on their ethics. This new spiritual life, generated in them by the Holy Spirit, set up a new relationship with God.

A new relationship with God

They became aware that they had become (what they were not before) *children of God*, that God had become their Father, and that they now possessed the life and spirit of God. They found it as natural to speak to God as a child does to its father, conscious that it is its father's child.

> You have received the spirit of sonship, by which we cry 'Abba, Father'. The Spirit himself bears witness with our spirit that we are children of God. (Rom 8:15–16 own trans.)

They became aware that the same Spirit that gave them spiritual birth *was now working in them*, expressing his desires, urging them to suppress their own sinful desires, leading them to behave ever more like their Father, so that they might mature and become grown-up sons of God: 'For all who are led by the Spirit of God', they said, 'are children of God' (Rom 8:14).

On one occasion Jesus expressed it this way:

> 'You have heard that it was said, "You shall love your neighbour and hate your enemy." But I say to you, Love your enemies and pray for those who persecute you, so that you may be children of your Father in heaven; for he makes his sun rise on the evil and on the good, and sends rain on the righteous and on the unrighteous. . . . Be perfect, therefore, as your heavenly Father is perfect.' (Matt 5:43–45, 48)

But how might anybody find either the desire or the power to behave like this? The early Christians explain what they found (and what all true Christians still find): the Holy Spirit, dwelling within them, supplied the desire and urge to behave like God, their Father, and not to give way to the hatred that they would have given vent to before. This is how they put it:

> Live by the Spirit, I say, and do not gratify the desires of the flesh. For what the flesh desires is opposed to the Spirit, and what the Spirit desires is opposed to the flesh; for these are opposed to each other, to prevent you from doing what you want. But if you are led by the Spirit, you are not subject to the law. Now the works of the flesh are obvious: fornication, impurity, licentiousness, idolatry, sorcery, enmities, strife, jealousy, anger, quarrels, dissensions, factions, envy, drunkenness, carousing, and things like these. I am warning you, as I warned you before: those who do such things will not inherit the kingdom of God.

By contrast, the fruit of the Spirit is love, joy, peace, patience, kindness, generosity, faithfulness, gentleness, and self-control. There is no law against such things. (Gal 5:16-23)

From this it becomes clear that *receiving the Holy Spirit and becoming a child of God did not turn them into robots.* They still had the choice whether to yield to the urgings of the Holy Spirit, or to give way to their own sinful impulses; and often this would involve a struggle. What, then, says somebody, is the advantage of having the Holy Spirit?

Consider an analogy. Lionesses, so we are told, take the young lions out with them when they go hunting, and the young lions learn to hunt by imitating the mother lions. The reason why this method of learning by imitation works is that the young lions already have their mother's nature and instinct in them, and imitation of their mother serves to develop it. But it would be no good sending a donkey out with the lionesses in the hope that it will learn hunting by imitating them! A donkey does not have lion life and instinct to start with.

So it is with people who have received the Holy Spirit and become children of God. It makes sense now, in a way that it did not before, to encourage them to imitate their Father, God, and to copy the behaviour of Jesus Christ (Eph 5:1-2, 25-28), because they now have the life and instinct of God within them which deliberate imitation and practice can develop and turn into mature and stable character.

Christians tell us that *however much they have to exert themselves with the Holy Spirit's help to conquer their sinful desires and urges, they do not find it slavery.* 'For you did not receive', they say, 'a spirit of slavery again to fall back into fear' (Rom 8:15). There are two reasons for this:

(*a*) They are not doing it to earn entry into God's family, but because they are already in his family.

A further analogy: Suppose a girl has inherited great musical ability from her father. She may find practising hard work, but at least she knows that she does not have to do it in order to gain a place as her father's child in her father's family. She does it because she is already a child of her father, loves her father, wants to please him, and enjoys music anyway.

(*b*) They are not doing it in fear that if they fail they will be thrown out of the family. God assures all his children that 'there is therefore now no condemnation for those who are in Christ Jesus' (Rom 8:1). They will never be rejected. There is no penalty: Christ has already borne that for them.

On the other hand the Christians are aware that *while there is no penalty, if they do wrong, there are consequences, and they will suffer loss.*

> Do not be deceived; God is not mocked, for you reap whatever you sow. If you sow to your own flesh, you will reap corruption from the flesh; but if you sow to the Spirit, you will reap eternal life from the Spirit. (Gal 6:7–8)

Let's illustrate that. Suppose God were to tell a Christian farmer to sow wheat in his field; but the farmer disobeyed God and sowed thistles.[1] If later he repented and confessed his sin, God would forgive him and there would be no penalty. But when the crop grew up it would still be a valueless crop. God would not do a miracle and turn thistles into wheat. Moreover the farmer would get no money for the crop; and he would have a lot of hard work to do in the following years to rid his field of the thistles.

(c) Christians are also assured that *the Holy Spirit will never forsake them*. On the contrary, as they abide in him, he intercedes for them according to God's will, and will not rest until they are finally brought fully to resemble Christ in character.

> Likewise the Spirit helps us in our weakness; for we do not know how to pray as we ought, but that very Spirit intercedes with sighs too deep for words. And God, who searches the heart, knows what is the mind of the Spirit, because the Spirit intercedes for the saints according to the will of God.

> We know that all things work together for good for those who love God, who are called according to his purpose. For those whom he foreknew he also pre-destined to be conformed to the image of his Son, in order that he might be the firstborn within a large

1 The point at issue is not whether God would give such a command or not; this is a simple way of illustrating the principles at work in much more serious matters of God's commands and whether we, his creatures, obey him.

family. And those whom he predestined he also called; and those whom he called he also justified; and those whom he justified he also glorified. (Rom 8:26–30)

CHAPTER 35

The Impact of the Coming
of the Holy Spirit
Part 2: A New Outlook on Reality

The coming of the Holy Spirit on the day of Pentecost produced profound changes in the early Christians' attitudes. One of the first to be noticed by the world at large was that receiving the Holy Spirit produced a transformation in attitudes to personal property.

A transformation in attitudes to personal property

Now the whole group of those who believed were of one heart and soul, and no one claimed private ownership of any possessions, but everything they owned was held in common. With great power the apostles gave their testimony to the resurrection of the Lord Jesus, and great grace was upon them all. There

> was not a needy person among them, for as many as
> owned lands or houses sold them and brought the
> proceeds of what was sold. They laid it at the apostles'
> feet, and it was distributed to each as any had need.
> (Acts 4:32–35)

We must be careful not to misunderstand these verses. They do not say or mean that every Christian property owner immediately sold all his properties, including his own house, and gave the proceeds to others. If he had, neither he nor his fellow Christians would have had anywhere to sleep or live in! What happened was something more profound. These people saw at once that if Jesus was risen from the dead, then he was indeed the Christ, the Son of God, and the rightful heir of everything. It was to him, therefore, that they surrendered their property. He did not have to threaten them to make them do it. They did it gladly. They reckoned that since their rightful Lord and Master had given his everything for them when he died on the cross, then the least they could do was to give everything they had to him. He became the owner of all their possessions.

That did not mean that they had to give them away to other people to control. They remained in charge, but now no longer as owners but as stewards of what belonged to Christ, and as such, responsible to administer it for the good of the Christian community at large. If urgent need arose among that community, and they had a spare property, they would sell it and give the proceeds to the apostles to distribute, or else distribute it themselves (Acts 5:1–4). No one thought of his goods as his own; they all held everything in trust on behalf of Christ for the good of the Christian community at large.

Now in those ancient days the Jerusalem Christian church was a tightly knit community in a pre-industrial society. Conditions in the large cities of the Roman Empire were already very different, and the administration of Christian social relief necessarily adapted itself to the local circumstances (see Acts 9:36, 39; 11:27–30; 20:33–35). Today the circumstances in which Christians exercise their stewardship of their material possessions are vastly more complicated still. But the basic underlying principle remains the same: since the resurrection of Christ no true Christian regards his possessions as belonging to himself, but to Christ, to be used under Christ's direction for the good of others.

A new evaluation of the human body

Receiving the Holy Spirit also produced a new evaluation of the human body.

The believer in Christ is given to know that his body has become 'a temple of the Holy Spirit' (1 Cor 6:19). This confers on his body a special sanctity, which the believer is responsible not to desecrate. Once more it is instructive to see how this fact is brought to bear on the believer's ethical behaviour. The New Testament does not say to the believer: if you manage to avoid fornication, your body could qualify to become a temple of the Holy Spirit. It puts it the other way round.

'Do you not know that your bodies are members of Christ? Should I therefore take the members of Christ

and make them members of a prostitute? Never! . . .
Or do you not know that your body is a temple of
the Holy Spirit within you, which you have from God,
and that you are not your own? . . . Shun fornication!'
(1 Cor 6:15, 19, 18)

Even after a believer receives the Holy Spirit, his body
remains mortal, subject to pain and decay, and will do so
until the Lord Jesus returns. But the Holy Spirit already
dwells in the believer's body and constitutes the 'firstfruits' of God's great work of redemption. That 'firstfruits'
is thus the guarantee that the full harvest will one day
come; and when it comes the believer's body will then
be redeemed and changed into a glorified, deathless and
eternal body such as the Lord Jesus already has (Rom
8:10–11, 23; Phil 3:20–21).

A new entity: the Body of Christ

The coming of the Holy Spirit has also brought into existence a new entity: the Body of Christ.

For just as the body is one and has many members,
and all the members of the body, though many, are
one body, so it is with Christ. For in the one Spirit we
were all baptized into one body—Jews or Greeks, slaves
or free—and we were all made to drink of one Spirit.
(1 Cor 12:12–13)

Look closely at this illustration of the human body
from 1 Corinthians. The thing that keeps all the members

of a human body alive, joined to each other and functioning properly, is that the same bloodstream carries the oxygen from the air to every member in the body. For that purpose two things have to be true simultaneously:

(*a*) the body has to be in the air—if it were cut off from an air supply it would die;

(*b*) the air has to be in the body—if there was air all round the body, but no air in the body, it would likewise die.

Now when somebody puts their faith in Christ, Christ places that person in the Holy Spirit (he baptises them in the Spirit) and at the same time he puts the Holy Spirit into that person (he makes that person drink of the Holy Spirit). So that person is now in the Holy Spirit, and the Holy Spirit is in that person. But that is also true of all believers in Christ the world through: all are in the same Holy Spirit and the Holy Spirit is in all of them. They thus form the Body of Christ, many members sharing the life of the Spirit, and joined by the Spirit into one living organism.

This is God's answer to the problems created by misdirected personality and excessive individualism. In the Body of Christ:

(*a*) no member, however weak and little gifted, is in fact unnecessary, or permitted to feel so (1 Cor 12: 15–20);

(*b*) no highly gifted member is allowed to feel that he does not need other less-gifted members (1 Cor 12:21–26);

(*c*) each member must use his gift, not to his own enhancement, but for the good of the whole, motivated by love (1 Cor 13).

And this consciousness of being a member in the Body of Christ bears in a very practical way on behaviour. No mentally healthy person would deliberately injure a member of his or her own physical body. And so, says the New Testament: 'So then, putting away falsehood, let all of us speak the truth to our neighbours, for we are members of one another' (Eph 4:25).

And finally, the coming of the Holy Spirit and the formation of the Body of Christ has brought about a new internationalism.

The new internationalism

In Old Testament times the Jews were directed, for certain good reasons, to keep very much to themselves. But the coming of the Holy Spirit on the day of Pentecost changed all that. If a Jew received the Holy Spirit and a Gentile received the Holy Spirit, they were, whether or not they realised it at the time, there and then incorporated as living members into the Body of Christ, which knows no national boundaries or social distinctions: 'For in the one Spirit', says the New Testament, 'we were all baptized into one body—Jews or Greeks, slaves or free' (1 Cor 12:13).

Now the Acts of the Apostles is at its most thrilling when it records in detail those crucial occasions when the old barriers that had separated nations were broken down and Jews and Gentiles came to accept each other as fellow members of the same Body of Christ. Acts tells us honestly that the Jewish Christians were at first a little reluctant to accept Gentile believers as equals in Christ;

but the miracle happened and they did. It would be worth reading the whole story (Acts 10:1–11:30); it is a watershed in world history.

On the other hand it tells us that in some countries and cities the local religion was so inseparably connected with their national and civic pride, that the Christian gospel was fiercely resented. The city of Ephesus was a case in point (see the long story at Acts 19:23–41). The chief object of worship for her citizens was the goddess Artemis. Now, Artemis was worshipped in many places in the ancient world. But in Ephesus the magnificent temple which they had built for her was one of the wonders of the world. They also had an image, which they claimed had fallen down out of heaven from Jupiter, the chief pagan god (it was probably a meteorite). Tourists visited the temple in large numbers and the local silversmiths made a lot of money by selling them miniature shrines of Artemis. When, therefore, the people of Ephesus began dimly to perceive that the Christian gospel and the doctrine of the One True God would undermine their pagan religion, they regarded it as an affront not only to their religion but to their national and civic pride as well. The whole city stampeded into the open-air theatre and for two hours on end shouted not simply 'Great is Artemis', but 'Great is Artemis of the Ephesians!' (Acts 19:28, 34).

Against this background it is illuminating to read the historically significant words that the Apostle Paul wrote a few years later to his converts in Ephesus. They mark the dawning of a new day in the history of Europe and of the world:

So then, remember that at one time you Gentiles by birth, called 'the uncircumcision' by those who are called 'the circumcision'—a physical circumcision made in the flesh by human hands—remember that you were at that time without Christ, being aliens from the commonwealth of Israel, and strangers to the covenants of promise, having no hope and without God in the world. But now in Christ Jesus you who once were far off have been brought near by the blood of Christ. For he is our peace; in his flesh he has made both groups into one and has broken down the dividing wall, that is, the hostility between us. He has abolished the law with its commandments and ordinances, so that he might create in himself one new humanity in place of the two, thus making peace, and might reconcile both groups to God in one body through the cross, thus putting to death that hostility through it. So he came and proclaimed peace to you who were far off and peace to those who were near; for through him both of us have access in one Spirit to the Father. So then you are no longer strangers and aliens, but you are citizens with the saints and also members of the household of God, built upon the foundation of the apostles and prophets, with Christ Jesus himself as the cornerstone. In him the whole structure is joined together and grows into a holy temple in the Lord; in whom you also are built together spiritually into a dwelling-place for God. (Eph 2:11–22)

CHAPTER

The Impact of the Second Coming of Christ

Part 1: Thinking, Living and Working in Hope

One cannot finally understand the power behind Christian ethics unless one takes into account the Christian doctrine of the second coming of Christ. Some people have argued that the doctrine of the second coming is some fairy-tale-like myth which popular imagination has woven around historic Christianity. They conclude, therefore, that one can safely discard or ignore it, in order to discover what is of solid and lasting worth in Christianity, that is, its ethics. But this theory cannot stand the test of sober examination of the New Testament.

It has been estimated that the second coming is mentioned in some 250 verses in the New Testament. Every writer in the New Testament refers to it; and some reference is made to it in every book of the New Testament.

Moreover, it is Jesus Christ himself who more than anyone else in the New Testament speaks about his second coming. He does so because it is an integral and indispensable part of his claim to be the Messiah. Throughout all the Old Testament prophecies it was the constantly repeated promise that when Messiah came he would put down evil, banish war, and judge the world in righteousness. This prospect filled generations of people with hope and jubilation (see, e.g. Ps 94, 96, 97, 98, 99; Isa 2:1-4). Naturally enough, therefore, when Jesus claimed to be the Messiah his contemporaries wanted to know when and how he proposed to fulfil these promises. He indicated quite clearly that he had no intention of executing the judgments of God on the world at his first coming (see the discussion in Chapter 25). But to have said that he had no intention of ever doing so would have totally destroyed his claim to be the Messiah. And of course he said no such thing.

On the contrary he said both publicly and privately, in straightforward language and in parable form, that he must first go away by death, burial, resurrection and ascension to heaven; that then his gospel would be preached throughout the world; and that finally he would return to set up the kingdom of God on earth by divine might (see, e.g. Luke 19:11-27; Matt 24:14). In fact the claim that he would come again was such an integral part of his claim to be the Messiah and the Son of God that he stated it before his judges at his trial. Having been put on oath by the high priest to tell them whether or not he was the Messiah, the Son of God, he answered in the affirmative and added: 'From now on you will see the Son of Man seated at the right hand of Power and coming on the clouds of heaven' (Matt 26:64). At that point they decided to crucify him for blasphemy. They understood precisely what he was saying. When therefore the apostles put to Jesus the question after his resurrection 'Are you at this time going to restore the kingdom?' he told them that the timing of his second coming was not theirs to know. Their immediate task was to get on with the evangelisation of the world. But at his ascension, as Luke the historian records, these same apostles were equally clearly told, 'This same Jesus, who has been taken from you into heaven, will come back in the same way you have seen him go into heaven' (Acts 1:6-11 NIV).

Luke was reporting what the eyewitnesses saw. Accordingly, the first Christians announced to the world in clear and direct terms that Christ would return to our world as literally (but with unimaginably greater splendour) as they had seen him being received up into the clouds.

Some people have suggested that Luke held a primitive and pre-scientific view of cosmology. They think that he imagined a physical heaven above a flat earth, below which was hell. And they say that Luke made up the story of the ascension to fit in with this primitive worldview. But there is no evidence whatsoever to support this view. It is even at odds with historical fact. We know that Luke was an educated man, a physician, living in a world which already knew the earth was round—over 200 years earlier Eratosthenes had even calculated its circumference. We also know that Luke was an historian of the first order. He was faithfully recording what the eyewitnesses actually saw—a literal ascension of Christ's physical body.

Of course, there have frequently been, and still are, misguided people who in spite of our Lord's clear words, confidently claim that they can predict the exact date of the second coming. Invariably and necessarily they are proved wrong. And there are others that will assert that Christ has returned, re-incarnated in some religious guru in some country or other. Jesus himself was careful to warn us against all such misunderstandings. When the second coming takes place, Christ says, no one will need to be told it has happened. It will be cosmic in its setting and universally visible (see Luke 17:22-37). But the misinterpretation of cranks does nothing to reduce the validity of the majestic promises of Christ or of the faith of all true Christians down the centuries to the present time.

But our task is to enquire about the impact that the second coming of Christ has on Christian ethics. Let us, therefore, consider some examples to show how pervasive it was in the lives of the early Christians.

A part of conversion and a part of life

The second coming of Christ formed both an element in conversion and the framework for subsequent living. Paul's evangelisation of Thessalonica in Macedonia (northern Greece) is recorded in Acts 17:1-9. In a letter which he wrote shortly afterwards to his converts in that city, he described what was involved in their conversion, thus:

> For the people of those regions report about us what
> kind of welcome we had among you, and how you

> turned to God from idols, to serve a living and true
> God, and to wait for his Son from heaven, whom he
> raised from the dead—Jesus, who rescues us from the
> wrath that is coming. (1 Thess 1:9-10)

Conversion, then, was not simply from one set of ethical rules to another, but from a false understanding of the universe to an acknowledgement of the truth about the universe and its personal Creator ('you turned to God from idols').

Furthermore, conversion involved a new goal and framework for life ('to wait for his Son from heaven').

Finally, belief in the second coming was not a form of escapism that encouraged people to abandon daily work, but an incentive to work all the harder and all the better. Daily work ceased to be a drudgery, wresting a living from impersonal Nature or a capricious universe in competition with an unprincipled, selfish, heartless society; it became a service gladly rendered to the living and true God whose Son had died to pay the penalty of sin and who would return as the final deliverer of his people. It is true, as we learn from Paul's second letter to these converts at Thessalonica, that some of them took the promise of the second coming as an excuse for not working and for abandoning their social duties. But this gave Paul the opportunity to point out that such behaviour was a total misunderstanding and indeed denial of the Christian faith (2 Thess 3:6-15). As Paul says elsewhere: 'Whoever does not provide for relatives, and especially for family members, has denied the faith and is worse than an unbeliever' (1 Tim 5:8).

An incentive to work

The second coming was itself a powerful incentive to diligent, devoted work. This is so *because it is at the second coming that Christ's disciples shall be rewarded* for the work they have done in Christ's name. We have already discussed this matter in Chapter 20, and we need not repeat it here. What we should notice now is that those rewards will be given not merely for 'spiritual' work and exercises, but also for ordinary daily work done in the name of Jesus and for him.

Examples:

(*a*) Hospitality to the poor (Luke 14:12–14).

(*b*) Daily work done in field, factory, office, or home when it is done 'wholeheartedly, fearing the Lord' (Col 3:22–25).

The second coming also acts as a restraint on employers and factory managers, etc., reminding them that they too have a Master in heaven, who will one day call them to account for the way they have treated the workers (Col 4:1).

And it constitutes a solemn warning of God's judgments that shall fall on those who have unjustly oppressed the workers (Jas 5:1–6).

The second coming is also a motivation to our work, *because at that time each believer will have to meet Christ and give account to him personally.* To see what this means we use an illustration.

A rich young man decides he would like to be a painter. He can afford to pay for his own lessons, so he goes to Florence, St. Petersburg and Paris to study under famous artists. But he becomes careless, wastes his time on parties, drink and amusements. He does poor work, and when he submits his paintings for examination, a group of experts whom he has never met and does not know personally, rejects them in his absence as substandard. He is disappointed, but he has no one to account to but himself.

A poor young man wants to be a painter. So his widowed mother works hard, and denies herself many comforts, in order to make enough money to send him to study under famous painters in Florence, St. Petersburg and Paris and to maintain him while he is there. He too wastes his time and does poor work. But when he submits his paintings for assessment, he is required to attend the examination in person, and sitting among the experts who criticize and eventually reject his work, he finds his widowed mother, whose love, money, work and sacrifice he has wasted. What will he feel like?

Now read carefully:

> For the grace of God has appeared, bringing salvation to all, training us to renounce impiety and worldly passions, and in the present age to live lives that are self-controlled, upright, and godly, while we wait for the blessed hope and the manifestation of the glory of our great God and Saviour, Jesus Christ. He it is who gave himself for us that he might redeem us from all iniquity and purify for himself a people of his own who are zealous for good deeds. (Titus 2:11-14)

These verses come after a detailed passage of ethical instruction (Titus 2:1-13). They list the pressures that God's grace exerts on believers to live responsible, just and

God-fearing lives. And among those pressures the greatest, perhaps, is this: the very grace of God that saves a believer from the penalty of sin, and assures him of a place with Christ in heaven, commits him to the certainty that one day he will meet Christ who gave himself to the suffering of the cross to free him from a sinful way of living and to turn him into an enthusiast for good works. What then, if when he faces the majestic Christ in all his glory, he has to admit that as far as he is concerned he has largely wasted the opportunities that Christ's sufferings bought for him? The Bible warns us that such a person will be ashamed before Christ at his coming (1 John 2:28).

In light of the second coming

Why do you think that the New Testament places such emphasis on the second coming of Christ?

Why is belief in the second coming not escapism?

If it is true that we each have to meet Jesus Christ personally, what practical effect do you think that belief should have in our lives?

CHAPTER 37

The Impact of the Second Coming of Christ
Part 2: A Purifying Hope and a Promise of Justice and Peace

It is fitting that, in our final chapter, we continue to investigate the ethical impact of the second coming of Christ. We have seen how the second coming was a very important element in conversion and provided a solid hope for the future in the context of which life was to be lived. In practical terms, the second coming was a powerful incentive to diligent work. We will now consider what it contributes to the believer's personal development—how it prepares us now for the life that is to come.

The great step forward

The second coming will bring to perfection the Christian's moral and spiritual development. It is made quite clear

How hard could it be?

To impress upon a believer how rigorous the course is, the New Testament uses metaphors drawn from athletics: *running* (1 Cor 9:24–26), *long-distance running* (Heb 12:1–3), *boxing* (1 Cor 9:26–27), *wrestling* (Eph 6:12). Each of these metaphors has a special point; consider with your students or group members what it is, by studying their contexts.

in the New Testament that conversion to Christ commits believers to a rigorous course of moral and spiritual development. They must aim not only to do better work than they did before, but to be better people than they were before.

Here is the Apostle Peter describing what this course of moral and spiritual progress involves:

His divine power has given us everything needed for life and godliness, through the knowledge of him who called us by his own glory and goodness. Thus he has given us, through these things, his precious and very great promises, so that through them you may escape from the corruption that is in the world because of lust, and may become participants in the divine nature. For this very reason, you must make every effort to support your faith with goodness, and goodness with knowledge, and knowledge with self-control, and self-control with endurance, and endurance with godliness, and godliness with mutual affection, and mutual affection with love. For if these things are yours and are increasing among you, they keep you from being ineffective and unfruitful in the knowledge of our Lord Jesus Christ. For anyone who lacks these things is short-sighted and blind, and is forgetful of the cleansing of past sins. Therefore, brothers and sisters, be all the more eager to confirm your call and election, for if you do this, you will never stumble. For in this way, entry into the eternal kingdom of our Lord and Saviour Jesus Christ will be richly provided for you. (2 Pet 1:3–11)

And here is the Apostle Paul describing the same thing:

Yet whatever gains I had, these I have come to regard as loss because of Christ. More than that, I regard everything as loss because of the surpassing value of knowing Christ Jesus my Lord. For his sake I have suffered the loss of all things, and I regard them as rubbish, in order that I may gain Christ and be found in him, not having a righteousness of my own that comes from the law, but one that comes through faith in Christ, the righteousness from God based on faith. I want to know Christ and the power of his resurrection and the sharing of his sufferings by becoming like him in his death, if somehow I may attain the resurrection from the dead.

Not that I have already obtained this or have already reached the goal; but I press on to make it my own, because Christ Jesus has made me his own. Beloved, I do not consider that I have made it my own; but this one thing I do: forgetting what lies behind and straining forward to what lies ahead, I press on towards the goal for the prize of the heavenly call of God in Christ Jesus. (Phil 3:7–14)

In all this the early Christians make it quite clear that the ultimate goal they have in mind is not simply to keep every ethical rule in the Bible. Their goal is much more personal than that: they are in love, so to speak, with the person of Jesus Christ, and their great aim and ambition is to be like him in character and behaviour (2 Cor 3:18; Rom 8:29). The great assurance given them by God, which keeps them persevering in their spiritual progress, is that when, at the second coming of Christ, they see him face to face, that glorious sight will complete the process and they will be for ever like Christ:

> Beloved, we are God's children now; what we will be has not yet been revealed. What we do know is this: when he is revealed, we will be like him, for we will see him as he is. (1 John 3:2)

But—and here comes the practical implication of that hope—anyone, says the next verse (3:3), who professes to have this hope of being eventually like Christ, will diligently set about the task of purifying his or her life, to make it more like Christ in the here and now. Moreover, 'being like Christ' is not some vague, sentimental idea: it means behaving like Christ behaved when he was on earth, and pursuing the same goals or righteousness as he pursued. The person who says they hope to be like Christ at his second coming but lives unrighteously and makes no attempt to be like Christ now, is simply not a true Christian at all. This, says the Apostle John, is how you can tell those who are genuine children of God, and those who merely say they are (3:3–12).

A promise of participation

The second coming of Christ guarantees to all believers participation in the coming reign of Christ. Consider what Paul said when addressing Christians in Corinth and Thessalonica:

> What I am saying, brothers and sisters, is this: flesh and blood cannot inherit the kingdom of God, nor does the perishable inherit the imperishable. Listen, I will tell you a mystery! We will not all die, but we will all be changed, in a moment, in the twinkling of an eye, at the last trumpet. For the trumpet will sound, and the dead will be raised imperishable, and we will be changed. For this perishable body must put on imperishability, and this mortal body must put on immortality. (1 Cor 15:50–53)

> But we do not want you to be uninformed, brothers and sisters, about those who have died, so that you may not grieve as others do who have no hope. For since we believe that Jesus died and rose again, even so, through Jesus, God will bring with him those who have died. For this we declare to you by the word of the Lord, that we who are alive, who are left until the coming of the Lord, will by no means precede those who have died. For the Lord himself, with a cry of command, with the archangel's call and with the sound of God's trumpet, will descend from heaven, and the dead in Christ will rise first. Then we who are alive, who are left, will be caught up in the clouds

> together with them to meet the Lord in the air; and so
> we will be with the Lord for ever. Therefore encourage
> one another with these words. (1 Thess 4:13–18)

A question had arisen in the minds of the Apostle Paul's recent converts at Thessalonica. Their question was this: granted that Jesus Christ was going to return one day, as he promised, and set up God's kingdom of justice and peace worldwide—what about those believers who died before Christ returned? Would they miss participation in that coming kingdom for which they had worked and suffered?

That is a kind of question that many people, and not just Christians, have had. There have been many great movements in the course of history that have set out to bring about world reform and an age of justice, peace and welfare for all. And they have called upon their followers to work, suffer, sacrifice and even die to help the movement gain momentum and attain its goal. But all such movements that were atheist in their basic belief have suffered from a fatal weakness: they have had to admit that the majority of those who work and suffer, and all of those who die, for the sake of the movement, would never see the wonderful new epoch for which they worked.

Then why should people work, suffer and die for the benefit of some future age that they will never see or enjoy? What comfort would it have been to the hundreds of thousands of people that have been murdered in recent generations in countries such as Rwanda and Cambodia, to name but two, to have told them that their deaths would somehow contribute to a paradise they themselves would never enjoy? To all the millions of people down the centuries who have suffered and died unjustly, or suffered and died for some good cause, atheism, by definition, offers no ultimate personal hope whatever. When such people sorrow, they sorrow, as Paul says, as those who have no hope.

It is different for Christians. They are certainly expected to work, suffer and if need be die, for Christ. But however long it turns out to be before Christ returns, every believer is guaranteed participation in his coming reign and in God's eternal kingdom. The passages quoted above explain how that guarantee will be put into effect. It is this that fills Christians with a sense of the worthwhileness of life and work, fills them with hope, and even in the face of sorrow and death puts a song of triumph in their hearts:

> When this perishable body puts on imperishability, and this mortal body puts on immortality, then the saying that is written will be fulfilled:
>
> 'Death has been swallowed up in victory.'
> 'Where, O death, is your victory?
>   Where, O death, is your sting?'
>
> The sting of death is sin, and the power of sin is the law. But thanks be to God, who gives us the victory through our Lord Jesus Christ.
>
> Therefore, my beloved, be steadfast, immovable, always excelling in the work of the Lord, because you know that in the Lord your labour is not in vain. (1 Cor 15:54–58)

A fitting place to stop

Much more could be said, and not only about the second coming. All of the events and people and ideas we have surveyed in the course of these chapters will repay further reading and study. The whole of the Bible, with its sweeping history, deserves more attention than one such book could possibly give it. Yet it is appropriate that our studies stop here, looking forward to that great future event to which the New Testament itself points. Ultimately, the Bible is not only an historical record through which God has revealed his dealings with people of the past, nor is it meant only to teach us how God works in the present. The Bible also points to what God will yet do, as he reveals what he wants people to become—to be like his Son, Jesus Christ. And here it is worth listening to a fuller quotation from the Apostle John as he writes to Christians in the first century:

> See what kind of love the Father has given to us, that we should be called children of God; and so we are. The reason why the world does not know us is that it did not know him. Beloved, we are God's children now, and what we will be has not yet appeared; but we know that when he appears we shall be like him, because we shall see him as he is. And everyone who thus hopes in him purifies himself as he is pure. (1 John 3:1–3 ESV)

Since the goal is deeply personal, what we have considered in these chapters can hardly be thought to be simply for our passing interest. Either what the Bible has to say about right, wrong and our responsibility as human beings before God is not true, and therefore is largely irrelevant, or else it is true. If it is true, then each of our destinies turns on the question of what we choose to do about it or, more accurately, what we do about Jesus Christ. That is no exaggeration for effect; it is simply the fact of the matter, taken on the Bible's own terms.

APPENDICES

APPENDIX

Fulfilled Prophecies about Jesus Christ

Here is a list of some of the predictions about the coming Messiah (Christ) made in the Old Testament, which were fulfilled in the New Testament.

THEME	PROPHECY	FULFILMENT
humanity	Genesis 3:15	Galatians 4:4
virgin birth	Isaiah 7:14	Matthew 1:18
descendant of Abraham	Genesis 22:18	Matthew 1:1; Galatians 3:16
descendant of Isaac	Genesis 21:12	Luke 3:34
descendant of Jacob	Numbers 24:17	Luke 3:34
of the tribe of Judah	Genesis 49:10	Luke 3:33; Hebrews 7:14
of the family of Jesse	Isaiah 11:1, 10	Luke 3:32
of the House of David	2 Samuel 7:12–14a, 16; Jeremiah 23:5	Luke 3:31; Acts 13:22–23
announced by messenger	Isaiah 40:3	Matthew 3:3

THEME	PROPHECY	FULFILMENT
born at Bethlehem	Micah 5:2	Matthew 2:1, 4–8; John 7:42
shall be God with us	Isaiah 7:14	Matthew 1:23
enter temple	Malachi 3:1	Matthew 21:12
enter Jerusalem on a donkey	Zechariah 9:9	Luke 19:35–37
his death for our sins	Isaiah 53:5	Mark 10:45; 1 Corinthians 15:3
his resurrection	Psalm 16:10	Acts 2:31
his ascension	Psalm 110:1	Acts 2:34; Hebrews 1:3

Notes
(i)   There are many more detailed prophecies about the death of Christ, some of which are discussed in Appendix B.
(ii) There are prophecies not yet fulfilled. For example, Daniel 7:13–14 predicts that Christ will return. Jesus repeated the prediction before his judges and was in fact crucified for it (Matt 26:62–66).

Appendix

Evidence for the Resurrection of Jesus Christ

If the keystone is removed from an arch, the arch will collapse. The whole existence of the arch depends on the keystone. In the same way, the whole of Christianity depends on the resurrection of Christ. If the resurrection did not happen, if the New Testament's records of it could be proved untrue, then the whole of Christianity would collapse. Nothing worthwhile could be salvaged from it.

We can see that ourselves, if we read the New Testament and observe how central the resurrection is to its preaching and teaching. But what is more significant is that the early Christians themselves were aware that if the resurrection of Christ was not a fact, then there was nothing in Christianity worth having. Take, for example, the Apostle Paul. Writing to his converts in Corinth he says: 'If Christ has not been raised, your faith is futile and you are still in your sins' (1 Cor 15:17).

It is easy to see why this is so. Central to Christianity is the gospel. The gospel, says the Bible (Rom 1:16), is the power of God unto salvation. But how does it work? By offering and effecting forgiveness of sins, reconciliation and peace with God, through the death of Christ on the cross. But the death of a mere man could not make atonement for the sins of the world. Only one who was the Son of God could do that. Now Jesus predicted not only that he would die for our sins, but also that he would rise again. His resurrection would finally prove he was the Son of God. But suppose Jesus did not in fact rise from the dead. His prediction would then be shown to be fake. We could no longer believe he was the Son of God. We should then have to regard his death as simply one more cruel death such as many men have suffered. In that case Jesus' death could not procure forgiveness of sins for mankind any more than any other man's death. Christianity would be left with no gospel to preach.

Again, Paul says about himself and the other Christian apostles and preachers:

> And if Christ has not been raised, then our proclamation has been in vain and your faith has been in vain. We are even found to be misrepresenting God, because we testified of God that he raised Christ—whom he did not raise if it is true that the dead are not raised. For if the dead are not raised, then Christ has not been raised. (1 Cor 15:14–16)

Here Paul tells us bluntly that if it were not true that Christ rose from the dead, he, Paul, and the other apostles would be convicted of being deliberate and despicable liars. For at the heart of their Christian gospel was their insistence that God had raised Jesus bodily from the dead, and that they had personally met, seen and spoken to him after his resurrection. How could anyone respect, let alone have faith in, Christianity, if its first propagators were a bunch of deliberate liars?

Some people suggest that if Paul were living today he would not insist on Christ's literal and physical resurrection, for he would know that many modern scientists and philosophers hold the theory that physical resurrection is impossible. But this suggestion is false. In the passage cited above, Paul tells us that many philosophers and 'scientists' in his own day held a similar theory that resurrection (of anyone at all) is simply impossible. Paul was fully aware of their views. But he held that the sheer historical occurrence of Christ's resurrection and his subsequent appearances, witnessed by many responsible eyewitnesses, himself included, outweighed—and in fact destroyed—the mere theory of the contemporary philosophers and scientists. But if, knowing all about their theories, Paul and his fellow apostles had deliberately concocted a story of Christ's resurrection, aware in their own hearts that they had not seen, handled and talked to the risen Christ, and that it was simply a myth which they themselves had fabricated; then they were nothing but religious hoaxers, worthy of contempt. And the Christian gospel would stand in ruins.

In light of this, it becomes important to know who it was that first told the world that three days after his burial, Christ's tomb was found to be empty.

Not the Christians but the Pharisees

Notice what is recorded in Matthew's Gospel:

> The next day, that is, after the day of Preparation, the chief priests and the Pharisees gathered before Pilate and said, 'Sir, we remember what that impostor said while he was still alive, "After three days I will rise again." Therefore command that the tomb be made secure until the third day; otherwise his disciples may go and steal him away, and tell the people, "He has been raised from the dead," and the last deception would be worse than the first.' Pilate said to them, 'You have a guard of soldiers; go, make it as secure as you can.' So they went with the guard and made the tomb secure by sealing the stone. (Matt 27:62–66)

> While they were going, some of the guard went into the city and told the chief priests everything that had happened. After the priests had assembled with the elders, they devised a plan to give a large sum of money to the soldiers, telling them, 'You must say, "His disciples came by night and stole him away while we were asleep." If this comes to the governor's ears, we will satisfy him and keep you out of trouble.' So they took the money and did as they were directed. And this story is still told among the Jews to this day. (Matt 28:11–15)

From this passage we see that it was the Jewish authorities who first let it be known that Christ's tomb was empty.

The Christians as yet said nothing to anybody (except among themselves); and it was to be another fifty days before, on the day of Pentecost, they publicly proclaimed that Jesus had risen from the dead (see Acts 1 and 2).

Why then did the Jews act before the Christians and announce the fact that the tomb was empty? *Because it was a fact!* And, as Matthew tells us, they had strong reasons for not trying to cover up the fact: what would Pilate have said if fifty days later he had discovered that the Jewish authorities had been involved in a cover-up? And they had urgent reasons for getting their explanation of the fact across to the public and gaining credence for it at once, if possible. For they knew that the Christians would presently claim the empty tomb as evidence that Jesus had risen from the dead. They felt they must get out ahead of the Christians: the first explanation on the market, would, they hoped, gain the most credence.

Now the Jewish authorities' explanation of the fact is self-evidently untrue. It is impossible to believe it. But that still leaves the fact of the empty tomb. How shall it be explained?

The records of the resurrection were written by Christians

Would it not be more convincing, some people say, if some of the records of the resurrection were written by non-Christians? At least, they would not be biased and prejudiced; and therefore their independent witness would be more impressive.

Perhaps so. But there are the following considerations.

First of all, in those early days people who became convinced that Jesus had risen from the dead, became Christians. It would be difficult indeed to find someone who was convinced of Christ's resurrection and yet did not become a Christian and so was able to give an 'unbiased' record of the evidence for the resurrection. The important thing to notice about the thousands who in those early days became Christians is that they were not Christians when they first heard the claim that Jesus was risen from the dead. It was the force of the evidence of his resurrection that converted them.

The conversion of Saul of Tarsus is a case in point:

> Meanwhile Saul, still breathing threats and murder against the disciples of the Lord, went to the high priest and asked him for letters to the synagogues at Damascus, so that if he found any who belonged to the Way, men or women, he might bring them bound to Jerusalem. Now as he was going along and approaching Damascus, suddenly a light from heaven flashed around him. He fell to the ground and heard a voice saying to him, 'Saul, Saul, why do you persecute me?' He asked, 'Who are you, Lord?' The reply came, 'I am Jesus, whom you are persecuting. But get up and enter the city, and you will be told what you are to do.' The men who were travelling with him stood speechless because they heard the voice but saw no one. Saul got up from the ground, and though his eyes were open, he could see nothing; so they led him by the hand and brought him into Damascus. For three days he was without sight, and neither ate nor drank. (Acts 9:1–9)

The case of Saul of Tarsus is special in many ways. But it is clear from the narrative that not only was he not a Christian: he was a positive and violent opponent of Christianity, and was out to destroy what he regarded as the fraudulent story of Christ's resurrection. But then the risen Christ appeared to him on the Damascus road. It was the reality of the risen Christ that converted him.

One cannot deny the historicity of his conversion. It was he who as the Apostle Paul did more than any other by his missionary travels, preaching and writings to establish Christianity in Asia and Europe. It was his writings that later transformed Europe at the time of the Reformation. And still to this day his writings exercise an enormous influence over millions of people. One cannot, therefore, ignore Paul's conversion; its effects have been so vast and so enduring. What, then, caused his conversion? He says that it was a personal encounter with Jesus after he rose from the dead; and, not surprisingly, his subsequent sermons and writings are full of the reality, the wonder, and the glorious implications of Christ's resurrection. If that resurrection was not in fact a reality, what other adequate cause can we posit for Paul's conversion?

But to get back to the question: why are there no records from the non-Christian contemporaries of the early Christians in support of the claim that Jesus rose from the dead? That question, as we have just seen, is rather unhelpful. A better question would be: where is the evidence from the contemporary opponents of Christianity that Christ had not risen from the dead? Many people at the time, of course, when they heard the Christians say that Christ was risen, immediately dismissed it from their minds as nonsense. Many still do. But the Jewish authorities in Jerusalem could not afford to do so. They had instigated his judicial murder; and in the first few weeks after Pentecost, when the Christians were daily proclaiming in the temple that Jesus was risen from the dead, and some few thousands in Jerusalem, including many priests, were getting converted, the authorities understandably made strenuous efforts to strangle Christianity at its birth (see Acts 2–9). They put the Christian apostles on trial, beat and imprisoned them, and tried (unsuccessfully) to suppress all preaching in the name of Jesus.

Then why did they not, in those first few weeks, do the one thing that would have stopped Christianity dead in its tracks? Why did they not produce the dead body of Jesus and put it on public display? They had all the panoply of State, including torture and help from the Roman governor, available to them to track down the body of Jesus if the Christians had, in fact, surreptitiously removed it. Why, then did they not produce the body?

'Because', said the Christians, 'they couldn't. The body was gone. Jesus had in actual fact been raised from the dead.'

Now the absence of this particular piece of negative evidence is surely significant. But in addition we must next ask: what kind of positive evidence did the first Christians put forward for the resurrection? To that question we shall now turn.

Exhibit A: **Physical evidence**

We first consider evidence from one of Christ's disciples, John. He says that when he first heard that the body of

Jesus was missing from the tomb, he went at once to examine the situation. He found that though the body was indeed gone, the tomb was not completely empty: the grave clothes in which Jesus had been buried were still there. Furthermore, there was something about the positioning and state of the grave clothes that convinced him that the only satisfactory explanation of what he saw was that a miracle had taken place and Jesus had risen.

Now, many of us will have read detective stories or else followed closely the evidence in the trial of some well-known person. Even if we are but amateurs, we can use our detective skills on the evidence that John gives us. But first let us assess the reliability of John as a witness.

The reliability of John as a witness

The question is: can we be sure that in reporting what he saw, John is being honest and not deliberately telling untruths? So let us ask: What motive would he have had for lying? He himself reports that on the evening of the day in which he found the tomb empty, he and his fellow disciples met in a room that was bolted for fear of the Jews (John 20:19). A few weeks later he was twice imprisoned and then beaten by the authorities for publicly preaching that Jesus was risen from the dead (Acts 4:1–21; 5:17–42). Then his fellow Christian, Stephen, was stoned to death (Acts 6:8–7:60). Later his own brother, James, was executed by King Herod for his belief in the risen Christ; and so severe was the general persecution that many Christians were obliged to flee for their lives from Jerusalem (Acts 11:19; 12:1–2). During the subsequent persecution by the emperor Nero, many Christians suffered horrible deaths.

And in his old age John himself was exiled on the island of Patmos (Rev 1:9). Are we to think, therefore, that having convinced many people of the resurrection of Jesus by telling lies about what he saw in the tomb, he was prepared to stand by and see them persecuted and executed for the sake of these lies which he had concocted; and then himself suffer imprisonment, fear of death, and exile for what he knew to be a lie?

Moreover a few pages earlier in his book he records Christ's words before Pilate: 'For this I was born and for this I came into the world, to testify to the truth. Everyone who belongs to the truth listens to my voice' (John 18:37). Is it likely that shortly after writing this, he deliberately falsified the record of what he saw in the tomb in order to bolster the claim of Jesus to be witness to the truth? If he did, he was a most despicable religious charlatan. But religious charlatans don't write books of moral power and spiritual beauty like the Gospel of John. You may think John was mistaken or self-deceived over what he saw in the tomb; but it is impossible to think that he was deliberate liar.

So let us now investigate (*a*) what he tells us about the way Jesus was buried; (*b*) what he saw in the tomb on the third day after the burial; and (*c*) what he deduced from what he saw. Then we shall be in a position to make up our own minds.

The way Jesus was buried

> After these things, Joseph of Arimathea, who was a
> disciple of Jesus, though a secret one because of his

fear of the Jews, asked Pilate to let him take away the
body of Jesus. Pilate gave him permission; so he came
and removed his body. Nicodemus, who had at first
come to Jesus by night, also came, bringing a mixture
of myrrh and aloes, weighing about a hundred pounds.
They took the body of Jesus and wrapped it with the
spices in linen cloths, according to the burial custom
of the Jews. Now there was a garden in the place
where he was crucified, and in the garden there was a
new tomb in which no one had ever been laid. And so,
because it was the Jewish day of Preparation, and the
tomb was nearby, they laid Jesus there. (John 19:38–42)

From these verses and from John 20:1 (and from Luke
23:53) we learn that Jesus was buried not in a grave dug
in the earth, but in a tomb hewn out of the rock face.
The entrance to the tomb and the space inside were big
enough, we learn (John 19:40–42 and 20:6–8), for at least
two adult people to enter, in addition to the corpse. The
dead body would not have been laid on the ground but
on a shelf hewn out of the wall of the tomb. The mixture of myrrh and aloes which Nicodemus brought would
have weighed at least 25 kg. This is not an exaggerated,
fairy tale figure, but usual for the burial of an honoured
and valued personage in the ancient Middle East.[1] Both
the myrrh (a fragrant resin) and the aloes (made of aromatic sandalwood) would have been used in powdered

1 About 35 kg of spices were used by a certain Onkeles at the funeral of
the Rabbi Gamaliel a little later in the first century AD ('Onkelos and Aquila'
in *Encyclopaedia Judaica*, 2007) and, according to Josephus, a much larger
quantity was used at the funeral of Herod the Great just before the start
of the first century (*Antiquities of the Jews*, 17.8.3).

form. The body of Jesus was wrapped in strips of linen cloth, interlarded with the spices. The head (see John 20:7) was bound round with a large face-cloth which, running beneath the jaw and then over the top of the head and round the front and back of the head, would have kept the jaw from falling open. The body would then be laid on the stone bench, at one end of which there would have been a shallow step to act as a cushion for the head.

What John and Peter saw in the tomb

> Early on the first day of the week, while it was still dark, Mary Magdalene came to the tomb and saw that the stone had been removed from the tomb. So she ran and went to Simon Peter and the other disciple, the one whom Jesus loved, and said to them, 'They have taken the Lord out of the tomb, and we do not know where they have laid him.' Then Peter and the other disciple set out and went towards the tomb. The two were running together, but the other disciple outran Peter and reached the tomb first. He bent down to look in and saw the linen wrappings lying there, but he did not go in. Then Simon Peter came, following him, and went into the tomb. He saw the linen wrappings lying there, and the cloth that had been on Jesus' head, not lying with the linen wrappings but rolled up in a place by itself. Then the other disciple, who reached the tomb first, also went in, and he saw and believed; for as yet they did not understand the scripture, that he must rise from the dead. (John 20:1–9)

It is clear that Peter, John and Mary Magdalene, in spite of all that Jesus had told them, were not expecting Jesus to rise from the dead. Otherwise, they would have been at the tomb to see it happen; and on finding the tomb empty, Mary would not have reported the fact to John in the words: 'They [some unknown persons] have taken away the Lord out of the tomb and we don't know where they have laid him.' And even when Peter and John heard Mary's report, they still did not grasp the implication that the Lord had risen from the dead, and explain it all to Mary. They simply ran to investigate what had happened. Grave robbing was a common practice at the time (the Roman Emperor Claudius, AD 41–54, issued a decree–a copy of which, engraved on stone, has been found in Palestine– forbidding it on pain of death). It could, for all Peter and John expected, have been that grave-robbers had removed the large stone that would have been used to cover the entrance of the tomb once the body had been placed inside, and had stolen the body in the hope of finding jewellery and other small valuable items buried with it (not to speak of the large amount of very expensive spices bound up with the extensive–and valuable–linen cloths).

Now when John first arrived at the tomb, he tells us that he did not go in, but peeped in from the outside. From that position the thing that immediately caught his eye was that, though the body was gone, the grave clothes were still there. The next thing that struck him forcibly (he mentions it twice, in v. 5 and again in v. 6) was that the grave clothes, that is, the linen cloths, were not only there: they were lying there. That is, they were not in a heap, they were not thrown all round the tomb (as they might have been if robbers had hastily torn them off the body); they were lying there still on the shelf just as they had been when the body was inside them, but flattened somewhat now that the body was gone.

Then Peter caught up with John, and in his characteristically impetuous manner (notice how uncontrived and true to life the narrative is) entered the tomb, and John with him. Now they could both see, what from outside the tomb John could not see, the position of the face-cloth that had been round Christ's head.

The immediately noticeable thing was that it was not lying with the linen clothes. It was twirled round upon itself just as it had been when it had been on the Lord's head; and it was lying by itself in a distinct place, presumably on the shallow step that had served as a cushion for the Lord's head.

What John deduced from what he saw
He saw and believed, says the narrative. Believed what? Not simply believed what Mary had told them about the body being missing. It would not have taken the presence, position and state of the linen cloths and the face-cloth to confirm Mary's story. John could just as easily have seen that the body had gone, if the grave-cloths had gone as well. Nor, so he tells us, did what he saw remind him of Old Testament Scriptures that indicated that the Messiah must rise from the dead, and so lead him to conclude that these Scriptures must have been fulfilled. At the time, he says, neither he nor Peter had realised that the Old Testament prophesied that Messiah must rise again. And what is more, he had not yet met the risen Lord, and did not do so until the evening of that day.

What he deduced from the presence, position, and state of the linen cloths and the face-cloth was that the body of Jesus had come through the grave clothes without unwrapping them, and had left them largely undisturbed, though somewhat collapsed. In other words a miracle had taken place. Christ's body had somehow gone and left the grave clothes behind. A resurrection, whatever that might turn out to mean, had taken place.

The reasonableness of John's belief
We can say at once that what John saw shows conclusively that the body had not been removed by grave robbers. They would not have taken the body and left the grave clothes and spices which were worth more than a dead body. And had they undone all the linen cloths and the face-cloth in order to get the body out, they would not have delayed in order to put the cloths back again just as they were before the body was taken; not when there was a posse of soldiers on guard outside, liable any moment to inspect the tomb (see Matt 27:62–66).

But suppose the impossible, that someone, friendly to Jesus, had managed under the very noses of the soldiers to break the seal on the tomb and roll away the stone, intent on removing Jesus' body for religious or sentimental reasons. It is conceivable that they would have removed the grave clothes from the body so as not so easily to be seen to be carrying a dead body through the streets. It is also conceivable that they might have put the grave clothes back to make it look to the soldiers on a casual inspection as though the body was still there. But they would not have left the stone rolled away and the tomb wide open! And we know from Matthew that when the soldiers did look into the tomb, they were not deceived into thinking that the body was still there (Matt 28:11–15). But all this unlikely speculation founders on the fact that if anyone friendly to Jesus had removed the body and buried it elsewhere for safekeeping, they would eventually have told the other disciples where it was.

So next suppose that someone had taken the body away and deliberately arranged the grave clothes to make it look as if a miracle had taken place. Who would that someone have been? The authorities in Jerusalem would certainly not have done any such thing. And, for reasons which we discussed at the beginning of this chapter, neither John, nor any other of the early Christians, would have perpetrated such a deceit; nor could have done with a posse of soldiers on guard.

Final conclusion
What John and Peter saw, then, when they went to the tomb early on the first day of the week, constitutes a powerful piece of physical evidence for the resurrection of Christ. And there was more to follow. In the evening of that same day Christ appeared to his disciples in the upper room, showed them his hands and his side (John 20:20); got them to handle him to see that he was not a disembodied spirit, but a body with flesh and bone; and called for food and ate it in their presence (Luke 24:36–43), and continued to appear to them in similar fashion for the next forty days. This cumulative physical evidence confirmed John's initial deduction from the grave clothes, and made the resurrection of Christ, not merely a theory that could

be deduced from lifeless physical evidence, but a personal experience of the living Lord.

But now we must investigate another kind of evidence for the resurrection.

Exhibit B: Psychological evidence

We cite here the striking fact that in the whole of the New Testament (as distinct from later decadent centuries) there is not the slightest hint that the early Christians venerated the grave of Christ or made a shrine of his tomb. This is remarkable, for the Jews of the time were in the habit of venerating the tombs of their famous dead prophets (see Luke 11:47–48); but the Christians built no shrine around Jesus' grave, nor made it a special place of pilgrimage or prayer. Nowhere in the New Testament is there the faintest suggestion that a visit to Jesus' tomb was of some spiritual benefit or efficacy. When from time to time in the course of his missionary journeys the Apostle Paul returned to Jerusalem, we read of his calling on the Christian leaders, of his visiting the Jewish temple, of celebrating Pentecost, but never of his paying a visit to the tomb of Christ.

And this is all the more remarkable because in the hours that followed the Lord's burial, the Christian women began to behave in a way that if unchecked would naturally have led to turning the tomb into a shrine of prayer and devotion to Christ. But something checked them. What was it? What power or influence was strong enough to overcome the natural psychological instincts that impel people, and women in particular, to cling to the relics of loved ones now dead? And what was it that stopped dead any superstitious tendency to imagine that the tomb of Christ possessed magical powers?

A reconstruction of events

All four Gospels are unanimous that the first Christians to visit Christ's tomb on the third day after his burial were a group of women from Galilee. Out of gratitude for what Christ had done for them, these women had followed him on his long, slow journey to Jerusalem, and had helped and supported him from their own resources. They could afford to do so, for they were comparatively well off. One of them, indeed, a certain Joanna, was the wife of a man called Chuza, who was the manager of King Herod's household (Luke 8:3). When Jesus was crucified, they stood watching at some distance from the cross along with others of Christ's acquaintances (23:49). And when he was buried by Joseph and Nicodemus, both wealthy men, these well-to-do women from Galilee were not afraid to join the little burial procession. They saw what tomb he was buried in, noted exactly where it was, and how the body was positioned in the tomb. They watched Nicodemus wrap 25 kg of aromatic spices in with the strips of linen that were bound round the body. But large and expensive as that amount of spices was, it was not enough for them. They wanted to express their own love and devotion to Christ. So they went back to the various places in Jerusalem at which they were staying over the Passover period (Joanna may well have been staying, with her husband, in Herod's Jerusalem palace); and there they prepared more spices and ointment (23:55–56).

Their intention was to return to the tomb as soon as the Sabbath day was over and reverently and affectionately anoint the body of Jesus still more.

But at this point we meet a difficulty that has caused many people to conclude, after a superficial reading of the Gospels, that their accounts of the resurrection of Christ contradict each other. That is not so. The difficulty arises simply because none of the gospel writers sets out to record everything that happened. Each writer selects from his particular sources what particularly interested him and fits it into the flow of his particular narrative; and in so doing he naturally omits or telescopes other events. But if we collect all that the four Gospels between them say about the women from Galilee, we can with care compile a coherent account of what they did and where they went on the day in question. The story goes like this:

When, at early dawn on the first day of the week, they arrived at the tomb, they were startled to find the stone already rolled away from the entrance (Luke 24:1-2). Some of them entered—they could scarcely have all got inside at once—and immediately shouted their alarming discovery to the others, that the body was gone. Whereupon Mary Magdalene did not wait to see what happened next—which was that after a while two angels appeared to the women inside the tomb and told them that Christ was risen (24:4-8). Mary ran off at once as hard as she could to the house where John and Peter were staying. Breathlessly she reported what seemed to her the obvious explanation, that someone or ones had removed the body from the tomb and that neither she nor the other women knew where they had deposited it. Thereupon, Peter and John immediately ran to the tomb. From the presence, state and position of the grave clothes John concluded that a miracle had taken place: Christ must have risen from the dead; and with that, he and Peter went back (directly or indirectly) to the house where they were staying, and waited to see what would happen next (John 20:1-10).

Mary, however, went back to the tomb. The other women, of course, had gone. They had in fact been so scared by the appearance of the angels and by the message the angels ordered them to take to the apostles that for a while they told nobody about it (Mark 16:8). Presently joy got the upper hand over fear, and they started out to go to the apostles, when the risen Lord met them and confirmed the message they were to convey (Matt 28:9-10). Whereupon they proceeded, not like Mary had done to the house where John and Peter were staying, but to a small upper room in Jerusalem which the (now eleven) apostles had hired as a place to meet in. There the women told their amazing story to the apostles who by this time had been joined by John and Peter.

Let's leave them there for a while and rejoin Mary. This is what happened as she stood looking into the tomb.

> But Mary stood weeping outside the tomb. As she wept, she bent over to look into the tomb; and she saw two angels in white, sitting where the body of Jesus had been lying, one at the head and the other at the feet. They said to her, 'Woman, why are you weeping?' She said to them, 'They have taken away my Lord, and I do not know where they have laid him.' When she had said this, she turned round and saw Jesus standing

there, but she did not know that it was Jesus. Jesus said to her, 'Woman, why are you weeping? For whom are you looking?' Supposing him to be the gardener, she said to him, 'Sir, if you have carried him away, tell me where you have laid him, and I will take him away.' Jesus said to her, 'Mary!' She turned and said to him in Hebrew, 'Rabbouni!' (which means Teacher). Jesus said to her, 'Do not hold on to me, because I have not yet ascended to the Father. But go to my brothers and say to them, "I am ascending to my Father and your Father, to my God and your God."' Mary Magdalene went and announced to the disciples, 'I have seen the Lord'; and she told them that he had said these things to her. (John 20:11–18)

Consider the following points:

1. Mary had originally come to the tomb that morning with the other women from Galilee to honour the body of Christ. Dead though it was, she could not let it go. She would express her love to the Lord as she anointed his body with costly ointment, and stifled the smell of the corpse with her fragrant spices.

2. Distraught at finding the body gone, her one thought now was to regain possession of it: though she did not refer to the body as 'it'; to her the dead body was still 'him'. It was all she now had of him. 'Tell me', she said to the man whom she supposed was the gardener, 'where you have laid him, and I will take him away.' For it was unbearable to her not to know where the body was and to be left with not even a relic of it, and not even a grave that she could venerate as his.

3. Suppose, then, the 'gardener' had showed her where the body was and she had taken it away. What would she have done with it? There is no doubt. She and the other women would have bought for it, or rather, him, the best tomb obtainable, no expense spared. Lovingly they would have buried him; and his grave would have become for them the most sacred place on earth. They would have made a shrine of it, venerated it, and visited it as often as they could.

4. But something happened to Mary that day in the garden that blew all such ideas clean out of her heart and head once and for ever. It must have been something very powerful to banish so completely and suddenly all the former psychological instincts and reactions. What was it?

5. It was that in the garden that day she encountered the living Lord Jesus, risen from the dead. Of course she abandoned the tomb! You don't venerate the tomb of someone who is alive and whom you have just met! You don't go to a tomb to pray to someone with whom you can have a direct living conversation!

6. But there was more to it than that. Mary's previous experience of Jesus had been wonderful; but death seemed to have destroyed it, leaving her nothing but a dead body: fragrant memories but a blighted heart. Now Jesus did a wonderful thing. He replaced that earlier experience with an utterly new, warm, vibrant, living relationship between Mary and God the Father, between Mary and himself, a relationship bound together by a life that not even Mary's eventual physical death could possibly destroy. 'Go to my brothers', said he, 'and say to them, "I am ascending to my Father and your Father, to my God and your God."'

Thereafter though still on earth, Mary knew herself bound to God and Christ in heaven by the indestructible power of eternal life already possessed, entered into, and enjoyed. So did all the other disciples. And so may all today who confess Jesus as Lord and believe in their hearts that God has raised him from the dead (see Rom 10:9).

In her new-found life and ecstatic joy Mary now went to convey the risen Lord's message to the other disciples. And this time she went, not to the house where John and Peter were staying, but to the upper room. There she reported to the Eleven and all the others that she had seen the Lord (Luke 24:10; John 20:18). That was more, of course, than Peter or John or any others of the Eleven had so far done; and Peter, much perplexed went off to examine the tomb once more (Luke 24:12). It was shortly after that—and before Christ appeared to all the apostles at once in the upper room—that he appeared to Peter (1 Cor 15:5, here called Cephas). The painful matter of Peter's recent denial of the Lord had to be cleared up: and it was better done in private.

After this the early Christians showed no further interest in the tomb where the body of Christ had lain. They had no reason to visit it—they knew that Jesus had risen.

Exhibit C: **The evidence of the Old Testament**

The writers of the New Testament tell us honestly that when on various occasions the disciples saw the risen Lord, some doubted (Matt 28:17). Sometimes the reason why they hesitated to believe was that it seemed too wonderful, too joyful, too good to be true. They did not want to believe it uncritically, only to find that it could not survive hard-headed examination (Luke 24:41). And then a miracle the size of a resurrection, when they first heard about it from the women who claimed to have met the risen Lord, seemed more likely to be the result of overheated imagination than hard, objective fact. But that kind of reluctance to believe was eventually swept away by the sheer concrete, tangible evidence of the risen Lord inviting them to touch him, sitting bodily with them and eating an ordinary meal (24:41-43).

But there was another form of unbelief, the cause of which ran deeper and had to be removed by somewhat different methods, as we shall now see:

> Now on that same day two of them were going to a village called Emmaus, about seven miles from Jerusalem, and talking with each other about all these things that had happened. While they were talking and discussing, Jesus himself came near and went with them, but their eyes were kept from recognizing him. And he said to them, 'What are you discussing with each other while you walk along?' They stood still, looking sad. Then one of them, whose name was Cleopas, answered him, 'Are you the only stranger in Jerusalem who does not know the things that have taken place there in these days?' He asked them, 'What things?' They replied, 'The things about Jesus of Nazareth, who was a prophet mighty in deed and word before God and all the people, and how our chief priests and leaders handed him over to be condemned to death and crucified him. But we had hoped that he was the one

to redeem Israel. Yes, and besides all this, it is now the third day since these things took place. Moreover, some women of our group astounded us. They were at the tomb early this morning, and when they did not find his body there, they came back and told us that they had indeed seen a vision of angels who said that he was alive. Some of those who were with us went to the tomb and found it just as the women had said; but they did not see him.' Then he said to them, 'Oh, how foolish you are, and how slow of heart to believe all that the prophets have declared! Was it not necessary that the Messiah should suffer these things and then enter into his glory?' Then beginning with Moses and all the prophets, he interpreted to them the things about himself in all the scriptures. (Luke 24:13-27)

The reason for the travellers' disillusionment

The two travellers on the road to Emmaus were disillusioned; and the reason was this. On our Lord's last visit to Jerusalem they had joined the large crowds who had genuinely thought that Jesus was the Messiah, whose coming was promised by God through the Old Testament prophets. Now from their (probably scant and superficial) knowledge of the Old Testament, they were expecting that the Messiah, when he came, would turn out to be a powerful military and political leader who would raise armies and lead the nation of Israel in a successful uprising against the imperialist forces of the Roman occupation. 'We hoped', they explained to the stranger who joined them on the road, 'that he was the one who would liberate Israel.'

But, of course, Jesus had done no such thing. Far from liberating the masses of Israel, he had been arrested, tried, condemned and crucified by a combination of the Jewish religious establishment and the Roman military governor. And the mockery that had gone on at the trial had made a public laughing-stock of Jesus' claim to be a king. At one blow the whole movement had come to nothing, like a pathetic, ill-organised, ineffectual peasant rising. What good was a political liberator who could not even save himself from being crucified? So the two travellers were going home in profound disillusionment.

Why at first could they not take in the fact that Jesus had risen from the dead? It was because, to their way of thinking, Jesus had not fulfilled the Old Testament's promises of a coming Liberator–King. Instead, he had been defeated, crucified, a failure. He was therefore not the promised Messiah. And that being so, the rumour that he had risen from the dead seemed not only incredible in itself but irrelevant into the bargain. If he wasn't the Messiah, what was the point of his being raised from the dead?

So what had to be done to make faith in the resurrection possible for them? Notice that at the beginning of his conversation with them the risen Lord did not attempt to convince them that he was Jesus. Indeed he first gently chided them because their reading of the Old Testament had been unduly selective. They had read the parts that appealed to them, about the promised coming of a Liberator–King. But they had overlooked, or not understood, or conveniently forgotten the parts that foretold that the Messiah would first have to suffer and die, and only after that would be raised from the dead and enter his glory. And so the stranger took them through the whole Old Testament and pointed out passages that either stated, or else clearly implied, this. The point of the lesson was obvious: if the Old Testament prophesied that Messiah must first suffer and die, then Jesus' sufferings and death, far from proving that he was not the Messiah, were strong evidence that he was. If, in addition, the Old Testament prophesied that after his death Messiah would live again and liberate his people and share with them the spoils of a great victory, then to do that he would have to rise from the dead.[2] The reports which the two travellers had heard from the women that Jesus was risen and that they had seen him, might therefore be true after all. The stumbling-block that had prevented their believing was removed.

The relevance of this incident to us
Still for us today one of the most important strands of evidence for the resurrection of Christ is that the Old Testament foretold, not only that the Messiah would rise from the dead, but that he would do so as an integral part of God's plan for the redemption of mankind. Notice the repeated emphasis on this fact in the Apostle Paul's great statement of the Christian gospel:

> For I handed on to you as of first importance what
> I in turn had received: that Christ died for our sins
> in accordance with the scriptures, and that he was

2 See the implication in Isaiah 53:8–12 that the Messiah would first suffer and die, and then rise from the dead. Likewise see Psalm 16 and compare with Acts 2:25–32.

buried, and that he was raised on the third day in
accordance with the scriptures. (1 Cor 15:3–4)

A report that some otherwise unheard-of ordinary individual had been raised from the dead unexpectedly and
for no apparent reason might well be difficult to believe.
We should all ask: 'Why him?' and 'What is the point of
it?' and 'How can we believe that such an extraordinary
exception to the laws of nature has taken place arbitrarily
and for no apparent reason?' Atheists, of course, believe
that the universe as a whole has come into existence for
no apparent reason. Its existence cannot be accounted
for: it is just an arbitrary, inexplicable, brute fact. Those
who believe in an intelligent Creator, however, would find
it difficult to believe that the Creator had overruled the
normal laws of nature arbitrarily to raise some obscure
individual from the dead for no apparent reason.

But Jesus was no ordinary person! He was God incarnate. Nor was his resurrection an isolated phenomenon. It
was part of the Creator's gigantic plan for the redemption
of mankind and for the eventual renewal of the universe.
Nor was the story of the resurrection invented by Christ's
disciples. God had had it announced through his prophets
and written down in the Old Testament centuries before
Jesus was born into our world. And it is still open to us
today to study the Old Testament seriously and see for
ourselves whether the birth, life, death and resurrection
of Christ match the Old Testament's God-given prophecies.

When Jesus had finished his rapid survey of the Old
Testament, the main difficulty in the way of the travellers'
believing was removed. But they still did not recognize

that the stranger was in fact Jesus risen from the dead. How, then, did they come to recognize him? We must look at that in detail because it raises a large general question.

How did they know it was really him?
What evidence convinced the disciples that the person who appeared to them claiming to be Jesus risen from the dead was actually Jesus and not some kind of impersonation?

> As they came near the village to which they were going, he walked ahead as if he were going on. But they urged him strongly, saying, 'Stay with us, because it is almost evening and the day is now nearly over.' So he went in to stay with them. When he was at the table with them, he took bread, blessed and broke it, and gave it to them. Then their eyes were opened, and they recognized him; and he vanished from their sight. They said to each other, 'Were not our hearts burning within us while he was talking to us on the road, while he was opening the scriptures to us?' That same hour they got up and returned to Jerusalem; and they found the eleven and their companions gathered together. They were saying, 'The Lord has risen indeed, and he has appeared to Simon!' Then they told what had happened on the road, and how he had been made known to them in the breaking of the bread. (Luke 24:28-35)

The two travellers invited the stranger to stay the night with them, and they sat him down to an evening meal. But still they had not recognised who he was. Then he took the bread that was on the table, gave thanks, broke it and began to give it to them. And in that instant their eyes were opened and they recognised him; and he vanished out of their sight. Later, when they returned to Jerusalem and recounted their experience, they explained that Jesus was recognised by them when he broke the bread.

What was there so special about his breaking of the bread? First, in taking the bread, breaking it, giving thanks and giving it to them in their own house, he was taking over the role of the host. That must have riveted their attention on him. Second, in that moment as he broke the bread they would have caught sight of the nail-prints in his hands. But there was more to it than that. Watching those hands break the bread the way he did, it would have evoked memories of what only the closest of Jesus' disciples could have known about. They would have heard from the eleven apostles before they left for Emmaus how at the Passover meal on the night he was betrayed Jesus had taken bread, broken it and uttered what then must have sounded very mysterious words, but words which no one ever had said to them before: 'This is my body which is given for you.' There had followed the (for them) devastating experience of the cross. But now they had listened to the stranger's exposition of Old Testament passages. These passages not only prophesied that Messiah would have to die and rise again, but also explained why: he would have to die for his people's sins, and indeed for theirs too. Now as they saw him with nail-pierced hands break bread and give it to them personally, his action carried profound overtones which no impersonator could have known about or invented. Its significance was utterly and uniquely peculiar to Jesus. They recognised him at once. It was unmistakably Jesus.

How do we know it was really him?

But what about those millions, like us today, who have never seen, and cannot see Jesus with our own two eyes?

> But Thomas (who was called the Twin), one of the twelve, was not with them when Jesus came. So the other disciples told him, 'We have seen the Lord.' But he said to them, 'Unless I see the mark of the nails in his hands, and put my finger in the mark of the nails and my hand in his side, I will not believe.'
>
> A week later his disciples were again in the house, and Thomas was with them. Although the doors were shut, Jesus came and stood among them and said, 'Peace be with you.' Then he said to Thomas, 'Put your finger here and see my hands. Reach out your hand and put it in my side. Do not doubt but believe.' Thomas answered him, 'My Lord and my God!' Jesus said to him, 'Have you believed because you have seen me? Blessed are those who have not seen and yet have come to believe.' (John 20:24-29)

Notice that Jesus did not rebuke Thomas for doubting. He respected his honesty. Jesus did not rebuke Thomas for demanding evidence before he would believe. And Jesus gave Thomas the evidence he asked for.

This reveals an interesting and important thing. Jesus had obviously heard Thomas speak and heard his demand for evidence even though Thomas was unaware of his presence at the time; for when he entered the room, without waiting for Thomas to say anything, he offered him the evidence he had earlier demanded.

That reminds us that at this very moment because Jesus is risen from the dead, he hears what we say and knows what we are thinking. And we may certainly express ourselves freely and say, if we really mean it: 'If Jesus is really alive, let him provide me with evidence that I can really believe; and then I will believe on him.'

But before we do so, let us ponder deeply what else Jesus said to Thomas: 'Because you have seen me, you have believed; blessed are those who have not seen, and yet have believed.' Evidence that can be seen with physical eyesight is not the only kind of evidence available that Jesus is alive. If it were, physically blind people could never see it. It is not, in fact, by itself the best kind of evidence. The evidence that is perceived by our conscience, heart and spirit, is far and away the best evidence. And no one ever speaks to our hearts like Jesus does. He says that he personally loves us and died for our sins according to the Scriptures, and has risen again according to the Scriptures; and that if we open our hearts to him, he will enter and fill them with his presence and love. If with conscience, heart and spirit we listen to him speaking the Bible to us as he did to the travellers, and if we come to see that his hands were nailed to the cross as he gave himself to death for us personally, we shall find that 'faith comes from hearing, and hearing through the word of Christ' (Rom 10:17 ESV). And we too shall find our hearts burning within us as he talks to us on life's journey and opens to us the Scriptures.

Further reading

Craig, William Lane. *Reasonable Faith: Christian Truth and Apologetics.* [1984] 3rd edn. Wheaton: Crossway, 2008.

Habermas, Gary R. and Licona, Michael R. *The Case for the Resurrection of Jesus.* Grand Rapids: Kregel Publications, 2004.

Keller, Timothy. *The Reason for God.* London: Hodder & Stoughton, 2008.

Lennox, John. *Gunning for God: A Critique of the New Atheism.* Oxford: Lion, 2011.

Strobel, Lee. *The Case for Christ : A Journalist's Personal Investigation of the Evidence for Jesus.* Grand Rapids: Zondervan, 1998.

Wright, N. T. *The Resurrection of the Son of God* (Christian Origins and the Question of God series Book 3). London: Society for Promoting Christian Knowledge, 2003.

Bibliography

See also reading list on p. 263.

Bailey, Kenneth. *Poet and Peasant*. Grand Rapids: Eerdmans, 1976.

Butterfield, Herbert. *Christianity and History*. London: Bell, 1949.

Craig, William Lane. *Reasonable Faith: Christian Truth and Apologetics*. [1984] 3rd edn, Wheaton: Crossway, 2008.

Gooding, David. *True to the Faith: Defining and Defending the Gospel in the Acts of the Apostles*. Coleraine, N. Ireland: Myrtlefield House, 2013.

Habermas, Gary R. and Licona, Michael R. *The Case for the Resurrection of Jesus*. Grand Rapids: Kregel Publications, 2004.

Hillyer, N., et al., eds. *The Illustrated Bible Dictionary*. Leicester: Inter-Varsity, 1980.

Homer. *Iliad*.

Hoyle, Fred. *The Intelligent Universe*. London: Joseph, 1983.

Josephus. *Antiquities of the Jews*.

Lennox, John. *Seven Days that Divide the World*. Oxford: Lion Books, 2011.

Lewis, C. S. *Mere Christianity*. [1952] London: Collins, 2012.

—. *Miracles: A Preliminary Study*. [1947] London: Collins, 1974.

NIV Study Bible. London: Hodder & Stoughton, 1985.

Plato. *Critias*.

Sartre, Jean-Paul. *Words*. London: Penguin, 1967.

Skolnik, Fred and Michael Berenbaum, eds. *Encyclopaedia Judaica*, 22 vols. 2nd edn, Detroit: Macmillan Reference, 2007.

Scripture Index

Scripture Index

368

Scripture Index

Scripture Index

Scripture Index

Scripture Index

The Quest for Reality and Significance

A Six Part Series
by David Gooding and John Lennox

We need a coherent picture of our world. Life's realities won't let us ignore its fundamental questions, but with so many opposing views, how will we choose answers that are reliable? In this series of books, David Gooding and John Lennox offer a fair analysis of religious and philosophical attempts to find the truth about the world and our place in it. By listening to the Bible alongside other leading voices, they show that it is not only answering life's biggest questions—it is asking better questions than we ever thought to ask.

Being Truly Human

The Limits of Our Worth, Power, Freedom and Destiny

In Book 1 – *Being Truly Human*, Gooding and Lennox address issues surrounding the value of humans. They consider the nature and basis of morality, compare what morality means in different systems, and assess the dangerous way freedom is often devalued. What should guide our use of power? What should limit our choices? And to what extent can our choices keep us from fulfilling our potential?

Finding Ultimate Reality

*In Search of the Best Answers
to the Biggest Questions*

In Book 2 – *Finding Ultimate Reality*, Gooding and Lennox remind us that the authority behind ethics cannot be separated from the truth about ultimate reality. Is there a Creator who stands behind his moral law? Are we the product of amoral forces, left to create moral consensus? Gooding and Lennox compare ultimate reality as understood in: Indian Pantheistic Monism, Greek Philosophy and Mysticism, Naturalism and Atheism, and Christian Theism.

Questioning Our Knowledge

*Can We Know What
We Need to Know?*

In Book 3 – *Questioning Our Knowledge*, Gooding and Lennox discuss how we could know whether any of these competing worldviews are true. What is truth anyway, and is it absolute? How would we recognize truth if we encountered it? Beneath these questions lies another that affects science, philosophy, ethics, literature and our everyday lives: how do we know anything at all?

Doing What's Right

*Whose System of Ethics
is Good Enough?*

In Book 4 – *Doing What's Right,* Gooding and Lennox present particular ethical theories that claim to hold the basic principles everyone should follow. They compare the insights and potential weaknesses of each system by asking: what is its authority, its supreme goal, its specific rules, and its guidance for daily life? They then evaluate why even the best theories have proven to be impossible to follow consistently.

Claiming to Answer

*How One Person Became the Response
to Our Deepest Questions*

In Book 5 – *Claiming to Answer*, Gooding and Lennox argue it is not enough to have an ethical theory telling us what standards we ought to live by, because we often fail in our duties and do what we know is wrong. How can we overcome this universal weakness? Many religions claim to be able to help, but is the hope they offer true? Gooding and Lennox state why they think the claims of Jesus Christ are valid and the help he offers is real.

Suffering Life's Pain

Facing the Problems of Moral and Natural Evil

In Book 6 – *Suffering Life's Pain,* Gooding and Lennox acknowledge the problem with believing in a wise, loving and just God who does not stop natural disasters or human cruelty. Why does he permit congenital diseases, human trafficking and genocide? Is he unable to do anything? Or does he not care? Gooding and Lennox offer answers based on the Creator's purpose for the human race, and his entry into his own creation.

About the Authors

David W. Gooding is Professor Emeritus of Old Testament Greek at Queen's University Belfast and a Member of the Royal Irish Academy. He has taught the Bible internationally and lectured on both its authenticity and its relevance to philosophy, world religions and daily life. He has published scholarly articles on the Septuagint and Old Testament narratives, as well as expositions of Luke, John, Acts, Hebrews, the New Testament's Use of the Old Testament, and several books addressing arguments against the Bible and the Christian faith. His analysis of the Bible and our world continues to shape the thinking of scholars, teachers and students alike.

John C. Lennox, is Professor Emeritus of Mathematics at the University of Oxford and Emeritus Fellow in Mathematics and the Philosophy of Science at Green Templeton College. He is also an Associate Fellow of the Said Business School, University of Oxford. In addition, he is an Adjunct Lecturer at the Oxford Centre for Christian Apologetics, as well as being a Senior Fellow of the Trinity Forum. In addition to academic works, he has published on the relationship between science and Christianity, the books of Genesis and Daniel, and the doctrine of divine sovereignty and human free will. He has lectured internationally and participated in a number of televised debates with some of the world's leading atheist thinkers.